# Your **Florida** LANDSCAPE

**A complete guide to planting and maintenance**

Trees, palms, shrubs, ground covers and vines

## Edited by

Robert J. Black

Kathleen C. Ruppert

UF/IFAS Cooperative Extension Service
University Press of Florida/Gainesville/Tallahassee/Tampa/Boca Raton
Pensacola/Orlando/Miami/Jacksonville

06  05  04  03  02  01    7  6  5  4  3  2

Layout and Design: Katrina Vitkus
Editor: Charles Brown
Indexer: Toni Funaro

**Library of Congress Cataloging-In-Publication Data**
Your Florida landscape: a complete guide to planting and maintenance /edited by Robert J. Black and Kathleen C. Ruppert.

p. cm.

ISBN 0-8130-1641-X  (pbk.)

1, Landscape gardening—Florida. I. Black, Robert J. (Robert John), 1942–. II. Ruppert, Kathleen C. (Kathleen Carlton), 1955–.

SB473.Y68    1998

635'.09759-dc21        98–25884

**Front cover captions**

Left top: Adam's needle (*Yucca filomentosa*)
Right top: Daylily (*Hemerocallis* spp.)
Left bottom: Southern Magnolia (*Magnolia grandiflora*)
Right bottom: Beach morning glory (*lpomoea pes-caprae*)

The University Press of Florida is the scholarly publishing agency for the State University System of Florida, comprising Florida A&M University, Florida Atlantic University, Florida International University, Florida State University, University of Central Florida, University of Florida, University of North Florida, University of South Florida, and University of West Florida.

University Press of Florida
15 Northwest 15th Street
http://www.upf.com

The Cooperative Extension Service is a partnership of county, state, and federal government which serves the citizens of Florida by providing information and training on a wide variety of topics. The Extension Service is a part of the University of Florida's Institute of Food and Agricultural Sciences with selected programs at Florida Agricultural and Mechanical University (FAMU). Extension touches almost everyone in the State from the homeowner to huge agribusiness operations in such areas as: food safety, gardening. child and family development, consumer credit counseling, youth development, energy conservation, sustainable agriculture, competitiveness in world markets, and natural resource conservation.

# Table of Contents

# Foreword

Florida's warm climate, 8,426 miles of indented coastline, and pleasing natural and man-made environments have established its world-wide reputation as an excellent place to live. As a result, Florida has grown to become the fourth most populous state in the nation with approximately 13.4 million residents. Most people moving into Florida are not familiar with its plants and growing conditions. The problem is further compounded by the state's limited water supply, wide variety of soil types, and abundant supply of insects and plant diseases.

This book, developed by scientists at the University of Florida's Institute of Food and Agricultural Sciences (IFAS), provides current information on how to plant and maintain trees, palms, shrubs, ground covers, and vines in the Florida landscape. For more horticultural information, Florida residents can contact their county Extension office (a list of county offices is included in GETTING HELP). To help disseminate this information, many county agents have developed master gardener programs. Florida Master Gardeners are adult volunteers recruited and trained by county Extension agents and other professionals to provide assistance in home horticulture programs.

As Florida's population grows and the dominant sector becomes more urban, the landscape maintenance industry installs and maintains more and more of the plants in landscapes. This book should be especially helpful for newcomers to this industry. Extension agents are available for consultation with commercial landscapers and can provide information on maintaining client landscapes.

At the present time there is an unprecedented awareness and concern for the environment and the preservation of natural resources. Our goal is to encourage the development of landscapes that do not pollute or waste natural resources. We believe this book provides you with the horticultural practices and techniques that can make this possible.

# Acknowledgments

In addition to the authors, we would like to express our special gratitude to reviewers Sydney Park Brown, Gregory L. Davis, Raymond H. Zerba, Jr., and Gary Knox.

For her assistance in editing, writing and photographing, we also would like to thank Donna Mitchell, a photographer and manuscript editor for the Department of Environmental Horticulture. Our student assistant, William G. Griswold, also contributed to this project with his computer and proofreading skills. Many other people have contributed, in various ways and sometimes unwittingly. They, too, have our deep appreciation. Without them, it would have been difficult if not impossible to have produced this book at all.

# Authors and Contributors

## Faculty and Staff of the Institute of Food and Agricultural Sciences

### University of Florida

**Michael J. Aerts, M.S.**
Assistant In Pesticide Information
Pesticide Information Office

**William J. Becker, Ph.D.**
Safety Specialist
Professor Emeritus, Agricultural Engineering

**Robert J. Black, Ph.D.**
Consumer Horticulture Specialist
Associate Professor, Environmental Horticulture

**Timothy K. Broschat, Ph.D.**
Tropical Ornamentals Specialist
Professor, Environmental Horticulture
Ft. Lauderdale Research and Education Center

**James L. Castner, Ph.D.**
Photographer
Entomology and Nematology

**Greg L. Davis, Ph.D.**
Landscape Horticulturist
Assistant Professor, Environmental Horticulture

**Bijan Dehgan, Ph.D.**
Plant Taxonomist
Professor, Environmental Horticulture

**Edwin R. Duke, Ph.D.**
Woody Landscape Specialist
Assistant Professor, Environmental Horticulture
Ft. Lauderdale Research and Education Center

**Robert A. Dunn, Ph.D.**
Nematologist
Professor, Entomology and Nematology

**Thomas M. Dykstra, M.S.**
Ph.D. Student
Entomology and Nematology

**Edward F. Gilman, Ph.D.**
Landscape Horticulturist
Associate Professor, Environmental Horticulture

**William G. Griswold**
Student Assistant
Environmental Horticulture

**Dale H. Habeck, Ph.D.**
Entomologist
Professor, Entomology and Nematology

**Dewayne Ingram, Ph.D.**
Former Woody Ornamentals Specialist
Environmental Horticulture

**Freddie A. Johnson, Ph.D.**
Entomologist
Professor, Entomology and Nematology

**Gerald Kidder, Ph.D.**
Soils Specialist
Professor, Soil and Water Science

**James W. Kimbrough, Ph.D.**
Mycologist
Professor, Plant Pathology

**Gary W. Knox, Ph.D.**
Woody Ornamentals and Water
Management Specialist
Associate Prof., Environmental Horticulture
North Florida Research and Education Center

**Philip Koehler, Ph.D.**
Entomologist
Professor, Entomology and Nematology

**Alan W. Meerow, Ph.D.**
Foliage and Nursery Crop/Tropical
Ornamentals Specialist
Associate Prof., Environmental Horticulture
Ft. Lauderdale Research and Education Center

**Donna Mitchell, B.A.**
Manuscript Editor and Photographer
Environmental Horticulture

**O. Norman Nesheim, Ph.D.**
Pesticide Information Specialist, Pesticide
Information Office
Professor, Food Science and Human Nutrition

**Jeffrey G. Norcini, Ph.D.**
Weed Management/Growth Regulation Specialist
Associate Prof., Environmental Horticulture
North Florida Research and Education Center

**Sydney Park Brown, M.S.**
Horticulture & Water Management Agent IV
Hillsborough County Extension Office

**Kathleen C. Ruppert, Ed.D.**
Environmental Horticulture Specialist
Assistant Prof., Environmental Horticulture

**Paul F. Ruppert, B.S.**
Biological Scientist
Entomology and Nematology

**Donald E. Short, Ph.D.**
Entomologist
Professor, Entomology and Nematology

**Gary W. Simone, Ph.D.**
Plant Pathologist
Associate Professor, Plant Pathology

**Karen M. Vail, M.S.**
Ph.D. Student
Entomology and Nematology

**Thomas H. Yeager, Ph.D.**
Woody Ornamental Specialist
Professor, Environmental Horticulture

**Raymond H. Zerba, Jr., M.S.**
Horticulture Agent IV
Clay County Extension Office

# CREATING the Environmentally Friendly Landscape

Florida's landscapes vary from those made up of cold hardy plants in north Florida to those composed of subtropical plants in south Florida. Within these variations, there are both formal landscapes and natural or informal landscapes. Although the plants and designs may differ, all landscapes perform the same important functions. A well-planned landscape enhances the beauty of a home and moderates the climate around it by protecting it from extremes of wind, heat, cold and glare. Furthermore, landscaping can increase a home's value by 15% and reduce home cooling costs by 30%.

The way we design and manage our landscapes has a significant impact on the environment of our state. We must learn sound landscape management practices if we are to protect our fragile environment and preserve our limited water supply.

Our goal at the University of Florida's Institute of Food and Agricultural Sciences (IFAS) is to encourage the development of landscapes that do not pollute or waste natural resources. Research-based information is used to develop landscaping techniques that conserve energy and water as well as promote environmentally safe and effective pest control.

Because plant placement, irrigation, fertilization and pest control interact with each other, the IFAS approach is to treat the landscape as a whole, interrelated system. For example, a landscape site has certain characteristics that usually govern which kinds of plants will grow well and how frequently they will require irrigation. Watering practices in turn influence how often fertilization is required which then affects the occurrence of pest problems.

One must weigh these and many other interrelated limitations and possibilities when making landscape decisions. By learning about your landscape site and planning before purchasing and planting, you can create a landscape that meets your tastes and needs while remaining environmentally friendly.

## Designing the Landscape

An environmentally sound landscape begins with a good design based on a solid assessment of your site (see *The Planting Site*). Whether designing a new landscape or renovating an old one, low maintenance should be the primary concern. A low maintenance landscape not only saves time and money, but also conserves water and energy. Low maintenance design is achieved through proper plant selection as well as the arrangement of the plants on the site.

If, for instance, you place plants together in beds instead of scattering them throughout the lawn, you greatly reduce the time required for mowing, watering and other maintenance practices. By grouping plants with similar water requirements together, water will not be wasted on plants that do not need it or withheld from plants that do. Moderately large beds in regular shapes are more efficiently irrigated than a larger number of small, narrow or irregularly shaped beds. If plants with high water requirements, like annuals, are located near the home or near a water source, they can be watered by hand or with a micro-irrigation system that drips, trickles or sprays water directly to the soil surrounding the root systems of the plants.

Large lawns are maintenance intensive and suitable only where sports and other outdoor activities demand a wear-resistant surface. A small area of turfgrass combined with ground covers and shrubs can be equally or more attractive and is generally a more environmentally friendly choice. Turf in narrow strips and on steep slopes is troublesome to mow and irrigate.

Trees, shrubs and vines should be placed to shade the home. Shading the windows on the east and west sides of a house provides the most benefit. Trees that are small (up to 25 feet) and medium (25 to 40 feet) in size, when mature, will provide shade within five years when planted within 20 feet of the home. A tree planted close to the home will shade for a longer period of time during the day and over a greater part of the summer than the same tree planted at a greater distance. (Trees should not be planted too close to a structure, however. See *The Planting Site* for details.) Shrubs can effectively block the long, low rays of early morning sun on eastern walls and late afternoon sun on western walls. Espaliered shrubs (trained to grow horizontally against a wall) can block a great deal of sunlight from striking and heating up the wall. With the help of a trellis or a lattice type support, vines can be trained to shade walls, windows and outdoor living spaces.

The outdoor compressor/condenser unit of the air conditioning system will use less energy if it and the surrounding area are shaded from direct sun during the entire day. A tree can shade the unit when the sun is overhead, while nearby shrubs can provide protection during the early morning and late afternoon hours. However, care must be taken not to block the conditioner's air flow. If the warm discharge air is prevented from escaping, the intake air temperature will be raised, causing the unit to operate less efficiently. All in all, the shade provided by plants in combination with good building insulation can reduce energy consumption in the Florida home as much as 30%.

## Plant Selection

A successful landscape requires plants appropriate to the specific site they will occupy. Light, exposure, soil, moisture and other conditions can vary significantly not only from one landscape to the next but even within a single relatively small landscape. Light levels may range from full sun exposure to dense shade; soil may vary from well-drained sand to poorly drained clay. You will need to analyze these and a variety of other factors (see *The Planting Site*) when making your plant choices.

Because healthy plants will establish more quickly and have fewer pest problems than those in poor health, examine plants at the nursery or garden store closely. Look for healthy, vigorous plants which are well-shaped and heavily branched. In most cases, foliage should be dense and free of spotting and yellowing. Avoid plants that are pot-bound, weed infested or show signs of pests or disease. See the chapters on plant selection in the sections on TREES; PALMS; SHRUBS, VINES and GROUND COVERS.

## Planting and Establishment

If a plant is to survive and thrive, it must be installed correctly. The planting hole should be two to three times the diameter of **but no deeper than** the plant's root ball. One of the most common causes of poor plant establishment is planting too deeply. When the plant is placed upright in the planting hole, the top of the root ball must be level with or even slightly higher than the surrounding landscape soil. The hole is filled with the soil taken from the hole. This soil is also used to construct a raised ring around the planting hole to hold irrigation water. After a thorough watering, a 2- to 3-inch layer of mulch is placed around the plant to reduce soil temperature fluctuations, conserve moisture, help control weeds and improve the appearance of the landscape. More specific instructions on planting and establishing trees and other plants are provided in the sections on TREES; PALMS; SHRUBS, VINES AND GROUND COVERS and in the chapter *Mulches for the Landscape.*

## Maintenance

How plants are cared for not only determines how well they grow but also has an impact on energy and water consumption and thus the environment. Apply enough water and fertilizer to keep the plants growing and healthy, but not so much as to waste water, encourage excessive growth and pollute lakes and waterways with fertilizer contaminated run-off.

## Watering

Landscape irrigation can account for up to 50% of a home's water use. Conservation practices such as stretching out the intervals between watering as long as possible, spot watering those plants which require frequent irrigation, watering in the early morning hours and applying 3/4 inch of water per application can significantly reduce water usage without jeopardizing the quality of the landscape. See *Conserving Water Through Landscape Design* for information on irrigation.

## Fertilization

Over-fertilization can have dire consequences for the landscape and the environment. Research has shown that several pest problems are increased when plants are overstimulated with excessive fertilizer. In addition, too much fertilizer promotes excessive growth. This greatly increases the amount of pruning required to keep the landscape attractive, which also leads to more yard waste. Finally, fertilizer-laden water may run into storm drains and eventually into rivers, lakes and bays. Algae in these bodies of water then grow so rapidly that the oxygen supply in the water is depleted, killing fish and other vital organisms.

When purchasing fertilizers, look for those which have at least 30% of the nitrogen in a water-insoluble form. These fertilizers provide nitrogen to the roots of plants for a long period of time and less escapes to pollute surface run-off water, lakes and waterways.

Most established landscape plants grow well with two or three fertilizer applications per year. For detailed information on fertilizing, see the section on SOIL, FERTILIZER AND PLANT NUTRITION.

## Pest Control

Millions of pounds of pesticides are used each year on landscape plants. Such widespread use of chemicals to control pests is not without risks. There is always a chance of environmental contamination, destruction of beneficial organisms, pest resistance and outbreaks of secondary pests.

Dealing with plant pests begins with selecting plants that have few pest problems. Avoid cultural practices such as over-watering and over-fertilizing that make lawns and landscape plants susceptible to pests. Frequently monitor your landscape for pests and know the difference between harmful and beneficial insects. (See section on INSECTS AND PESTS). If a pest problem is detected, spray only the affected plant or plants. Blanketing the landscape with pesticides is wasteful and can be environmentally damaging.

Try to use insecticides which are safe for the environment and the people who use them. Products such as refined horticultural oil, *Bacillus thuringiensis*, and insecticidal soaps are environmentally safe and effective against most of the insect pests encountered in the landscape. For more information, see the section on INSECTS AND PESTS.

### Recycling Leaves, Clippings and Other Maintenance Leftovers

Grass clippings, leaves and pruning clippings all contain valuable nutrients and should be recycled back into the landscape either as mulch or as compost. Grass clippings are generally best left on the lawn where they will quickly decompose and provide nutrients to the lawn. For details on mulching and composting, see *Mulches for the Landscape* and *A Guide to Composting*.

## Summary

The environmentally friendly landscape is a common sense approach to landscape design and maintenance which conserves energy and water, recycles yard wastes and reduces inputs of fertilizers and pesticides into the environment. The environment is our responsibility, and we must each do our part if we are to preserve Florida's natural beauty for generations to come.

— *Robert J. Black*

# THE PLANTING SITE
## Planning Before Planting

A beautiful landscape owes its success to many types of care and considerations. Chief among them is a keen assessment and understanding of the particular conditions of the landscape site. No matter how attractive and healthy the plants chosen or how well tended once they are in the ground, if they are not suited to the site they may well prove a serious disappointment. Among the factors to be taken into account are the planting site's climate and microclimates, the amounts of direct and indirect sunlight received throughout the day, exposure to wind and, in coastal areas, salt, various characteristics of the soil and the underground environment and, of course, manmade components like utility lines, signs, fences and buildings.

Thought must also be given to how the plants chosen will relate to each other. A good landscape is both aesthetically and ecologically harmonious, combining plants with complementary forms, growth patterns and survival requirements. Take time to evaluate your landscape site and envision what it will need and how it will look during different stages and seasons.

## Climate
### Cold Hardiness and Heat Tolerance

Florida's weather varies significantly from one part of the state to another and, as a consequence, plants that flourish in one locale may do poorly or fail altogether in another. To help determine which plants will succeed in your area, locate the **hardiness zone** in which you live (Figure 1). A plant that is adapted to your hardiness zone is one that can tolerate the lowest winter temperature your zone **usually** experiences. To find

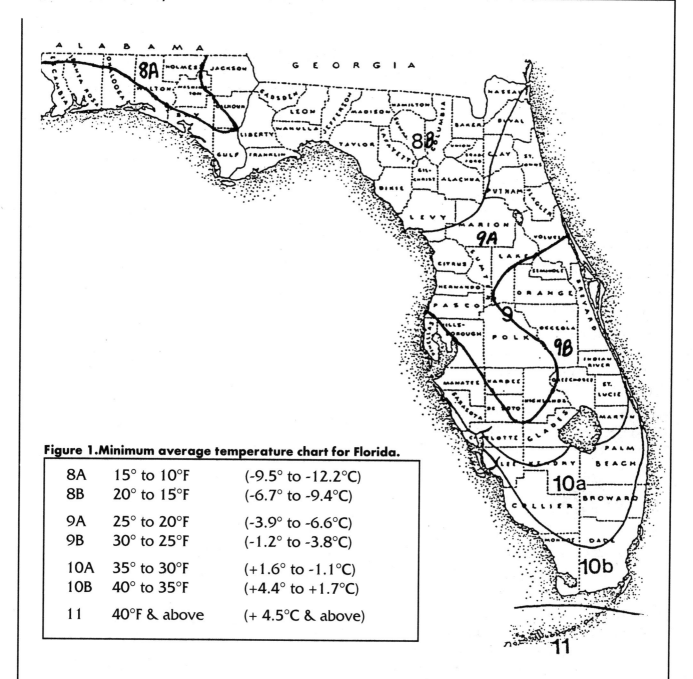

**Figure 1. Minimum average temperature chart for Florida.**

| | | |
|---|---|---|
| 8A | 15° to 10°F | (-9.5° to -12.2°C) |
| 8B | 20° to 15°F | (-6.7° to -9.4°C) |
| 9A | 25° to 20°F | (-3.9° to -6.6°C) |
| 9B | 30° to 25°F | (-1.2° to -3.8°C) |
| 10A | 35° to 30°F | (+1.6° to -1.1°C) |
| 10B | 40° to 35°F | (+4.4° to +1.7°C) |
| 11 | 40°F & above | (+ 4.5°C & above) |

which plants are adapted to your hardiness zone, consult a reliable book, computer program or list from a garden center. Your county Extension agent is also a good resource for this information. A number of reference books will also indicate how far south a given plant can grow (i.e. its heat tolerance). This is especially good to know if you live in central or south Florida.

You may wish to plant an occasional specimen that is outside the range for your region, just to see how it will fare. An arboretum or a botanical garden near you may be testing the cold hardiness or heat tolerance of a number of different species should you be interested in seeing the responses of a broader range of plants.

## Microclimates

In addition to the larger climate that governs your community and your site, plants will be affected by little pockets of weather specific to certain parts of your property. Also, taller plants will have a totally different microclimate than those at or near ground level. These microclimates may vary by several degrees, a difference that can mean life or death in cold weather.

Microclimates are influenced by sun exposure, existing vegetation and nearby buildings. Take note of the differences on your site, keeping in mind that, in general, minimum winter temperatures occur on the north side of a house and maximum summer temperatures are reached on unshaded western exposures. Southern exposures will be the warmest during the winter; on the south side of a house, temperature fluctuations in a given day in winter can be dramatic and may predispose plants to winter damage by stimulating new growth that can't tolerate a sudden drop in temperature.

Tree canopies protect neighboring plants by reducing their radiant heat loss. In winter, the microclimate beneath a tree may be several degrees warmer than the surrounding air, and this small increase in temperature could keep some plants alive. Furthermore, the tree's shade during the early morning slows the rate of thaw and can reduce the amount of cold damage to some species. Building overhangs, arbors and fences may provide similar kinds of protection.

# Above Ground Site Analysis
## Exposure to Sunlight

All plants require some amount of sunlight, but some species need many hours of full sun while others do best largely in shade. Before choosing plants for your landscape, observe how many hours of sun and shade various parts of the site receive. Remember to take into account that the angle of the sun changes with the time of year and that you will probably have more hours of direct sun in summer than in other seasons.

Plants requiring full sun (e.g. junipers) will need at least 6 hours daily of direct sun and will often produce the best form and growth if they receive sun all day. Most large trees grow best in full sun, while some small trees do better in sites that are shaded part of the day.

Plants that can tolerate full sun to partial sun/partial shade will need 3 to 4 hours of direct sun. Shade loving plants will adapt to sites with less than 2 hours of direct sun or with filtered sun/filtered shade. Some shade loving plants can tolerate direct exposure to early morning sun but may suffer if directly exposed to 2 or more hours of mid-day or afternoon sun.

## Wind

Wind increases the amount of water loss from a plant to the atmosphere. This may not be a problem if roots can expand into the surrounding soil uninhibited by compacted soil or by structures such as curbs, sidewalks, patios, buildings and streets. However, the root systems of plants growing in confined situations (for instance, cutouts in city sidewalks) dry out the soil quickly, and the plants are then susceptible to wind desiccation. Plants in very sandy, well-drained soils are likewise vulnerable.

Well-managed irrigation can partially overcome such water deficits but may be difficult to accomplish in highly urbanized sites. The best way to manage water loss on a windy site is by selecting species tolerant of drought. If soil on such a site is poorly drained, select a species that can tolerate both drought and wet soil.

## Salt

Air-borne salt can affect plants' twigs and foliage or, after being deposited on the ground, their roots. Plants within a quarter of a mile of salt water coastlines should possess some degree of tolerance to salt spray. Those exposed to direct spray along the dunes will need to be highly salt tolerant. Salt tolerant plants are often deformed by direct exposure to salty air, but they can survive and grow. Salt sensitive plants grow poorly or die when exposed to salty air.

## Overhead Power Lines

For over 50 years utility companies have been trying to get both home gardeners and professional landscapers to plant the right tree in the right place. Ultimately, the consumer foots the bill for the hundreds of millions of dollars that are spent on pruning or removing trees that were planted too close to power lines.

Plant only trees that are small at maturity directly under or within 6 feet of overhead lines. When planting between 6 and 50 feet of a utility line, size at maturity is still a critical issue. Remember that a tree with a wide spreading canopy must be planted further from the wire than a tree with a narrow, more upright canopy. For example, if a planting site is 20 feet from a power line, the tree selected should be one that at maturity will have a canopy that is less than 40 feet in diameter.

## Buildings

If planting under the eaves of a building, be aware that plants will receive little or no rainfall if the building has gutters. The soil may then become too dry to support good root growth unless irrigation is regularly supplied. If a building has no gutters, water running off the roof may supply plants in the immediate vicinity with several hundred inches of rainfall every year instead of the usual 50 to 60 inches. Unless soil is well drained, be sure to install plants that can tolerate wet soil conditions for extended periods. Locate plants so that water cascading off a roof will not land directly on the plants. During heavy storms, such runoff can physically pound a plant causing extensive damage. Remember, too, that areas directly under the eaves of buildings will be shaded longer than adjacent areas.

Most **shrubs and vines** can be planted to within a foot of a building as their roots will not grow large enough to damage the foundation. Plants with an upright habit such as heavenly bamboo (nandina) are suited for close planting. However, it is best to plant shrubs with a round, oval or spreading habit at least 3 feet out from a wall (or fence). This will prevent the shrubs from becoming one sided and appearing jammed against the building when mature.

**Trees** are most stable when they develop a uniform root system distributed more or less evenly in every direction from the trunk. When roots meet a building wall, they are deflected laterally and possibly downward in well drained soil. The one-sided and unbalanced root system that develops as a consequence can reduce the wind firmness of the tree. Large-maturing trees planted within 10 feet of a one- or two-story building can blow over, especially if wind comes from the building side of the tree. Trees growing in compacted, poorly drained soil are most at risk because they develop few, if any, deep roots to help keep them upright.

Above-ground, if planting within 10 feet of a building, a tree with a narrow canopy is likely to be the most appropriate choice. The tree may be of any height, though a small tree is preferable. One will see examples to the contrary, but planting a large-maturing tree closer than 15 feet to a building is not the best idea. If a large, wide-spreading tree is planted 15 feet or more from a one- or two-story building, a symmetrical canopy can be developed by training branches to grow over the building. The tree will then be more resistant to windstorms than one with an unbalanced canopy. Trees planted near buildings over two stories tall need to be far enough away to allow nearly symmetrical canopy development. If closer planting is required, trees with a narrow canopy are the best choices.

## Signs

To prevent conflicts between signs and plants, use small trees near tall signs and large trees near low signs. While large-maturing trees may obscure a low sign for several years, over time the lower branches can be removed to thin the lower canopy. When correctly pruned and trained, a tree can frame and draw attention to a sign.

## Existing Trees

When young trees or shrubs that require full sun are planted under or near the canopy of established trees, they will bend in the direction of the sunlight and become deformed. Without adequate light reaching a plant from all sides, the tendency is to become one-sided. Although the plant is not necessarily damaged by this, it can be unsightly. Shade tolerant plants are a better choice for planting in the shade of established trees.

## Below Ground Site Analysis

Soil and below ground characteristics that significantly affect the growth and well-

being of plants include soil pH level, drainage capacity, depth of topsoil, salinity, distance to the water table and rooting space limitations. Recent surveys show that most people do not take these factors into consideration when selecting plants, and this may in turn account for why so many plantings fail.

Soil of good quality is precious and should not be wasted. When deciding to build on a site, advanced planning (before construction starts) enables you to identify and preserve good soil. Make provisions to save and store high quality soil for use when construction is completed. Do not permit this soil to be taken away or buried. Work with contractors to prevent excessive soil compaction in areas where trees will be planted. These areas can be isolated with heavy fences and fines levied for violations.

More frequently one must select plants for a site where construction has already been completed and the soil and ground modified. Equipment operations may have done damage such as turning a moderately well drained clay soil, that would have been capable of supporting tree growth, into poorly drained pools of mud. Simply layering soil over the compacted soil will not promote good plant growth. Compacted soil needs to be broken up and mixed with loose soil.

Landscapes in highly urbanized areas will need more soil tests and site evaluation than will older or undisturbed sites. Poor quality subsoil is sometimes substituted for topsoil, and rubble or other debris is often mixed with soil. Examine soil throughout the planting site and test each different type you find. A shovel or backhoe is used to collect soil data at the site. Some county Extension offices can perform limited soil testing; others have no testing facilities. Complete soil tests can be obtained through the Soil

Testing Lab at the University of Florida's IFAS in Gainesville (see GETTING HELP) or through a private soil testing lab. Some, but not all, counties can provide a soil survey of the county through the United States Department of Agriculture Natural Resources Conservation Service. These surveys include aerial views and detailed information regarding soil types and various characteristics such as soil texture, height of the water table, rock layers, drainage and native vegetation.

## Soil pH

A soil's level of acidity or alkalinity is rated numerically and known as its pH. The higher the number the less acidic and more alkaline the soil. Soil pH levels govern the availability of nutrients to plants and also affect the activity of soil microorganisms.

Nearly all plants can grow in soils with a pH between 5.5 and 7. If soil pH is less than 5.5, check with local specialists regarding proper species selection. Parts of coastal Florida, especially south Florida, as well as many urban areas throughout the state have soils with pH levels of 7 or higher. In soil this alkaline, micronutrient deficiencies develop in plants such as the gardenia, azalea, ixora, camellia, sweet gum, red maple, queen palm and royal palm, to name a few. If soil pH is above 7, choose plants that are adapted to alkaline (high pH) soil. Few plants grow well in soils with a pH above 8.5.

The most important component of a soil test is the pH, so don't try to guess the level. A pH test should be conducted in several areas of the planting site, wherever the soil color or texture appears distinctly different from elsewhere on the site. Due to the limestone sub-base under pavement, soil pH is often higher close to driveways, parking lots and sidewalks. It may be lower or higher next to a building due to the sand or other materials used near the footings. **Soil pH may vary too much across the site to permit planting of the same species or cultivar over the entire landscape.**

To collect soil samples for testing, use a trowel or shovel to dig about 10 to 15 small holes **in each area** of the site. Remove a slice of soil from the side of each hole from the surface down 6 inches deep. (You may also use a soil coring device to collect samples.) Mix the slices (or cores) of soil from the 10 holes together in a clean jar or plastic bag and take a subsample to a lab for testing. (Contact the county Extension office for assistance.) The test report you receive may include corrective measures for adjusting pH. (For more information see *Soil pH and Landscape Plants*).

When digging soil cores, take note of the color and texture of the soil in each. Indicate on your landscape sketch which areas contain loose soil and which contain dense clay or other types of soil as this information will affect your irrigation frequency when landscaping is completed.

## Soil Texture

While soil texture is not in itself a growth limiting factor, it does indicate other soil attributes that influence plant growth. For example, clay with its dense texture often drains poorly if the terrain is flat or the soil has been compacted by heavy equipment. When planting in clayey soil, you must know whether drainage is poor or good to select plants that are adapted to the level of moisture that will prevail. On the other hand, many sandy soils drain quickly and if irrigation will not be provided on a regular basis after plants are established, drought resistant species should be chosen for the site.

Nitrogen, potassium and other essential elements are leached more quickly through sandy soils. These elements can migrate below the root zone which will affect fertilization management. A controlled, slow-release fertilizer is recommended for sandy soil. (Soluble fertilizers leach quickly.) Consider choosing a species native or adapted to a sandy soil type. Such plants may be more tolerant of soils with a lower nutrient content.

## Compacted Low Oxygen Soils

Compacted and poorly drained soils contain little oxygen, which plant roots need in order to survive and grow. Though some plants tolerate soils with low oxygen, most die, grow poorly or eventually succumb to a disease or insect problem when planted in soil that is too compacted or too wet during certain times of the year. Although any type of soil can become compacted, compacted clay offers plants the most difficult challenge.

To check for compaction and drainage, dig several holes at least 18 and preferably 24 to 30 inches deep in each section of your planting site. Soil that is difficult to dig may be compacted; if a pick axe must be used, soil is probably too compacted for planting without taking remedial measures. If the soil is fairly easy to dig with a shovel, it is probably not compacted.

Fill the holes with water. If water stands in a hole for a day or more, soil is too compacted for good drainage. Another method for determining if soil is poorly drained is to smell it. A sour smell and a gray color indicate low oxygen content. Occasionally, the sour smell may be strong enough to detect while standing near a dug hole. More often, a soil clump must be broken open close to your nose to detect the smell.

If plants that cannot tolerate wet roots must be planted on a site with a high water table or poor soil drainage, a mound known as a **berm** can be created to elevate the plants' root systems. Although its use may be the only option, making a berm is not an ideal solution because of the various problems it entails. Successful use of this landscaping technique requires intelligent advance planning.

First, the berm should be made from the same topsoil found in the surrounding landscape. If none is available, an equivalent or better grade of topsoil may be used. The berm must be created with its sides gradually sloping away from the planting(s). If sides are too steep, irrigation will run off the soil quickly and could wash it away from the roots, leaving them exposed. This could cause plant death.

The soil of the berm will dry faster than the soil in the surrounding landscape, leaving plants and turf on the berm susceptible to pests and environmental stress. The berm requires more frequent irrigation; however, unless it has a system of its own, the surrounding landscape will be overwatered. Because of these various difficulties, the use of berms for strictly decorative purposes is discouraged.

Compacted and poorly drained soils may be improved by tilling. A ripping tool, which is dragged behind a bulldozer, can be used to loosen soil on a large site. An experienced operator is required. Do not use the tiller or ripping tool under the drip-line of trees and shrubs or you will cause serious damage to their root systems.

## Subsurface Compacted Layers

Soil that has been loosely spread over a compacted soil creates special challenges.

Roots often grow only in the loose soil and fail to penetrate the compacted subsoil. The resulting shallow root system can create unstable and potentially hazardous large trees. Consequently, only small and medium sized trees are recommended for planting where less than 2 feet of loose soil will be spread over compacted subsoil.

In landscapes with subsurface compacted layers, the lowest areas are likely to be wet during certain times of the year. Within a day or two after a significant rainfall, evaluate the site and decide if choosing plants tolerant of wet sites will be necessary. If this kind of evaluation is conducted during a drier time of the year, you may mistakenly conclude that your drainage is fine.

## Artificial Soil Horizons

Most soils in urban areas and many in suburban landscapes have been disturbed by heavy equipment before planting. Poor quality subsoil with a fine texture, high clay content or high pH is often brought to the surface. Construction debris and other soils from other sites may be layered on top of one another creating an artificial soil profile or horizon. This structure disrupts the flow of water through the soil and can create poorly drained areas. You can suspect a drainage problem if there are abrupt changes in soil color as you dig a hole. If soil is mixed with bricks, concrete or other construction debris, consider replacing the soil or sifting out the debris.

## Soil Salinity

Some soils in coastal areas have a high salt content. If you are unfamiliar with the area or suspect that salts could be a problem, have the soil tested. If the electro-conductivity (E.C.) of the soil is over 1 mmho per cm, then salt content is too high for many plants. You will then need to select plants that have good tolerance for soil salts.

Irrigation water may also be salty. When using well water along the coast, have it tested. If conductivity (E.C.) of irrigation water is above 1 mmho per cm, poor growth in some trees and plants may result. If good water is not available, choose salt tolerant plants or those that have been growing well in your area with the same irrigation water.

## Other Soil Contaminants

Have an expert perform an environmental audit on the site if you have reason to believe that the planting site contains contaminants such as petroleum waste products, heavy metals or other potentially hazardous residues. Not only could these contaminants cause poor plant growth, they could prove dangerous to people and animals.

## Soil Depth

In the ideal planting site, the layer of soil above bedrock would be at least 5 or 6 feet deep. Dig a hole to learn the depth of your soil layer. If bedrock comes close to the surface or for other reasons there is little soil, trees that are small to medium sized at maturity are the best choice for planting. Large maturing trees planted in shallow soil are likely to form large surface roots which can disrupt foundations, driveways, sidewalks, curbing and gardens. Furthermore, large trees with shallow root systems can topple over in storms.

## Distance to the Water Table

Below ground variations of a planting site and the surrounding terrain affect the distance between the soil surface and the top of the water table in a given locale. In central and south Florida, the water table may be a few feet below the soil surface but more than 50 feet down in other areas. The distance to the water table often varies throughout the year; you may find that the water table that was within inches of the surface in one season has dropped several feet below it during another season. For the purposes of plant selection, sites with water within a foot or two of the soil surface during part of the year should be treated as poorly drained.

To determine the distance to the water table, use a shovel or a 4-inch auger to dig several holes 2 to 3 feet deep around your planting site. Wait for 2 hours. If water appears in the hole, the water table is high, suggesting a need to select plants that tolerate wet sites. If the distance from the soil surface to the surface of the water is less than 18 inches, only small- or medium-sized wet site trees are recommended. (Large maturing trees will adapt to wet sites by developing shallow root systems and can then become unstable in storms. The possible exceptions are trees that grow with submerged root systems, such as bald cypress and black gum.) If no water appears in the hole, you need not take the water table into consideration in choosing plants for that site.

## Underground Utilities

Before any digging or planting, the location of underground electric, telephone and television cables as well as water, sewer and gas lines must be determined. In Florida, the telephone company often can provide you with a single toll free number that will notify all companies at once before you dig. However, this needs to be done several days before the digging is to take place. Digging holes without regard for underground utili-

ties risks serious personal injury as well as damage to the lines. The person(s) causing the damage must pay for repairs.

Trees that are large at maturity should be planted at least 12 feet from major underground utility lines; the rule of thumb is to plant as far away as possible. No tree should be planted directly on top of a utility line as it might be damaged or need removal if the line needs servicing.

Medium to large-maturing trees planted near septic tanks and drain fields can cause damage with their roots. (Though the roots of small maturing trees and shrubs can also invade septic tanks, they seldom cause extensive problems.) To be safe, plant a tree at least as far from a potential underground trouble spot as the diameter of its canopy at maturity. For example, a tree expected to produce a canopy 40 feet in diameter should be planted 40 feet from a septic tank or drain field.

## Site Preparation and Soil Amendments

Many planting sites need to be prepared before planting begins. Preparations may include grading, tilling of compacted soil, installation of irrigation or other utilities, the addition of gutters to a roof to control runoff during heavy rains, terracing to retain runoff, amending soil or other projects that will affect the nature or viability of the planting site.

Grading the soil to achieve the aesthetically desired land form is the first step to take in preparing the site. Adequate surface drainage that directs water flow away from structures and planting beds and into an appropriate water path for the area must also be achieved at this stage.

Compacted soil may be loosened by plowing or tilling. However, such cultivation under the canopy of trees or shrubs may cause serious damage to the root system as roots are located within one foot of the soil surface. Instead, a 3 to 5 inch layer of mulch over compacted soil can help promote root growth and aid in plant establishment by providing a loose medium for root growth.

Most landscape soils are not modified with soil amendments prior to planting, and the plants grow well. However, amendments may serve to adjust the soil pH to a desirable range (although the effect is usually temporary) or to add nutrient elements or to temporarily increase organic matter. Because it promotes rapid root growth, composted organic matter is a good amendment for large planting beds containing groups of shrubs. However, individual planting holes for trees and shrubs usually do not need amendments. In the occasional special case, the soil in a small area may be replaced entirely with a suitable topsoil. This can be costly and is therefore reserved for instances where chemical residue or excessive compaction has rendered existing soil unsuitable for plants. Research is ongoing as to whether amendments such as humic acid, polymers and absorbents help establish or maintain woody landscape plants.

— *Edward F. Gilman*

# CONSERVING WATER
# Through Landscape Design

Water is the lifeblood of plants. It is required for seed germination, plant growth, photosynthesis, nutrient transport and temperature control. Water also maintains turgidity, which enables leaves to retain their shapes.

The average volume of rainfall in Florida ranges from nearly 52 inches on the central and northern peninsula to almost 65 inches in the panhandle west of Tallahassee and along the southeast coast below Lake Okeechobee. More than half of Florida's total annual rainfall is concentrated in the central and southern peninsula between June and September. During the winter and spring, lack of rainfall may seriously compromise plant development. Soils with a limited capacity to retain moisture must be irrigated during periods of low rainfall. Even during the rainy season, evapotranspiration (water loss from plants and soil) occurs between showers and may mandate supplemental watering.

As Florida's population grows and becomes more urbanized, the demand on limited water resources steadily increases. Saltwater intrusion into freshwater wells has further reduced the state's available water supply. Home gardeners, as well as all other water users, must practice water conservation. One of the best ways to conserve water is to design or modify the landscape to reduce its water requirements.

## Landscape Styles

The traditional or conventional landscape is characterized by large areas of turf accented by flower beds and manicured trees and shrubs. This type of landscape is typical of the cool, temperate regions of the northeastern United States and was brought to Florida by people moving here from the North. Unfortunately, the traditional landscape is not well adapted to Florida's sandy and porous soils, hot sub-tropical climate, and well-defined wet and dry seasons. In Florida, traditional landscapes require large amounts of water and maintenance.

In response to drought and limited water resources, a number of new landscaping ideas have evolved which reduce water and maintenance requirements while still providing aesthetically pleasing landscapes. For instance, the concept of natural or ecological landscaping involves plant selection that is based on the climate and environment of the area as well as the particular characteristics of the site. Exposure, light intensity, soil pH, soil aeration, soil mineral analysis, site drainage and irrigation water quality are all site characteristics that will affect levels of necessary maintenance as well as the viability of plantings. Proper plant selection based on site characteristics will enhance the plants' likelihood of becoming established in the site and reduce incidences of low vigor, disease and death.

Native species are often preferred for natural landscapes but plant selection should take into consideration the microclimate and topography of the site (See *The Planting Site*). In some cases, native plants will not be the most appropriate choice because microclimate and topography have been significantly altered by development. Parking lots become deserts, retention ponds and waterways mimic swampland and large structures create areas of artificial shade. The microclimatic features of the developed site will determine which plants will be most effective in the landscape design. For example, plants adapted to wet soils should be used in waterways and spillways, low spots, retention ponds and areas with poor drainage while drought-tolerant plants can be placed in windy, dry or exposed areas or in plantings on berms or against unshaded south or west walls of buildings.

Since natural landscaping is a rather abrupt change in American landscaping philosophy, home gardeners may find it difficult to alter their conceptions of what a landscape should look like. One way to satisfy the desire for a traditional landscape within the framework of water conservation and low maintenance is to use the **oasis** approach to landscape design. This involves placing the showiest plants with the highest water and maintenance requirements in those areas that will have the greatest visual impact (i.e. entries, patios, courtyards, viewpoints). Because they require the most water, the oasis areas will have the most elaborate irrigation systems.

Other areas with less traffic or less visibility, such as the sides of buildings, service areas and the more remote parts of the landscape, are well suited to plants that require little water or maintenance. The transition zone between these natural expanses and the oasis areas can support plants that require more water and maintenance than the natural landscape but less than the oasis areas.

The oasis concept improves water management practices because it concentrates water resources in plantings close to main use areas; such concentration may also reduce installation costs as the system is likely to be closer to water lines.

## Other Aspects Of Design

In addition to these larger landscape philosophies, certain design practices will also help conserve water. Plants with similar water requirements can be grouped together in the landscape and the irrigation zoned so that each group receives only the amount of water it requires. This way, a plant is not over or under watered to meet its neighbor's needs.

The use of mulches will also reduce maintenance and water use. A 2- to 3- inch layer of mulch should be used in planting beds to reduce evaporation from the soil surface, moderate soil temperatures and suppress weeds. Mulches can sometimes replace turf or ground covers in areas that require extensive watering or where coverage is incomplete. In such situations, mulches have the additional benefits of requiring less maintenance and no water. On slight inclines, mulch can control erosion as well. (See *Mulches for the Landscape*.)

Some Florida municipalities now supply the irrigation systems of homes and businesses with reclaimed water. Reclaimed water is highly tested wastewater that is safe for most irrigation needs. Reclaimed water may contain small amounts of nutrients which some users say reduces the need to fertilize. Depending on the area, hooking into a reclaimed water system may be considerably cheaper for constructions in new developments than for existing homes. The cost of installation may soon be offset by the savings on the water bill. Often users of reclaimed water are billed a small flat monthly fee and a substantially lower water consumption fee. Owners of golf courses and industrial parks have long realized the substantial savings to be had from using reclaimed water.

Although home plumbing can often be modified to permit recycling of grey water (from tubs, showers and non-kitchen sinks) for one's own home irrigation, such conversions may require special permitting in Florida. Untreated grey water, even when obtained only from bathtub and bathroom sink drains, can contain fecal coliform bacteria. Water from kitchen sink drains generally contains oils, fats and grease which cause unpleasant odors and can attract pests. Laundry water may contain chlorine or boron, which can damage plants. Grey water from laundering diapers should never be used.

In areas with sandy soil, terrain that drains rapidly, or under other conditions that make it difficult to supply any or enough water,

drought-tolerant plants are a good alternative. Such plants are adapted by nature to withstand long periods without water.

Finally, windbreaks formed by walls, fences, trees, shrub beds or hedges will reduce wind velocity and thereby greatly diminish evaporation during irrigation and evapotranspiration from the plants themselves. Properly constructed, windbreaks can cut wind velocity 75% to 85% and are highly recommended for areas that experience steady or frequent and gusty winds.

## When to Water

Variables such as plant species, soil type, time of year and weather conditions determine when and how much plants should be watered, consequently it is difficult to offer specific watering procedures. However, the following guidelines should provide some general information.

Irrigate only when plants need water. Follow local water restrictions which may dictate irrigation days and hours. During the summer, established plants need no water for 3 to 5 days after a rainfall or a water application that distributes at least 3/4 inch of water. You can wait much longer during the winter or when watering soils of finer texture, such as muck or clay.

Many landscape plants demonstrate their need for water by wilting. If they continue to wilt during the evening, water them the following morning. Some herbaceous plants, such as impatiens and coleus, typically wilt during the heat of the day. Even though the soil contains adequate moisture, the root systems of these plants cannot absorb water from the soil fast enough to replace the water vapor lost through the plants' leaves and stems. If the plants do not recover during the cooler hours of the evening, water them early the following morning.

Some plants show no early symptoms of drought stress. If drought conditions continue, however, they may exhibit injury symptoms such as leaf drop and/or browning of leaf margins or tips. Plants should be watered before the appearance of injury symptoms, since at this stage of drought stress they may become severely damaged or even die.

Plants in sandy soils exposed to full sunlight may need water every 3 to 5 days. The same plants placed in some shade or in soils of finer texture may need water only once a week, perhaps less often.

Landscape plants should be watered early in the morning when wind and temperature levels are low. Irrigating during the late morning, at midday and during the afternoon usually results in increased water loss from evaporation. With overhead irrigation systems, unequal water distribution caused by the stronger winds at these times of day is also more likely. Watering at night is not advised as this practice can encourage the development of disease.

When you decide it is time to water, be sure to comply with local and regional water regulations. In many areas, irrigation is allowed only on certain days or during specified hours. Also check local weather channels for rain forecasts before irrigating. Monitor local rainfall with a simple rain gauge, and install and maintain an automatic rain switch on automatic irrigation systems. You will save water by following these guidelines.

## How Much Water to Apply

When watering, soak the soil thoroughly. Frequent, light sprinklings waste water and do little to satisfy the water requirements of a plant growing in hot, dry soil. Plants watered in this way often develop shallow root systems, increasing their susceptibility to damage if watering is interrupted for a few days.

For most of Florida's sandy soils, 1/2 to 3/4 inch of rainfall or irrigation is sufficient to wet the root zone. Because not all soils and plants are alike, however, some adjustments in the amount of water applied may be necessary. To determine when a hose-end or in-ground sprinkler system has delivered 3/4 inch of water, place cans or cartons at intervals within the spray pattern (as shown in Figure 2) and continue watering until the average water level in the cans reaches 3/4 inch.

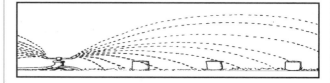

**Figure 2. Measure water levels in containers placed in a sprinkler's spray pattern to determine amount of water being applied.**

## Watering Methods

The most efficient and effective watering method currently in use is microirrigation, which is also known as drip or trickle irrigation. Microirrigation supplies small quantities of water directly to a plant's root system via plastic tubing located on or below the ground surface. Low-pressure emitters (i.e. nozzles that drip, spray or sprinkle) are attached to the plastic tubing and slowly release water into the soil around a plant. Wetting only the root zone results in dramatic water savings, limits weed proliferation and accelerates plant growth. Microirrigation kits are available at many home and garden stores, and individual components of a system can be purchased at irrigation supply stores. More sophisticated systems can be designed and installed by a professional. Irrigation supply stores also carry what are known as retrofit kits for converting existing irrigation systems to microirrigation.

When microirrigating, you need to know which kind of emitter to install in a given location. With drip emitters, water will move laterally in sand only 10 to 12 inches from the source point. Drip emitters are ideal when such precision is desirable or for narrow strip plantings, such as along hedge rows. Because drip emitters are frequently placed under mulch or buried in the soil, clogging may occur and is difficult to detect. Because the action of drip emitters is not readily apparent, it is also difficult to know whether the system is irrigating excessively due to accident or oversight. Frequent inspection is required to ascertain that the drip emitters and the overall system are functioning. Likewise, all irrigation systems should be inspected periodically to assure proper operation.

On the whole, spray-jets (either micro-sprayers or micro-sprinklers) are more desirable than drip emitters for most Florida landscape applications. Because they can cover areas 3 to 20 feet in diameter, fewer emitters are needed. Not only is their action visible, but the greater flow rate of water through spray-jets (10 to 20 gallons per hour versus the drip emitter's .25 to 2 gallons per hour) makes them less susceptible to clogging. Through the use of a deflector plate, micro-sprayers create a fan-shaped distribution of fine water droplets. These fan-jets perform well when used for directional spray and confined area applications. Shaping vanes known as spokes can be added to the deflection area to create streams of water called spoke-jets. A spoke-shaped application pattern works well for a single tree. A deflection cap will confine the application to areas 2 to 5 feet in diameter. Some manufacturers have added spinner devices to create a sprinkler effect. These micro-sprinklers have more uniform water distribution than the fan-jets or spoke-jets and can provide excellent coverage.

Regardless of the emitter style, clogging can be a problem if the water supply is not filtered at the point it enters the irrigation system. It is especially recommended that water from wells be filtered. The safest and easiest way to maintain the emitters in a microirrigation system is to keep a small supply of clean back-ups on hand. Clogged devices can be easily replaced with clean units and then placed in a small container of the cleaning fluid appropriate for the clogging material. Periodic flushes of poly pipe laterals should remove accumulated precipitates and biological growths.

With other systems, water should be applied only as fast as the soil can absorb it. Using a hose with water pressure at full force can do more damage than good. Fast-flowing water runs off quickly, carrying away soil and exposing plant roots to direct sunlight. Watering with sprinklers is more efficient. Whether using a sprinkler attached to a hose or an automatic sprinkler system in the ground, the efficiency of the system depends on how well it is managed. A hose-end sprinkler may be placed anywhere in the landscape and allowed to run until it has delivered 3/4 inch of water. If the sprinkler is moved too soon, water will not reach the root zone. If the sprinkler runs too long, water will pass through the root zone and be wasted.

Sprinkler systems may be operated with a time clock or soil sensor; they may also be manually controlled. Scheduling irrigation with a time clock is easy but wasteful. The time clock turns on the system in rain or sunshine, irrespective of whether the plants need water. Soil-moisture sensors often require a lot of maintenance to remain accurate. A sprinkler system may be manually controlled by setting the time clock to the "off" position and switching the system on when the plants need water. The automatic position on the time clock is useful when you are away from home for more than a few days. By installing a shutoff device that overrides the system when rain falls, you can make the clock operate even more efficiently.

## Drought-Tolerant Plants

Using drought-tolerant plants is another way of conserving water in the home landscape. In areas where it is difficult to apply enough water, such as on sandy soil or terrain from which water drains rapidly, drought-tolerant plants offer an alternative. They are also a good choice in areas of the yard that cannot be easily reached with a hose.

## Tips for Conserving Water

- Control all weeds. Weeds use water that would otherwise be available for desirable plants.

- Reduce the number of fertilizer applications. Fertilizer promotes plant growth, increasing the need for water.

- Don't over prune. This leads to plants with too much tender growth demanding more water. Also, prune less frequently.

- Confine planting times to the season of the year when water demands during establishment will be least.

- Apply wetting agents to the soil to allow it to absorb water uniformly and to prevent dry spots.

- Use 2 to 3 inches of mulch on entire beds of shrubs, trees, annuals and herbaceous perennials.

- Extend the number of days or weeks between water applications to the longest suitable interval.

- Water less frequently but soak deeply to encourage deep root growth.

- Cull plants that are growing poorly. Don't waste water caring for marginal or undesirable plants.

- Use reclaimed water in your irrigation system if you live in an area that provides it.

- Adjust hose-end or in-ground sprinklers to avoid spraying water into gutters or onto sidewalks, driveways and streets. With automated systems, make test runs at least weekly to be certain the system is operating properly. When systems run only in the early morning hours, you may not know when they malfunction.

- Keep sprinkler heads clean to ensure uniform water distribution.

- Use rain shut-off devices to shut a system down during rainfall.

- Check hose and faucet washers annually, replacing them when worn.

*— Robert J. Black and Gary W. Knox*

# MULCHES
# for the Landscape

A mulch is any material applied to the soil surface for protection or improvement of the area covered. Mulches are usually applied around plants to beautify plant beds, to modify the soil environment and to enhance plant growth. The mulch material may be organic, such as bark, wood chips, leaves, pine needles, grass clippings or other biodegradable matter. Inorganic mulches do not decompose and include gravel, pebbles, ground rubber tires, polyethylene film and woven ground cloth.

## Benefits of Mulching

Mulch, when correctly applied, has the following beneficial effects upon the soil and plants:

- Mulches can prevent loss of water from the soil by evaporation. Moisture moves by capillary action to the surface and evaporates if the soil is not covered by a mulch.

- Mulches suppress weeds when the mulch material itself is weed-free and applied deeply enough to prevent weed germination or to smother existing small weeds.

- Mulches can maintain a more uniform soil temperature. The mulch acts as an insulator that keeps the soil cool under intense sunlight and warm during cold weather.

- Mulching will prevent crusting of the soil surface, thus improving the absorption and movement of water into the soil while at the same time reducing erosion.

- Mulching can prevent soil splash, which not only stops erosion but keeps soil-borne disease from splashing up onto a plant.

- Mulches composed of organic materials can improve soil structure. As mulch decays, the material becomes topsoil. Decaying mulch may also add nutrients to the soil.

- Mulches can add to the beauty of the landscape by providing a cover of uniform color and interesting texture to the surface.

- Mulched plants will produce roots in the mulch that surrounds them. These roots are produced in addition to the roots that a plant produces in the soil. As a result, mulched plants have more roots than unmulched plants.

## Organic Mulching Materials
### Yard "Trash"

Florida law prohibits disposal of pine needles, leaves, grass clippings and plant trimmings in lined landfills. These leftovers are usually placed at curbside and collected separately from the rest of our garbage for municipal disposal by burning, composting, or burial in an unlined landfill. Much of this yard trash can be recycled at home as mulch with the added advantage of retaining for your landscape the nutrients found in these organic materials. At-home recycling is also more efficient and helps save tax dollars otherwise spent in transporting and disposing of the yard trash.

Pine needles, leaves and grass clippings can be used as mulch either alone or in combination with each other. Of the three, pine needles are the best mulching material. They are attractive, not easily removed from beds by wind or rain and don't mat down excessively. However, they rarely last more than 6 months due to rapid decomposition. Leaves can be used alone as a mulch but tend to blow away in windy locations and are easily washed from beds during heavy rain showers. Leaves do best as a mulching material when they are shredded. Grass clippings are the least desirable mulching material. They are easily transported by the wind, decompose very rapidly and pack down to form a mat that can exclude air and water from the root zone. They should be spread thinly over the ground, mixed with other mulching materials or, best of all, composted with other yard waste. Plant trimmings such as twigs and small branches should be shredded before they are used as a mulch. A mechanical chipper/shredder is needed for this process.

Leaves, grass clippings and prunings are readily available in many landscapes and thus are a very inexpensive source of mulch. However, there is some reluctance to use them because they are not as attractive as some commercial mulch materials. This problem can be overcome by adding a thin layer of a more uniform mulch over the recycled materials. Some people also worry that weed seed may be distributed with home-made mulch. If this is a concern, yard clippings may be partially composted. In the composting process, the compost pile heats and inactivates most weed seed. However, after partially composting yard trash, use a rake to select out the larger particles (i.e. over 1 1/2 inches) for mulch. The use of smaller particles as mulch could smother roots of landscape plants by reducing soil aeration.

## Cypress Mulch

In spite of being expensive, cypress mulch is a very popular mulching material. Much of its popularity is due to its attractiveness and longevity. Cypress mulch appears to have a high water-holding capacity that may reduce the amount of water reaching the plant root zone. However, once the mulch is thoroughly wet, it buffers the soil against soil-water evaporative losses. When dry, cypress mulch repels water, making it difficult to wet, particularly if it is on a mound or slope.

With a new awakening to the importance of protecting Florida wetlands, recharge areas and wildlife habitat sanctuaries, the harvesting of cypress solely for use as mulch is now being discouraged. This has led to the evaluation of alternative materials and the growing of certain species specifically for mulch.

## Pine Bark

Pine bark makes an attractive, usually dark-colored landscape mulch. It can be purchased in various particle sizes, from shredded to large-size particles 1 1/2 to 3 inches in diameter (called "nuggets" or "chunks"). Shredded pine bark doesn't float away like nuggets.

## Wood Chips

Wood chips are obtained when the bark is removed from logs of pine, eucalyptus, melaleuca and other trees. This material contains bark and pieces of wood of various sizes and makes an attractive mulch. Because the wood will decompose more rapidly than the bark, a wood chip mulch does not last as long as one composed solely of bark.

## Straw

Straw can be used as a mulch but it is not attractive, decomposes rapidly, and may contain seeds that will germinate and produce weeds in the landscape.

## Pecan Shells

Pecan shells make a long lasting, attractive, dark brown mulch that is effective in retaining moisture in the soil. Availability is usually limited to areas where pecans are processed.

## Peanut Hulls

Peanut hulls can be obtained in areas where peanuts are processed. Because of their light color they are not as attractive as other mulching materials. They also may contain weed seed and lesion nematodes.

# Inorganic Mulching Materials

## Gravel, Pebbles & Crushed Stone

Gravel, pebbles and crushed stone are permanent, fireproof and may be colored to blend in with the features of the home, patio or landscape. When used near a lawn, there is some danger that lawn mowers will pick up and throw the stones. These materials reflect solar radiation and can create a very hot landscape environment during the summer months.

## Ground Rubber Tires

A relative newcomer to the consumer market, mulch made of ground rubber tires claims never to need replacing as it does not decompose. Its effectiveness as a mulch is still being evaluated.

## Plastic Film

Black polyethylene film is very effective in preventing weed growth. However, clear or translucent plastic film will not suppress weed growth because light penetrates the film. Cover plastic film with a layer of mulch such as wood chips or pine needles to reduce heat absorption and to mask its artificial appearance. Plastic films are not recommended for poorly-drained areas as they may cause the soil to remain too wet, which could result in root disease problems. They are also not suited for steep slopes as rain water will wash away organic matter applied over them.

## Woven Ground Cloth

Materials woven of either plastic or fabric are available in various lengths and widths. The fabric materials are treated to resist decomposition. Unlike the plastic films, woven materials allow water and air to move through them. They are very effective in controlling most weeds, although sedges and some grasses grow up through the holes in the fabric. They do little to prevent water loss from the soil or moderate soil temperature.

Fabric ground cloths need to be fastened down so they will not be pushed up by perennial weeds. Better moisture, temperature and weed control can by obtained by adding several inches of another mulching material on top of both the plastic and the fabric ground cloths.

## Where to Use Mulch

Mulching is an extremely important practice for establishing plantings as it helps to conserve moisture in the root ball of the new plant until its roots have grown out into the adjacent landscape soil. Without the competition for water and nutrients from turf and weeds, the growth rate and health of trees and shrubs increases. Mulch also helps to prevent tree trunk injury by mowers and line trimmers. Mulch entire beds of shrubs, trees, annuals, herbaceous perennials and/or ground covers.

In addition to benefiting plants, mulch can be employed as a ground cover for walks, trails, driveways, and play and natural areas. This makes less impact on tree roots than would hard concrete surfaces. By allowing for more even water percolation, it is also less disruptive to drainage patterns on a site. Light weight mulch such as pine straw or grass clippings can be used temporarily to cover low-growing tender plants to protect them from frost injury. Organic mulch can also be composted and used as a soil amendment.

## When and How Often to Mulch

Mulch can be applied around established plants at any time. Newly-set plants should be mulched immediately after they are planted, then thoroughly watered. Fall is an excellent time to collect fallen leaves and pine needles as mulch.

Organic mulches will gradually decompose and need replenishing to function effectively as a mulch. Shallow plant roots grow up and into moist mulch and they will die if the mulch is allowed to decay or wash away. How often mulch needs to be replenished will depend on the mulching material. Grass clippings and leaves decompose very rapidly and need to be replenished frequently. Other organic mulches such as cypress mulch and pine bark break down very slowly and need only be replenished to maintain a 3-inch depth. Once plants in a ground cover or shrub bed have formed a solid mass by

touching one another, the mulching requirement is reduced. The plants create their own mulch by dropping leaves, flowers and fruit. Leaves from surrounding trees also may fall in the beds and provide additional free mulch.

Most organic mulches will change from their original colors to a weathered grey color with age. There are several ways of restoring color to mulches. One approach is to apply a thin (1 inch or less) layer of fresh mulch to the surface of the existing mulch (never exceed 2 to 3 inches total depth). This approach is labor intensive, expensive and can result in an excessively thick mulch layer. Another approach is to shallow rake the existing mulch to restore a freshly mulched appearance. Because roots grow up into the mulch, care must be exercised when raking so that roots are not torn up or otherwise disturbed. A third choice is to use a mulch colorant. Mulch colorants are dyes that are sprayed on the mulch to restore its color. Manufacturers claim they are harmless to both plants and animals, but applicators should use them cautiously as they can cause skin and eye irritation. Dyes may also stain sidewalks and other surfaces.

Inorganic mulches such as gravel, pebbles and stones are considered permanent mulches and rarely need replenishing. Still, small particles will eventually move down into the soil, and a thin layer of new material may need to be added. To maintain a neat appearance, leaves and other debris need to be regularly removed from the surface of inorganic mulch.

## How to Apply Mulch

Spread a layer of mulching materials over the entire plant bed. When mulching individual trees planted out in lawns, create a circle of mulch about 2 feet in diameter for each inch of trunk diameter. (Measure trunk diameter 6 inches up from the ground.) Increase the size of the mulched area as the tree grows.

Pull mulch 2 to 3 inches away from the stems and trunks of plants. If mulch is placed too close, the high moisture environment it creates will increase the chance of stem or trunk rot which can result in plant death. Keep mulch pulled 6 to 12 inches back from the walls of buildings. Subterranean termites, which are found throughout Florida, nest in the soil and feed on wood and other materials that contain cellulose. Because termite treatments are applied to the soil around houses and buildings, keeping mulch pulled back from walls will prevent termites from using it as a bridge to cross treated soil.

## How Deep to Apply Mulch

The amount of mulch to apply will depend on the texture and density of the mulch. Many wood and bark mulches are composed of fine particles and should not be more than 2 to 3 inches deep after settling. Excessive amounts of these fine-textured mulches around shallow-rooted plants can suffocate their roots causing yellowing of foliage (chlorosis) and poor growth. Coarse-textured mulches such as pine needles and pine bark nuggets allow good air movement through them and can be maintained as deep as 4 inches.

Mulches composed solely of shredded leaves, small leaves (i.e. the size of oak leaves) or grass clippings should never be deeper than 2 inches. These materials have flat surfaces and tend to mat together, restricting the water and air supply to plant roots. Rather than raking, which can damage the root systems that have grown into the mulch, punching the mulched area

with a pitchfork will counteract the suffocating effects of matted mulches. This method should not be used where plastic or woven ground cloth has been laid down under mulch as the holes left by the pitchfork will give weeds a growth path. Instead, rake the surface of the mulch gently to ventilate the mulch.

## How Much to Buy

If you are going to buy mulch, you need to calculate the area and the desired depth of coverage to determine how many cubic feet of mulch you should purchase. Bulk quantities of mulch are sold in cubic yard volumes.

First, determine the square foot measurement of the shrub or tree area(s) to be mulched. For instance, if you have a shrubbery border 4 feet wide and 25 feet long, the area to be mulched equals 100 square feet (4 feet x 25 feet = 100 square feet).

Next, if you are going to apply mulch 3 inches deep to this area, convert the 3 inches to a fraction of a foot. Three inches divided by 12 inches equals 1/4 foot. Multiply this fraction by the square foot measurement of the area to be covered. In this example, you will need 25 cubic feet of mulch (1/4 foot x 100 square feet = 25 cubic feet).

One cubic yard measures 3 feet by 3 feet by 3 feet which equals 27 cubic feet. In the example just given, the 25 cubic feet you need is 2 cubic feet less than one cubic yard. Before you purchase mulch in bulk and buy an entire cubic yard, compare the cost with purchasing your mulch in smaller units. Bagged mulch is available in volumes such as 1.25 cubic feet or 2 cubic feet. In the shrubbery example given above, you will need 20 bags of mulch if you buy the 1.25 cubic foot bags (25 cubic feet ÷ 1.25 feet =

20 bags). If you purchase the 2 cubic foot bags, you will need 12.5 bags (25 cubic feet ÷ 2 cubic feet = 12.5 bags). You will therefore end up buying 13 bags.

However, as discussed above, remember that you will be pulling mulch 2 to 3 inches away from the stems and trunks of plants to lessen the chances of stem or trunk rot. Consequently, whether the shrubs are single or multi-stemmed, you will not need all of the mulch determined above; the calculations did not include either the area used by the stems and/or low branches, or the extra 2 to 3 inches around the stem(s). This means you can purchase less mulch than the calculations indicate. If you are using an organic mulch and buy more bags than you need, return the extras for a refund if possible as organic mulches will decompose in the bag. Inorganic mulches may be stored.

— *Robert J. Black, Edward F. Gilman, Gary W. Knox and Kathleen C. Ruppert*

# A GUIDE to Composting

The environmentally friendly landscape will have a spot for a compost pile. Although pine needles, leaves, clippings and other plant materials left over from landscape maintenance are often suited for use as mulch (see *Mulches for the Landscape*), they can also be converted to compost. During the composting process, the high internal temperatures of the compost pile will kill most weed seeds and pathogens. A properly tended compost pile does not smell bad, and properly prepared and applied compost will return valuable nutrients to the landscape and/or garden.

Composting yard trash and other organic household wastes (see Table 1) not only provides the home gardener with a free, high quality soil amendment but also conserves the energy and money consumed by disposal companies and their equipment. Composting is both a sensible and an environmentally positive practice.

**Table 1. What and what not to use in the compost pile.**

**DO USE**
Yard and garden waste[1]

| | |
|---|---|
| Leaves and twigs | Weeds and other garden waste |
| Chipped and shredded branches | Grass clippings (which also do good if left on |
| Small wood chips | the lawn) |

Kitchen waste

| | |
|---|---|
| Fruits and vegetables, including peels and seeds | Coffee grounds and tea leaves |
| Egg shells and nut shells | |

Other materials

| | |
|---|---|
| Hay or straw | Sawdust and woodshavings |
| Hair | Manure (but not from humans or pets) |
| Seaweed (rinsed) | |

**DO NOT USE[2]**

| | |
|---|---|
| Meat, bones and animal fats | Dairy products |
| Oils and oily scraps (such as leftover salad with dressing, baked goods containing oil or fat, etc.) | |

[1] Keep disease-ridden clippings and prunings out of the compost pile.
[2] These items are slow to decompose and may attract animal scavengers or other pests.

A little space, time and effort are required to make and maintain a compost pile. Though a variety of compost bins can be purchased or fabricated and a number of other composting aids are available commercially, successful odor-free composting can be achieved with nothing more than a pitch fork, a water supply, your composting materials and the information that follows.

## How Compost Happens

Organic materials break down and become compost thanks to the efforts of a host of living organisms. Conditions in the compost pile determine which organisms are multiplying and doing the work. The types of organisms present in turn affect how fast the composting process happens and whether there is any smell. Fortunately, the fastest and best composting method is also the odorless one.

The bacteria that go to work in the initial stages of decomposition arrive in the compost pile on the organic matter you place there. If you structure and maintain your compost pile so as to keep it aerobic (oxygenated), certain groups of bacteria are activated with such intensity that they ultimately produce enough heat to kill pathogens, parasites and most weed seeds. A compost pile is kept oxygenated by turning it frequently with a pitch fork.

While the compost pile needs to be kept moist, too much air is lost if moisture content is over 60%. (Anaerobic or oxygen-deprived conditions invite the bacteria that cause the compost pile to smell.) If you can squeeze drops of water from a handful of your compost, it is too wet. The compost pile must not be too dry, either. Bacteria start to become dormant when moisture is less than 40%. Your compost materials should feel moist to the touch. Water each

layer of material as you build your pile, and be sure your pile (or the bin it is in) is constructed in a way that allows for drainage.

In addition to oxygen and water, the microbes doing the composting require a balanced diet, preferably one that contains about 30 parts carbon to 1 part nitrogen (a C:N ratio of 30:1). The trick with a compost heap is understanding the carbon:nitrogen content of each of your ingredients (see Table 2) and then creating a recipe that incorporates the necessary amounts of oxygen, moisture, carbon and nitrogen. And, remember, the smaller the pieces your compost materials are in, the more surface area for the bacteria to work on and the faster the composting process. Using a chipper/shredder on twigs and branches larger than 1/4 inch in diameter, fibrous palm fronds and leaves, especially waxy types such as oak and magnolia, will help speed up decomposition. Whole fruits and vegetables will also compost faster if cut into small pieces before going into the compost pile. (A shovel makes quick work of chopping up large kitchen scraps.)

The compost pile will go through several phases. Different types of bacteria that thrive in different temperature ranges are largely responsible for the early stages of the decomposition process. While each of these types is present in the compost pile at any given moment, their numbers will increase or decrease depending on how favorable conditions are for the particular type. Given enough oxygen, the right amount of moisture and a favorable C:N ratio, there is a natural progression of each type needed. **Cryophilic** (also called **psychrophilic**) **bacteria** function in temperatures as low as 0° F but are most efficient around 55° F. The heat they give off or an increase in the ambient temperature makes the pile hospitable to the **mesophilic bacteria**, which do most of the decomposition work and thrive between 70° F and 90° F. In the wake of the mesophiles, **thermophilic bacteria** take over. They work at temperatures ranging from 104° F up to 200° F and, left undisturbed, can turn fresh and partially decomposed organic matter to a rich, dark brown color in 3 to 5 days.

At mid-range temperatures, organisms known as actinomycetes also become active in great number. Hardly larger than bacteria, actinomycetes are fungi that announce their presence with greyish cobwebby growths and a pleasant, earthy smell. While bacteria and actinomycetes predominate in the early, warm stages of the compost pile, other microbes, fungi and invertebrates also take part in the composting process. Some are active in the heating cycle, but most prefer the cooler temperatures of later decomposition. These include mushrooms and other fungi, beneficial nematodes, mold mites, springtails, wolf spiders, centipedes and millipedes, sow bugs, ground beetles, worms and snails. See *Insects and Other Organisms* for more information on some of these organisms.

# Making and Maintaining a Compost Pile

The space for a compost pile must measure at least 3 feet in each direction: side to side, front to back and from the ground up. The best location will be a partly sunny spot that is well drained, protected from drying winds and near a source of running water. Remember to consider accessibility and aesthetics. Try to make it easy to get materials to and from the compost pile. Though a compost pile is not necessarily an eyesore, it's not much to look at, either, and you may want to screen it from view.

The compost pile itself can be maintained with or without any housing. Very effective bins can be made from wood pallets, wire or concrete blocks stacked to allow for ventilation. Commercially made bins offer various features related to looks and convenience. Whether home-made or store-bought, a bin should be sturdy and allow for drainage and easy turning. Remember that an area **no less** than 3 feet by 3 feet by 3 feet is required for composting.

**Table 2. Carbon to nitrogen ratios of various compost materials[1].**

| MATERIAL | CARBON TO NITROGEN RATIO |
|---|---|
| Grass clippings | 20 to 1 |
|    if young, tender grass | 12 to 1 |
| Weeds and spent garden plants | 20 to 1 |
| Rotted (bagged) manures | 20 to 1 |
|    if fresh (caution: has smell) | 14 to 1 |
| Seaweed (rinse before adding) | 19 to 1 |
| Fruit and vegetable waste | 35 to 1 |
| Leaves | 60 to 1 |
| Straw | 100 to 1 |

[1] An overall Carbon:Nitrogen ratio of 30:1 is desired.

Begin the compost pile by alternating layers of nitrogen-rich materials (those with a lower carbon to nitrogen ratio) with those that have a high carbon to nitrogen ratio (see Table 2). (Adding large amounts of seed-bearing weeds or diseased plants is not recommended for compost that is to be used in a garden.) Apply water to each 3- to 4-inch layer. Or, mix all the ingredients together and water. The compost material should be wet, but not so wet that you can squeeze water from it. In hot or dry weather, check the pile daily to see if it needs more water.

Every 3 to 5 days (or when the internal temperature rises to 140°F or drops below 100°F), turn the pile with a pitchfork or shovel. When the pile no longer generates any heat and its material is dark brown to black with no identifiable plant parts, the compost is mature and ready to use.

## How to Use Compost

Compost may be used as a soil amendment in landscape beds and vegetable gardens. Compost not only adds small amounts of nutrients to the soil, but also:

- makes soil easier to cultivate
- helps sandy soil retain moisture
- aerates and improves drainage of clay soils
- increases the buffering capacity of the soil
- increases the biological activity of earthworms and other soil organisms
- allows the soil to hold more plant nutrients for longer periods of time
- in some cases reduces soil pests such as nematodes.

— *compiled by Donna Mitchell*

# INTEGRATED Pest Management

Americans spend millions of dollars each year on pesticides and pest control services. Here in Florida, where our subtropical climate provides the perfect haven for insect pests, diseases, weeds and nematodes, our use of pesticides probably exceeds the nation's average.

Concerns about health and ecological impacts are causing us to reconsider how and where pesticides are used. The old approach of routinely blanketing the landscape with pesticides has been replaced with a strategy called **integrated pest management** or **IPM**. IPM relies heavily on correct gardening practices, careful monitoring of the landscape and use of biological controls. While pesticides remain part of an IPM program, care is taken to select the safest ones and apply them only to affected plants. Production agriculture is successfully adopting IPM, and homeowners and landscape professionals can do the same. In the process, pesticide use can be dramatically reduced.

## Practicing Integrated Pest Management

Begin by planting a combination of different plants, particularly native species. The idea is to create an ecosystem whose diversity invites the natural balance of birds, beneficial insects and other wildlife that help keep pests under control. The good health of the landscape is also essential as pests are attracted to stressed and weakened plants. Use native species that are adapted to their environment and prepared to flourish under conditions that can stress or even kill exotics. Keep plants strong and healthy by building healthy soil with compost (see *A*

*Guide to Composting*), manure and organic fertilizer (which will last longer in the soil and is less likely to run off into streams, lakes or storm drains). A vigorous and diverse landscape is your first and most important defense against pests.

Here are some other common sense ways to practice IPM:

**Remember the "right plant/right spot" rule.** A plant growing in adverse conditions is prone to disease and insect problems. No amount of spraying will make pests go away as long as the site conditions are unfavorable. An example of the wrong plant in the wrong spot would be grass in dense shade or an azalea in full sun.

**Observe planting dates.** Vegetables and flowering annuals have short life spans and can only be grown during specific seasons. Growing these plants out of season spells failure. Avoid, for instance, planting petunias, a winter annual, in May or a fall/winter vegetable like cabbage, in July.

**Avoid excessive fertilizer and water.** Moderate amounts of both maintain the quality of your lawn and landscape. Too much will invite insects and diseases such as root rots, chinch bugs and brown patch disease. Like pesticides, excess fertilizer can find its way into lakes, rivers and streams, either by run-off or by leaching (being flushed down through the soil).

**Mow and prune properly.** Leaves, not fertilizer, provide food to plants. Leaves capture the sun's energy and convert it to food for growth and flowering. Mowing grass too short and shearing too much foliage from shrubs will weaken them and invite pest problems. Learn the mowing and pruning practices that apply to the turf and plants in your landscape.

**Scout your lawn and landscape frequently.** Walk around your yard and look for spotted or yellowing leaves. Frequent scouting allows you to identify and treat problems before they get out of hand. (See the introduction to *Insects and Other Organisms*.)

**Get to know "key plants/key pests."** By scouting your landscape, you will soon learn to recognize which of your plants are problem prone. These key plants may have particular pests (key pests) that plague them on a recurring basis. Learn about the life cycles and natural enemies of key pests like lacebugs on azaleas and caterpillars on oleander.

**Use mechanical pest control methods.** Most diseases and insect problems can be reduced or eliminated by hand-picking or pruning off affected leaves or plant parts. The heel of your shoe can be an effective form of pest control!

**Protect beneficial organisms.** Broad spectrum pesticides such as dursban, diazinon, malathion, rotenone, pyrethrum and Sevin kill many kinds of insects, good and bad. (Note that so-called organic pesticides like rotenone and pyrethrum are as lethal to beneficials as some inorganic pesticides.) Purchase biorational pesticides such as insecticidal soaps, horticultural oils and *Bacillus thuringiensis*. These materials are less harmful to beneficials and are safe for people, animals and the environment. Learn to recognize beneficial insects such as lady beetles, lady beetle larvae, lacewings, earwigs and many more (see the list in *Insects and Other Organisms*).

**Tolerate a few pests and a little damage.** Attempting to maintain a pest-free landscape is impractical and a waste of time and money. It also wipes out the food source of beneficial organisms. A few bad guys are necessary to keep the good guys around. Meanwhile, most plants can survive very well even after losing as much as 25% of their leaf surface.

**Buy knowledge, not pesticides.** If a professional company maintains your lawn and landscape, insist they apply pesticides only as needed and only to affected plants. Request spot treatments of problems, and don't allow routine blanket sprays. **Remember that with pesticides, more is not better.** Ask for an IPM option that includes a scouting service. Pay for expertise, not chemicals.

— *Sydney Park Brown*

# THE TRUTH About Trees

Numerous misperceptions about trees and their care abound and are passed around. Following are some truths about trees and tree care which include discussions based on current research findings.

## Tree Roots

### Most trees do not have taproots.

The deep roots that grow directly beneath the trunks of some trees are known as taproots. Taproots may develop on some trees in the woods in well-drained soils. Taproots generally do not form on trees planted in urban landscapes nor do they develop when the soil is compacted or the water table is close to the soil surface. Some oaks and pines will develop taproots when planted in sandy, well-drained soils.

### Roots grow far beyond the edge of the branches.

A tree growing in the woods has a root system reaching well beyond the outer perimeter of its branches, often to a distance from the trunk equal to the tree's height. Roots on trees and shrubs planted in a landscape grow to about 3 times the branch spread within 2 or 3 years after planting.

### Damaging roots on one side of a tree may cause branch dieback either on that side only or at random throughout the crown.

Unless the trunk is twisted, roots on one side of a tree such as oak or mahogany generally supply the same side of the crown with water and nutrients absorbed through the roots. When roots on one side of a tree are injured, branches on that side will often drop leaves. When trees such as the maples and rosewood receive damage on one side of the root system, branch death may occur anywhere in the crown of the tree.

### Root pruning does not stimulate root branching all the way back to the trunk.

Roots are often pruned before moving a tree in hopes of creating a denser root ball. However, most root growth after root pruning occurs at the end of the root just behind the root pruning cut, not further back toward the trunk. This means that you should dig the root ball of a recently root pruned tree several inches beyond where it was root pruned. If root pruning will be conducted only once before transplanting, do it 6 to 10 weeks before moving the field-grown or landscape tree. Some quality tree nurseries root prune each year to prepare a tree for transplanting.

### Roots circling around inside a container do not continue to grow in a circle once the tree is planted in the landscape.

Unless the container is specially designed, roots frequently circle within the perimeter of a container several times before the tree is planted into the landscape. The portion of the root which grew in the container does not straighten out, but new growth on this root will usually not continue to circle. Circling roots should be cut at planting to prevent eventual girdling and strangling of the trunk.

### Most roots are in the top 3 feet of soil. The finer roots are concentrated in the top foot of soil.

Most tree roots are located within the top 3 feet of soil. In well-drained soil, some roots grow 10 feet or deeper directly beneath the trunk. However, because the majority of the fine roots are concentrated in the top foot of soil, minor soil disturbances can injure or remove a large portion of the absorbing roots on a tree. Especially vulnerable are trees growing near construction sites.

# Construction Around Trees

**Injuries inflicted by heavy equipment during construction (or at any other time) can cause major and permanent damage to the tree.**

Because a tree does not replace injured tissue (heal) like an animal does, a wound or injury to its trunk, branches or roots permanently reduces the tree's capacity to fend off insects, disease or other potential stresses. Many roots are destroyed when heavy equipment operates over the root system. Even one pass over the root system with a bulldozer, earth scraper or other piece of heavy equipment can cause significant root damage. Equipment should not be permitted to operate within the dripline of trees which are to be saved.

**To save a tree during construction, do not disturb soil beneath the branch dripline.**

Because 50% of a tree's root system is located between its trunk and its dripline, sturdy fences should be constructed at the dripline to prevent equipment and vehicles from operating in or crossing over this sensitive area. Tree roots extend much further than the dripline. However, it is usually not practical to protect the entire root area. Protecting the area within the dripline and good irrigation management are the most important measures in helping prevent construction related tree decline.

**Grading to prepare a site for laying sod or planting shrubs can harm trees.**

Since many of a tree's fine roots are located close to the soil surface, changing the soil grade by as little as 6 inches can cause extensive damage to its root system. Design your landscape to fit the existing grade. If significant grade changes must be made close to a tree, the best course may be to remove the tree and plant several younger, healthy trees. However, a certified arborist

may be able to devise a system to save trees on construction sites.

**Building a tree well around the trunk of a tree will not help save a tree from the effects of fill soil.**

Never remove soil from or add a large amount of soil to the area within the dripline of a tree. Three or four inches of soil can be added to small areas under the tree provided the added soil has a coarser texture than existing soil. Building a wall (commonly called a tree well) several feet from the trunk then adding more than 3 or 4 inches of soil outside the well often kills the tree by suffocating most roots growing beyond the tree well. If a tree well is to be used, construct it no closer to the tree than the dripline and grade the soil outside of the well to prevent runoff water from entering the well. Success has been reported in several cases where gravel was spread over an existing grade, and vertical vent pipes were installed every 10 feet to supply the roots with oxygen. Coarse textured fill soil was then carefully spread over a soil-separator fabric that had been placed over the gravel. Hire a certified arborist to conduct this specialized work.

**If a tree survives the first 2 to 4 years following construction, it may still die from construction related injuries.**

Trees may decline quickly or slowly after construction of a building. Often, branches begin dying within a year or two due to severe root damage. The tree may be dead within 3 or 4 years. However, it is not uncommon for trees to show a slow decline over a 5 to 15 year period. Even if a tree does not show obvious signs of decline for many years, branches may quickly lose leaves and begin a rapid decline following a drought period. A year or two later, the tree may be dead.

# Tree Trunk and Branch Structure

**A trunk with a crook in it is just as strong as a straight one.**
Trunks with slight doglegs, crooks or bends are not weaker than those which are straight. This is a normal development on many trees, especially oaks. Healthy trees will grow out of this condition, and the trunk will appear straighter as it grows larger in diameter.

**Branches that remain smaller than half the trunk diameter are more securely attached to the tree than are larger branches.**
Branches growing in a horizontal orientation are usually smaller in diameter and well secured to trunks. Branches with diameters that are large in proportion to the trunk can become poorly attached. A branch growing in an upright manner parallel to the trunk becomes a second trunk, and the tree is said to have a double leader. Double leaders often form included or embedded bark in the crotch. This can be dangerous because the tree can easily split during a storm.

**Topping a tree creates a dangerous tree.**
Topping or rounding over is the practice of shearing off the top of a tree, thus removing branches and stems without regard to tree structure. Topping creates a hazardous tree because the wood inside the cut branch begins to decay. The cut stub is open and susceptible to decay organisms. The sprouts which grow in response to topping are not well secured to the topped branch, and they can easily split from the tree as they grow larger. When reducing the size of a tree, use a technique called drop-crotching. This involves pruning a branch back to a living branch that is at least half the diameter of the cut branch.

**A tree with multiple leaders (trunks) can become hazardous to people and property as the tree grows larger.**
Never allow large maturing trees to grow with multiple upright leaders. These trees may look handsome when young but can become hazardous as they grow older. Always prune large-maturing shade trees so that leaders or branches are spaced 18 to 36 inches apart along the main trunk.

# Pruning Trees

**Trees do not heal, but they are capable of isolating injured tissue from healthy wood.**
When trees are injured, they do not replace the cells lost in the injury. The swollen callus tissue developing around a trunk wound or pruning scar is simply closing over the injured tissue, not healing it. In order to stay alive, a tree must seal off injured tissue from its healthy portions. The storage capacity and functions of the injured parts are forever lost. Additional injuries seal off more wood, which further reduces the supply of available energy and can cause the tree to slowly starve.

**Never make a flush cut.**
Though standard practice was once to prune a branch flush with the trunk, extensive research has shown that this practice injures the trunk, is extremely detrimental to tree health and shortens a tree's life. Flush cuts make a tree more susceptible to frost cracks, heat injury, root problems, cankers and sprouting. Always cut to the outside of the branch collar. Usually located at the base of the branch and easily seen, the collar is the swelling where the branch meets the trunk. When properly done, a branch can be removed in its entirety without injury to the trunk.

**Rapid, thick callus growth around a pruned branch does not indicate the branch was pruned properly.**

The callus forming around a pruning scar often forms rapidly, regardless of the pruning technique. This tissue should form a ring or donut-shape if the branch was removed properly. If the callus is elongated or oval-shaped, the branch may have been pruned too closely to the trunk. Despite rapid callus formation around a pruning cut or injury, extensive wood rot can develop inside the tree.

**Wound dressings and pruning paints do not prevent wood rot.**

Wound dressings do not prevent wood decay behind a pruning cut. They provide no benefit to the tree. Some research indicates that wound dressings actually promote decay in certain situations. If pruning paints or wound dressings are to be used for cosmetic purposes, apply only a very thin coat. Only proper pruning practices prevent wood rot.

## Planting Trees

**Trees should be planted no deeper in landscape soil than they were in the nursery.**

Trees and shrubs should be planted at the same depth or slightly higher than they were in the nursery field soil or container medium. This allows for the quick root growth crucial to tree and shrub establishment. Planting too deeply slows root growth which can lead to poor establishment or death.

**Transplanted trees do not benefit from amending the backfill soil.**

The soil removed from the planting hole should be used to fill in around the root ball. No amendments need to be added to the backfill soil, since it does not improve sur-

vival or growth after planting. After transplanting, apply a layer of mulch 2 to 3 inches deep around the base of the tree and out to the dripline. Pull mulch back 2 to 3 inches from the tree trunk.

**Trees should not be pruned at transplanting to compensate for root loss.**

Pruning shoots and branches to compensate for root loss on transplanted trees is not recommended. The signal that initiates root regeneration originates in the shoot tips. Pruning removes shoot tips and can reduce root regeneration. Begin corrective pruning 1 year after planting. Correct major structural defects at planting if the tree will not be pruned for several years.

## Fertilizing Trees

**Established trees do not need to be fertilized with nitrogen in order to maintain their health.**

Because their root systems grow into fertilized shrub beds and lawn areas, established trees in a maintained landscape usually receive enough nitrogen fertilizer for moderate growth. In most instances, additional nitrogen is not necessary to maintain healthy trees. Some trees with micronutrient deficiencies respond to applications of minor elements. Other plants, especially palms, benefit from a slow-release potassium fertilizer. Phosphorus is rarely needed in a landscape fertilizer.

**Tree fertilizer does not need to be injected into the soil.**

Tree roots grow among lawn and shrub roots, many within the top 12 inches of soil. Fertilizer spread over the surface will reach tree, shrub and turf roots in adequate amounts. Soil injection may be beneficial in preventing fertilizer runoff on compact soils, slopes and berms.

**Fertilizing in the fall generally does not stimulate growth in the fall.**

Though crape myrtle and some other plants may grow in the fall in response to fall fertilization, many trees and shrubs will not respond to a fall application of fertilizer until the following year. Fall is an excellent time to fertilize trees and shrubs.

**Tree fertilizer is not tree food.**

Trees manufacture their own food. Fertilizers supply some of the elements necessary for trees to produce glucose, proteins and other materials that might be considered food, but fertilizer itself is not tree food.

— *Edward F. Gilman*

# HOW TO
## Select a Tree

Tree selection begins with choosing a species appropriate to your planting site (see *The Planting Site*). However, site conditions and maintenance capabilities will also dictate other choices, such as the size of tree to plant, its root ball characteristics, the method by which it was grown and the tree's structure. By examining nursery stock and asking questions of nursery personnel, you will greatly increase your tree's chance of surviving and flourishing.

Trees must also be selected for quality. Savings in cost at the expense of quality can result in trees that perform poorly in the landscape. Quality can be determined through thoughtful inspection. Quality factors to evaluate include root ball size and structure, trunk form and strength, branch structure and evidence of injury, disease or poor cultivation methods.

## Choosing the Right Tree Size

Table 3 outlines the important criteria for selecting trees for a planting site. Following these guidelines will also help you choose the appropriate size of tree.

Water must be supplied on a regular basis to newly planted trees; smaller trees will require regular irrigation for several months following planting, larger trees for much longer. If you cannot meet the watering requirements of a given tree, choose it in a smaller size (see Table 8, *Care During the Establishment Period*).

Site drainage also affects the size of tree you choose. On poorly drained sites, smaller trees with shallower root balls often do better than large nursery trees. A nursery tree is considered large if its trunk is more than 2 inches in diameter. (See Table 5 caption for where to take trunk measurement.) The larger root balls of big trees can become submerged in water on a poorly drained site. This will kill the roots at the base of the root ball and stress the tree, slowing the rate of establishment and thus making it more sensitive to pests, disease and drought injury. If large trees are absolutely necessary for a poorly drained site, select trees especially grown with a shallow root ball (see next section) or plant in a shallow hole to keep roots above the water level (see *Planting a Tree*).

## Root Ball Characteristics

The shape, depth and size of a tree's root ball is determined by the way the tree was produced in the nursery. Trees grown directly in the ground are called field-grown. The structure of the root ball of a field-grown tree depends on the soil type in which it grew, the water and drainage conditions in the field and the method used to dig up or harvest the tree. Trees may also be grown in containers that are made in sizes, shapes and materials that affect the structure of the root ball.

On many sites, the natural shape of a tree root system will be shallow and wide. This root ball structure is duplicated by growing trees in low profile containers, which are short and wide, or under field conditions where the subsoil is compacted or the water table is high. Low-profile root balls (Figure 3, left) are well suited to planting in poorly drained sites or compacted soils. Where soil is well aerated and well drained, root balls of any shape may be planted.

## Methods of Tree Production

When a tree will be planted in a well drained site and receive regular irrigation, the way it was produced is of little consequence. However, when watering will be infrequent, the method by which a tree was grown or harvested will affect its chances of surviving transplant (Table 4).

## Field-grown Trees

Field-grown trees that have been properly harvested and hardened off are strong and sturdy. They are good choices for any kind of site and usually the best choice for sites where watering will be infrequent or irregular. Compared to trees grown by other methods, the root ball of a harvested field-grown tree is larger and capable of more water storage, thus making it slower to dry out. The root balls of field grown trees are also much heavier than those of container grown trees, making them significantly harder to handle.

Field-grown trees that receive drip irrigation and fertilization near the base of the trunk during the first several years in the nursery's field will develop fine root growth near the trunk. This denser root system contributes to a healthy root ball.

Field-grown trees should be hardened off before going to market. By dealing with an established, reliable nursery, you minimize the risk of buying a field-grown tree that has not been hardened off. Hardened off trees

**Table 3. Comparing small-sized with large-sized nursery trees.[1]**

| CRITERIA | SMALL | LARGE (more than 2" trunk diameter) |
|---|---|---|
| Landscape establishment period | quick | slow |
| Irrigation period after planting | brief | extended |
| Susceptibility to drought | for a brief period after planting | very sensitive for a long time |
| Cost of nursery stock | inexpensive | expensive |
| Number of trees planted per dollars spent | large | small |
| Pruning needs[2] | high | moderate |
| Suitability for compacted or poorly-drained sites | well-suited | could be poorly-suited |

[1] This table applies regardless of the ultimate (or mature) height of the trees.

[2] Assuming good quality trees were purchased.

**Table 4. Choosing trees by production method**

| Production method | Root-ball weight | Need staking? | IF: Irrigation after planting is: | THEN: Root and trunk growth is: | AND: Survival is: |
|---|---|---|---|---|---|
| Plastic container | light | frequently | frequent | good to excellent | excellent |
| | | | infrequent | fair to good | fair |
| Fabric container | light to moderately heavy | usually | frequent | excellent | excellent |
| | | | infrequent | good** | good** |
| Balled-in-burlap | heavy | sometimes | frequent | excellent | excellent |
| | | | infrequent | good** | good** |
| Bare-root | light | usually | frequent | excellent | excellent |
| | | | infrequent | good** | good** |

* There is little research comparing bare-root trees with trees produced by other methods.
** Survival is good for trees hardened off in the nursery by pre-digging or root pruning several weeks to several months before planting. Survival and growth is only fair for fabric container-grown and balled-in-burlap trees dug and immediately transplanted in the landscape without frequent irrigation.

have had their roots pruned several weeks or months prior to being dug up. In the hardening off period, the newly harvested tree slows down the growth of its leaf shoots and can even drop leaves. Meanwhile, the root ball is regenerating new roots to replace those severed in pruning, and the tree is undergoing chemical changes that may make it hardier. During this time, the tree needs frequent and carefully managed irrigation, something a good nursery is equipped to handle. (Remember, a freshly dug tree which is not hardened off should not be planted in the landscape unless its special irrigation needs can be met. Certain palms such as the cabbage palm are exceptions to this rule and do not require hardening off.) Once they have been hardened off, field-grown trees are more tolerant than container grown trees of being transplanted into dry landscape soil.

When field-grown trees are harvested, their root balls are **balled-in-burlap**. That is,

burlap is wrapped around the root balls and secured with nails, string or wire. The root ball of a balled-in-burlap field-grown tree is fairly durable but care should be exercised to avoid breaking or crushing roots in transport and handling. (See "Preparing and Setting the Root Ball" in the chapter *Planting a Tree* for instructions on planting trees that have been balled-in-burlap.)

## Bare-Root Trees

As the name suggests, bare-root trees are sold with roots that are not encased in soil. They are field-grown, hardened off trees and are not commonly found in the Florida market. If their roots are kept shaded, moist and cool until planting, bare root trees should perform as well as container grown or balled-in-burlap trees. (See "Preparing and Setting the Root Ball" in the chapter *Planting a Tree* for further information on handling bare root trees.)

## Container-grown Trees

Container-grown trees have smaller root balls and many times more fine roots than similarly sized field-grown trees. For a variety of reasons, container-grown trees dry out more quickly, making them more sensitive to drought injury in the period following planting. (While trees planted from containers are more susceptible to desiccation and death if they do not receive enough water, they are less so than freshly dug trees that have not been hardened off.)

Root growth into landscape soil from container-grown trees appears to lag behind that of hardened off field-grown trees. The reason for this is not entirely clear but is probably related to the greater water stress experienced by container-grown trees following planting. Few trees planted from containers receive enough water following planting to encourage a swift rate of establishment.

Container-grown trees regenerate roots more slowly than hardened off field-grown trees. Shoot growth on container-grown trees appears to be similar to that of hardened off field-grown trees if sufficient irrigation is supplied until trees are established.

**Fabric containers or fabric bags** are made of a heavy flexible fabric especially designed for this growing method. Trees are planted in the fabric containers which are then planted into the ground. Small diameter roots penetrate the walls of the fabric containers and enter surrounding soil. However, these roots will be removed automatically when the tree is dug up by the nursery operator. The root balls of trees grown in fabric containers are about 50% smaller but contain about the same amount of roots as field-grown trees. Consequently, their root systems are denser than those of similarly sized field-grown trees. While their smaller size makes them easier to handle, they are

also more fragile and dry out faster than the root balls of field-grown trees that are balled-in-burlap.

Like field-grown trees, trees grown in fabric containers must receive carefully managed irrigation after digging and need to be hardened off in the nursery before planting into the landscape. The fabric container is cut from the root ball of the tree, which is then usually put in a plastic container before being sent to market. Some nurseries grow trees in fabric containers above ground. When this is the case, the trees will probably transplant more like container grown trees.

Trees are most commonly grown in **plastic containers** that are placed either above ground or, more recently, below ground and inside permanently installed containers with specially designed drainage holes. This latter method, known as pot-in-pot, insulates the root system and should produce roots that are more uniformly distributed than those found in above ground containers. Whether a containerized tree is grown above or below ground should not affect how it transplants, but few comparative tests on the subject have yet been published.

In a moist, humid climate like Florida's, containers are usually filled with an artificial or soil-less growing medium composed of one or more materials like bark, peat, compost and sand. These media are generally coarser than soil, which permits them to drain quickly and which, in turn, helps prevent root rot. Because of this rapid drainage, containerized trees require daily or more frequent irrigation in the summer.

When a container-grown tree is transplanted, moisture is drawn out of the container's growing medium into the more finely textured landscape soil causing the root ball to dry out even faster than it did in the container. To maintain optimum growth after planting, container trees should be watered at least as often as they were in the nursery. In the summer in Florida, **daily** irrigation (where soil is well drained) may be required for a number of weeks or months after planting, especially for trees whose trunks are over 2 inches in diameter. Watering can be tapered off as roots grow out into the landscape soil. (See *Care During the Establishment Period* for detailed watering instructions.)

**Standard plastic containers** have smooth sides and are about as deep as they are wide. Roots of trees in these containers frequently grow along the outside of the root ball and eventually encircle it. At the time of transplanting, all circling roots should be separated and straightened or cut (See Figure 15). This will prevent the roots from eventually girdling and strangling the trunk of the growing tree. (See "Checking the Root Ball for Defects" further on in this chapter and "Preparing and Setting the Root Ball" in the chapter *Planting a Tree*.)

**Low-profile containers** are short and wide, creating similarly shaped root balls (Figure 3, left) that are especially well suited to poorly drained sites and compacted soil. Circling roots pose less of a problem on trees grown in low-profile containers; if such roots do develop, they are far from the trunk. However, circling roots may be present if the tree was grown in a smaller container when it was young.

**Air-pruned containers** are designed with many holes in the sides and/or bottom of the container. Some are bottomless. Air entering the holes kills root tips growing outward and thus controls the growth of circling roots. Tip growth is forced inward, creating a root system that is superior to those on trees grown in standard containers.

**Copper-coated containers** have their inside surfaces coated with a copper compound

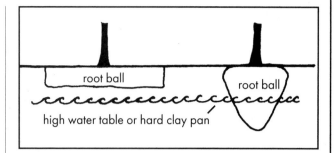

**Figure 3. Low profile root ball (left) and standard root ball (right).**

that prevents the formation of circling roots and thus creates a superior root ball. Early tests show that after planting into the landscape, trees grown in copper coated containers show root elongation and growth of shoots and trunk at rates similar to or slightly greater than those of trees grown in conventional containers.

## Nursery Collected Native Trees

Nurseries sometimes harvest trees from natural settings and replant them in fields for further cultivation. Generally, collected trees are dug with a tree spade, which is a tractor-sized piece of equipment.

Research on laurel oak in Florida indicates that the root balls on collected trees were similar to those on field-grown trees that hadn't been root pruned prior to transplanting. The only significant difference was that collected trees had slightly less fine root mass than trees grown in the nursery. They often had thinner canopies until they became established. The collected trees grew more slowly after transplanting than did trees produced by other methods, but all of them survived.

## Collecting Native Trees on Your Own

Before taking a tree from its natural setting, you will need to know the identity of the specimen you are collecting. You will want to be certain you are not harvesting a tree or plant that is protected or for some reason undesirable (i.e. invasive, poisonous, prone to overgrowth or otherwise noxious). Not infrequently, permits are required for removal of plants from the wild.

Secondly, you will need to learn the specific cultivation requirements of the species you are collecting. Most trees will need daily irrigation for several weeks after transplanting. As with nursery grown stock, your site and maintenance capabilities must be adequate for the tree's needs both at the time of transplant and establishment as well as at maturity.

## Checking the Root Ball for Defects

Some root ball defects are obvious, others require careful observation and inspection to discover. Because the health of a tree's root ball is critical to its ultimate survival, you may wish to patronize nurseries that allow you to remove trees from their pots (or will remove them for you) in order to examine the root balls. You will also want a nursery that knows what cultivation methods were used to grow their stock. Tree roots deformed within the first several months of propagation in the nursery can doom a tree, but the consequences of such root deformations may not become evident until the trees are older. A thorough inspection before planting will help prevent future disappointment.

One defect can be easily diagnosed without removing soil or the growing medium from the root ball. Remove any stakes from the tree and simply push the trunk back and forth once or twice while holding the root ball still. The trunk on a tree of good quality

**Figure 4. A good tree trunk bends and does not move in the soil (left) while a poor quality trunk bends little and pivots at or below the soil line (right).**

will bend along its length but will not move in the soil or medium (Figure 4, left). The trunk on a tree with a defective root system will pivot at its base before it bends or will appear to be loose in the root ball (Figure 4, right). A tree with this defect may not develop enough stability to hold itself up.

Next, check for the location of the top layer of the tree's roots, which should be very near the surface of the soil. Slip your fingers along the trunk and down into the soil until you feel the first root growing from the trunk. This should be no more than an inch or two below the surface of the soil. Sometimes trees have been planted too deeply either in the ground or in containers (Figure 5, right). Sometimes a nursery's cultivation equipment throws soil around the trunks of field-grown trees, raising the soil level. Whatever the cause, the raised soil level can hinder the tree's establishment in the landscape or can cause its decline several years later. If for some reason you are compelled to plant a tree with a raised soil level, remove all soil to expose the topmost root in the root ball. Plant the tree so that this root is just below the soil's surface (Figure 5, left). In extreme cases, you may have to remove as much as six inches of excess soil.

Check the main roots close to the tree's trunk. Using your fingers or a garden hose, go down about 4 inches and remove the soil or growing medium about 3 inches out all around the base of the trunk. This will not hurt the tree. With one-gallon sized root balls, you need only remove the media immediately adjacent to the base of the trunk. You are looking for kinked or circling roots close to the trunk and near the soil surface. If circling roots are tight up against the trunk, do not purchase the tree. Circling or kinked roots less than about one third the trunk diameter can be cut at the point where they begin to circle. This may temporarily slow growth but should have a positive impact on future tree survival and growth.

To further inspect the root ball of a **container grown tree**, first check the bottom of the container for escaping roots. There should be no evidence of escaping roots larger than about one-fifth the diameter of the trunk of the tree. (Smaller escaping roots may be cut off with little harm to the tree.) If the larger

roots exist and need to be cut to remove the tree from the container, the tree could suffer decline and leaf drop.

Once you have checked the container's bottom, lay the tree on its side. You should be able to simply slide the container off the root ball. If not, gently push the bottom of the container while holding the rim to loosen the root ball from the container. If this does not free the root ball, the tree may be pot-bound.

Once the tree is out of the container, the root ball should stay together but be somewhat pliable. You should be able to pick the root ball up and gently place it back in the container without its losing much medium. If the tree has many roots circling around the outside of the root ball or the root ball is very hard, it is said to be **pot-bound** or **root-bound**. A mass of circling roots on the outside of a root ball can act as a physical barrier to root penetration into the landscape soil after planting. The circling roots can also choke and kill the tree as it grows older. Do not purchase pot-bound plants.

With trees that are **balled-in-burlap**, note whether the root ball has been secured tightly with pins, twine or wire. A loose or droopy root ball indicates that the tree was not properly cared for and may perform poorly after planting. The tree's trunk should be sturdy in the root ball; if the trunk is

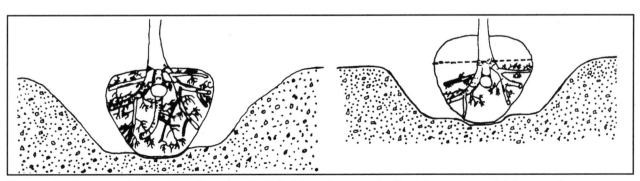

**Figure 5. A properly dug, quality root ball (left) and a root ball with excess soil (shown above dashed line) over major roots (right).**

unstable or needs a stake to prevent it from falling over, the root system may be inferior. Purchase is not recommended.

**Bare-root** trees should have living, small-diameter roots growing from the larger roots. The insides of living roots are whitish and wet.

## Root Ball Size

The American National Standards Institute recommends minimum root ball sizes for field-grown trees based on a tree's trunk diameter or height (see Table 5). In addition, Florida Grades and Standards makes minimum container size recommendations for trees grown in containers above ground and in fabric containers (Table 5). Trees with undersized root balls could perform poorly in the landscape.

## Trunk Form and Structure

### Trunk form

Strong trunks are thickest near the ground and taper up (Figure 6, left). They do not require stakes to support them. Trees that were staked overly long in the nursery may not develop proper trunk taper (Figure 6, center) and may fall over when stakes are removed (Figure 6, right). The trunks of these trees are often the same diameter at the

**Table 5. Recommended minimum root ball sizes and minimum and maximum trees heights for nursery trees.**

| | Minimum root ball diameter (inches) | | | Minimum tree height (feet)[2] | | | |
|---|---|---|---|---|---|---|---|
| Trunk caliper[1] (inches) | Field-grown shade trees[2] | Field-grown small trees[2] | Fabric container-grown trees[3] | Minimum container size (gallons)[3] | Standard trees | Slower-growing tree species or cultivars | Maximum tree height (feet)[2] |
| 0.5 | 12 | — | — | 1 | 5 | 3.5 | 6 |
| 0.75 | 14 | 16 | — | 3 | 5 | 4.5 | 8 |
| 1.0 | 16 | 18 | 12 | 5 | 6 | 5.0 | 10 |
| 1.25 | 18 | — | 14 | 7 | 7 | 6.0 | 11 |
| 1.5 | 20 | 20 | 16 | 15 | 8 | 7.0 | 12 |
| 1.75 | 22 | 22 | — | — | 9 | 7.5 | 13 |
| 2.0 | 24 | 24 | 18 | 20 | 10 | 8.0 | 14 |
| 2.5 | 28 | 28 | 18 | 25 | 11 | 9.0 | 15 |
| 3.0 | 32 | 32 | 20 | 45 | 12 | 9.5 | 16 |
| 3.5 | 38 | 38 | 24 | 65 | 13 | 10.0 | 17 |
| 4.0 | 42 | 42 | 30 | 95 | 14 | 10.5 | 18 |
| 4.5 | 48 | 48 | 36 | 95 | 14.5 | 11.0 | 18.5 |
| 5.0 | 54 | 54 | 36 | 95 | — | — | — |

[1]Trunk diameter (caliper) is measured 6 inches from the ground unless the trunk is more than 4 inches in diameter. If so, measure trunk diameter 12 inches from the ground.
[2]American National Standards Institute (ANSI Z60.1, 1990) used by American Association of Nurserymen. Note: Small trees 2, 3, 4, or 5 feet tall need root balls 10, 12, 14, or 16 inches.
[3]Florida Grades and Standards, 1997.

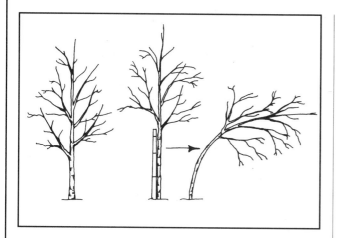

**Figure 6.  Good trunk taper (left) and poor trunk taper (center and right).**

ground as they are several feet up the tree. This is a sign that the trunk may be weak.

To test for trunk strength, take the tree into an open area and remove all stakes. If the tree is in leaf and it remains erect, it is probably strong enough. If possible, simulate rainfall by wetting the foliage with a hose. This weighs the branches down and further tests the sturdiness of the trunk.

Trunk strength is more difficult to evaluate when the tree is dormant (i.e. not in leaf); if the tree can stand erect without stakes and is otherwise satisfactory, buy it with the understanding that you may have to reduce the length of some of the branches if the trunk or branches droop over after leaves emerge.

## Single trunk trees

Trees with one trunk are usually considered stronger than their multi-trunk counterparts and are more durable in the landscape. Certain small trees such as crape myrtle, Japanese ligustrum, wax myrtle, guava and other ornamentals usually grow with several trunks but can be trained in the nursery to one trunk.

A tree that will grow to be more than 40 feet tall should have a single trunk well up

into its canopy (Figure 7, left), but the trunk does not have to be arrow straight. A slight bend, subtle dog-leg or zig-zag is acceptable (Figure 8, top left). A tree that forks in its top half (Figure 8, top right) should have one of the trunks removed before planting. If the trunk forks in the lower half of the tree, is unusually bent or has a severe dog-leg (Figure 8, bottom), then it should not be planted.

Trees with a single trunk are usually more appropriate for planting along streets and near walks and are also easier to train so that branches grow well overhead of vehicles and pedestrians (Figure 9, upper and lower right). Lower branches and entire trunks on multi-trunked trees often have to be removed several years after planting because they obstruct pedestrians and traffic (Figure 9, upper and lower left). This often disfigures the tree and compromises tree health.

## Multi-trunk trees

Small multi-trunk trees (i.e. under 30 feet tall at maturity) have a definite place in the landscape. If their several trunks originate

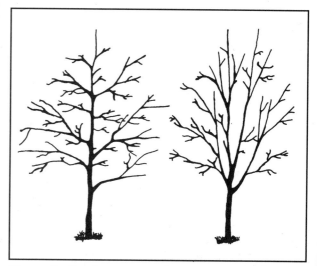

**Figure 7.  For large maturing trees, a single trunk tree with evenly spaced branches (left) is better than one that is multi-trunked or has branches clustered together (right).**

close to the ground, they make nice specimens, especially those trees that have attractive, showy bark or trunk structure.

Trees with several trunks often develop embedded bark in the crotches (Figure 10, left). Embedded bark appears as a crease running several inches to many feet down from the crotch. Bark is pinched into the crease. This condition can cause one of the trunks to split from the rest of the tree during a storm or even on a windy day. When a major branch or trunk splits, the character and health of the tree may well be significantly altered.

A multi-trunk tree is well formed if it has wide branch angles, trunks and branches less than half the diameter of the main trunk and no embedded bark (Figure 10, right).

## Trunk size and tree height

The American National Standards Institute and the Florida Grades and Standards for trees recommend minimum and maximum heights for nursery grown trees based on the diameter of the trunk (Table 5). Trees taller than the recommended height may have a weak trunk. Trees shorter than the recommended height that are not slow-growing or dwarf varieties may have root defects or other problems. These are best avoided unless the cause for the slow growth can be determined.

## Branch Size and Arrangement

Branches should be distributed along the trunk (Figure 11, left), not clumped toward the top (Figure 11, right). Branches in the lower half of the tree help distribute the stress placed on the trunk when the wind blows. At least half of the foliage should originate from branches on the lower two-thirds of the tree.

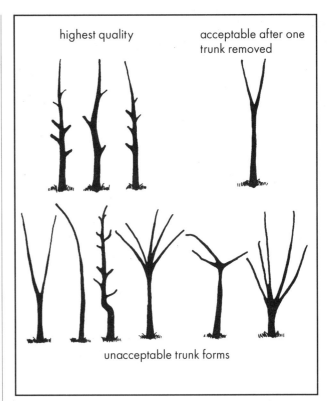

**Figure 8. Look for single trunks (top left) on large maturing trees. Remove one trunk on trees that fork in the top half (top right). Avoid other trunk forms (bottom).**

Branches that are less than half the diameter of the trunk and those with a "U" shaped crotch (Figure 10, right) are stronger than those that grow larger than half the trunk diameter and those with a "V" shaped crotch (Figure 10, left).

Branch arrangement and spacing is especially important on trees that will be large (i.e. over 40 feet at maturity). On saplings with trunk diameters of less than 2 inches, the main (or largest diameter) branches should be about 6 inches apart. Smaller sized branches can be closer than this. Although most branches on these sapling size trees will be removed as the tree grows, it is best to avoid trees with branch arrangements like those shown in the lower half of Figure 12. Trees with this inferior branch arrangement could split apart when they get older if they are not properly pruned.

Trees with trunk diameters between 2 and 4 inches might have one or two branches that will be permanent branches. Permanent branches should be spaced at least 18 inches apart and should not have bark embedded in the branch crotches (Figure 10). Trees with trunks larger than 4 inches in diameter are likely to have several permanent branches which should also be at least 18 inches apart. Choose trees with a branch arrangement similar to that illustrated at the top of Figure 12.

Branch arrangement and spacing is less crucial on trees that will be small at maturity. Simply look for those with a pleasing branch arrangement that will fit the needs of the planting site.

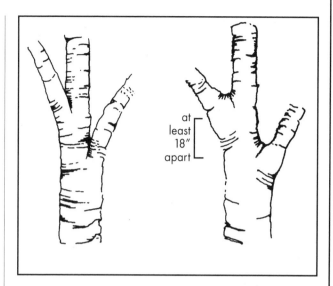

**Figure 10. Weak, "V" shaped branch crotch with bark embedded (left) and stronger, "U" shaped crotch (right).**

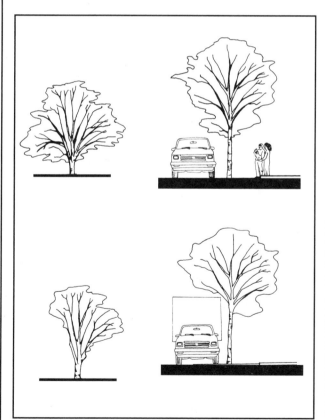

**Figure 9. Single trunk specimens (upper and lower right) are preferable to those that are multi-trunked (upper and lower left) for planting along sidewalks and streets.**

## Canopy Uniformity and Fullness

A tree's canopy is the overall form its foliage takes (Figure 13). Most people find trees with uniform canopies more attractive than those that are unbalanced. However, on nursery sized trees the canopy's uniformity is far less important than trunk form and branch arrangement. For example, a tree with a somewhat irregular canopy, a single trunk and good branch arrangement is superior to a tree with a double trunk and a uniform canopy. The canopy on the superior tree will fill in as the tree grows. Nevertheless, if the canopy is flattened, one sided or very unbalanced (Figure 13, bottom row), consider selecting another tree.

A thin canopy does not necessarily indicate poor quality. Many tree species appear open when young, then fill in as they grow in the landscape. Others are full of foliage even when they are small. Trees such as evergreen oaks usually lose most or all of their leaves for a brief period in the spring.

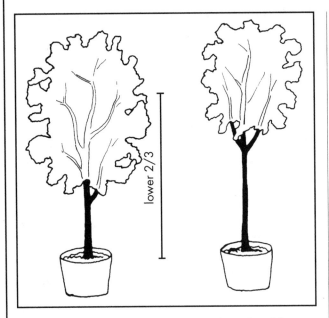

**Figure 11.** Half of a tree's branches should originate on the lower two-thirds of the trunk (Left). Poorer quality trees have no branches along the lower half of the trunk (Right).

This is normal. Remember, too, that recently dug trees will have dropped some leaves and may present thin looking canopies. Ask questions in order to judge whether a thin canopy is due to poor growing conditions in the nursery or is a natural characteristic of the tree.

## Signs of Disease and Injury

Examine a tree's leaves, trunk and branches for evidence of disease, pest infestation or other injury. Not only do you want to select a tree that is healthy, you also want to avoid exposing the other plants in the landscape to a contaminated specimen.

### Pests and disease

Many mites and insect pests are tiny and/or well camouflaged. Look carefully at both sides of a tree's leaves, especially if the foliage is speckled or spotted. Speckling may be the result of a generally harmless

leaf spot disease. Spotted foliage may also be an indication of sunburn or chemical injury or possibly an infestation of scales, spider mites, lacebugs or some other pest that sucks sap from the foliage. Such pests may be visible upon close inspection. Do not purchase trees with these pests. If you are not certain of the cause of leaf speckling or spotting, ask the nursery manager.

Because their color is often similar to that of twigs and branches, the presence of scale insects is one of the more difficult infestations to detect. Look for raised ridges or bumps on the tree's twigs. To determine if these are scales or a normal part of the tree, pick several off with your fingernail. If the bump is a normal part of the tree's bark, you will have exposed the green or white tissue

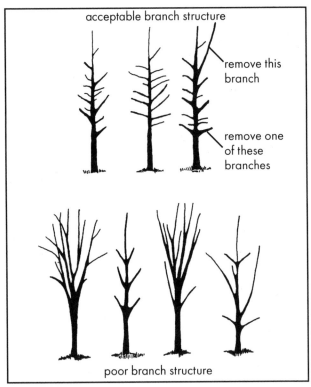

**Figure 12.** On large-maturing trees, the biggest branches should be evenly spaced along the trunk with some larger than others (top left and center). If two large branches are opposite each other, remove one (top right). Remove vertically oriented branches (top right). Trees with clustered branches, few branches or with all branches opposite each other (bottom) may not be durable.

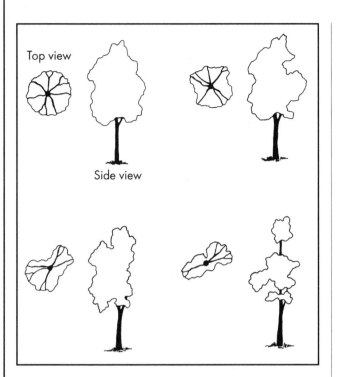

**Figure 13. Uniform canopies (top row) and inferior canopy uniformity (bottom row).**

that grows beneath the bark. If, however, the bump was a scale insect, the twig's bark will have remained more or less intact and no exposed tissue will be evident. Scale insects are easier to see when they are on foliage because their color is usually quite different from that of the leaves. Do not plant trees with scale infestations as the stress of defending against the infestation may prove excessive in the vulnerable period following transplant.

Except in their dormant season, nursery trees should have foliage to the ends of all their branches. Dead tips indicate problems that need further investigation. If the tree is dormant and has no leaves, scrape several of its twigs with your fingernail. If the tissue revealed is greenish or white, the twig is alive. Dry brown tissue indicates that the twig or branch is dead from that part out to the tip. This condition is known as **die-back**. As a rule, trees with die-back should not be purchased.

## Injuries and cultivation damage

Avoid trees with scars and other open wounds along the trunk. (If there is material covering the trunk, remove this **trunk wrap** to inspect the trunk, then replace it if needed to help prevent damage during shipment to the planting site.) Open pruning wounds are fine if they are small, but the presence of large open pruning wounds could indicate a poor or unplanned pruning program at the nursery. Small broken branches should be pruned back to healthy tissue. Trees with large broken branches should usually be left at the nursery. Do not purchase trees with bark stripped down the trunk from an improper pruning cut.

Evaluate old pruning cuts as well. Properly made pruning cuts are round in cross-section while improperly made cuts are often oval. Properly made pruning cuts indicate that the nursery has high pruning standards and is capable of growing high quality trees.

Check for injuries to the trunk from stakes rubbing against it, and be sure the tree was not harmed in the nursery by stake ties that were left on for too long. By the time of purchase, a tree should usually be able to stand without stakes.

Leaves should be colored like those of other trees of the same type. If leaves are smaller, lighter colored or yellower than others, the tree may lack vigor and grow poorly.

Major branches should not have bark embedded in the crotch (Figure 10, left side). Embedded bark indicates that the branch is not well attached to the trunk and could separate from the tree as it grows older.

Be sure a tree's root ball is free of weeds before planting. Weeds will slow the establishment rate of the tree and may spread out into the surrounding landscape.

— *Edward F. Gilman*

# PLANTING a Tree

## Care Before Planting

How a tree is handled between the time it leaves the nursery and the time it is planted will affect its health and even its chances of survival after planting. Before purchasing plants, decide how to provide the appropriate transportation to the planting site and the correct storage if the tree will not be planted as soon as it arrives at the site.

## Transportation

Never pick up a tree by the trunk; always lift and carry it by the root ball. Never drop a tree as this will disrupt contact between fine roots and soil which must be in intimate contact with each other if the roots are to absorb water.

Root balls in plastic containers or boxes are more resistant to rough handling than those in fabric containers or balled-in-burlap. With the latter, be sure that burlap is secured tightly or soil within the root ball could shift, causing cracks in the root ball and root breakage. A cracked root ball dries out quickly. To reduce water loss during shipping, some nurseries shrink-wrap plastic around the root balls of trees that are balled-in-burlap.

When taking a tree home in your car, don't let it get wind whipped by lashing it to the roof or letting foliage hang out the windows or the trunk. Exposure to such wind causes rapid moisture loss and could also result in severe damage to the foliage. The tree also needs protection against extreme temperatures, so don't let the car stand in the sun.

When transporting trees commercially, arrange for the use of a closed truck that can guarantee keeping the trees in temperatures under 100 degrees. (This will require air conditioning if the truck stands in the sun.) Trees that are shipped in open trucks lose more water through their foliage and twigs and can arrive at the planting site in poor condition. Many nursery operators cover trees with a fabric or cloth designed to reduce wind damage to the foliage.

Be sure trees are irrigated prior to loading. Trees may be shipped either standing or lying down as long as they are well secured and can not fall or roll around. Rolling or other movement during shipping can crack the root ball and break roots.

Some nursery operators routinely spray trees that are in leaf with anti-transpirants before shipping. Anti-transpirants may reduce water loss during shipping, but may also hinder photosynthesis for several weeks after planting, slowing root growth and thereby lengthening the establishment period. There is no scientific evidence to support the use of anti-transpirants and with careful handling and proper aftercare, they are probably not needed.

## Storage and irrigation at the planting site

If trees cannot be planted the day they arrive at the planting site, they will need a holding area that is shaded and screened from the wind. Depending on how the root balls are contained, specific irrigation requirements will need to be met, so establishing the holding area in advance of the arrival of the trees is strongly advised.

After trees leave the nursery, they should continue to receive the same amount of water at the same frequency the nursery provided. **Container-grown trees** in Florida often receive daily irrigation in all but the coolest months and may be watered twice a day in the summer. Ask the nursery operator for the applicable irrigation schedule.

Container grown trees dry out very quickly. Even one day without water can cause significant root death, depriving the tree of vigor and magnifying the stress of the establishment period. Several days without water could mean death. **Any plastic coverings used to protect the tree's foliage or roots during transport should be removed as soon as the tree reaches the holding area. Plastic coverings can allow temperatures to build to lethal levels.**

**Balled-in-burlap trees** should have their root balls surrounded by soil, compost, mulch or sawdust as soon as they arrive in the holding area, especially if they have roots growing through the burlap. This will help prevent root desiccation and will also facilitate the absorption of water by the root ball. **If the root balls have been enclosed in a layer of plastic, either remove the plastic or provide complete protection from direct sun. Plastic coverings can allow temperatures to build to lethal levels.** As with container-grown trees, follow the nursery's irrigation schedule. Water will roll off the surface of the root ball if it is applied too fast. A drip emitter or other low volume irrigation head will deliver water slowly enough to permit absorption by the root ball, though large root balls may need more than one emitter for thorough coverage. A hose or sprinkler may also be used as long as a thorough wetting can be achieved. Do not allow root balls to stand in pools of water after they have been saturated.

Keep **bare-root trees**, especially their roots, covered with moistened burlap and in the shade prior to planting. Fine roots can dry out and die if exposed to direct sun for even a few minutes. Spray roots with water often enough to keep them moist; how often will be determined by the weather and the characteristics of your holding area. Remove damaged or broken portions of the roots with a sharp hand pruner.

# Planting

Trees must be planted at the right depth and receive the right amount of water if they are to establish themselves and flourish. Planting too deeply and under- or over-watering are among the most common and serious planting errors.

## How Deep to Plant

In **well-drained soil**, the planting hole should never be dug any deeper than the height of the root ball (Figure 14a). This means that the soil at the bottom of the hole is left undisturbed. Setting the root ball on loosened soil will cause the tree to settle and sink too deeply into the soil. In well-drained soil, you want to locate the topmost root in the root ball so that it will be level with the soil surface (Figure 14b). Check to be sure that there is not an excess layer of soil (or container media) already covering the root ball. (This sometimes happens in the nursery. See "Checking the Root Ball for Defects" in the previous chapter, *How to Select a Tree*.) As little as half an inch of excess soil over the root ball can inhibit or prevent water from entering the root ball, especially on trees planted from containers. Only mulch should be placed over the root ball.

In well-drained soil, the planting hole should be at least two times and preferably five times wider than the root ball. Roots will grow more quickly into loosened soil, thus speeding up the tree's establishment time.

In **poorly drained or compacted soil**, take extra precautions to ensure that roots are not suffocated by the water saturation typical of these soils. The top quarter to third of the

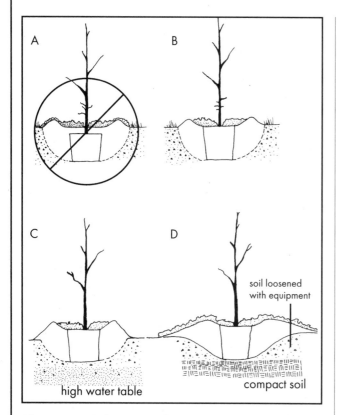

**Figure 14. (A) Never plant trees or shrubs too deep. (B) In well-drained soil, the topmost root in the root ball should be even with the soil line. In poorly-drained (C) or compacted (D) soil, install the root ball slightly above the grade.**

structure of this type root ball is more likely to remain above the standing water level. (See "Compacted Low Oxygen Soils" in *The Planting Site.*)

Loosening compacted soil before planting can dramatically increase the rate of root growth and root penetration into the landscape soil. Establishment time is sped up, reducing the period of the tree's vulnerability to pests, disease and drought. Loosen the soil 15 to 20 feet or more in diameter around the area where the tree will be planted (Figure 14d). If the compacted area is substantial, a ripping tool can be attached to the back of a large tractor or bulldozer and the soil ripped 18 to 36 inches deep. Disk to smooth the soil after it is loosened.

root ball should be planted higher than the surrounding soil and irrigation managed accordingly. Dig the planting hole only two-thirds the height of the root ball and, after planting, mound soil to create a gentle slope down from the top of the root ball (Figure 14c). The planting hole and resulting mound should be at least five times wider than the root ball. This technique will help prevent the top portion of the root ball from becoming saturated during rain or irrigation and will keep at least that portion of the root ball above standing water at all times. The top of the root ball may dry out quickly in summer on some sites, so be prepared to irrigate accordingly. Consider planting a low-profile root ball (see *How to Select a Tree*) on a poorly drained site. The shallower

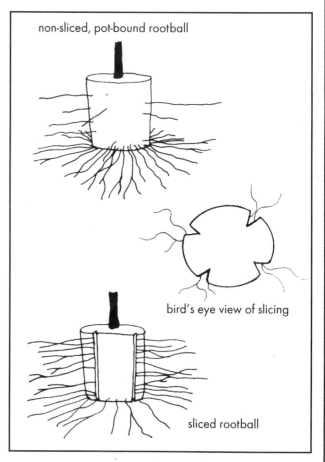

**Figure 15. Slicing the root ball on a container-grown tree.**

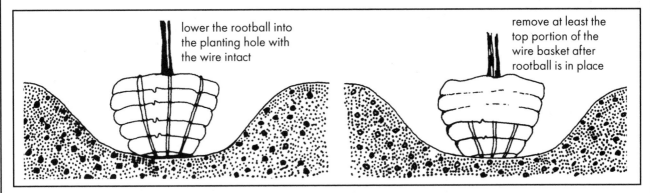

lower the rootball into the planting hole with the wire intact

remove at least the top portion of the wire basket after rootball is in place

**Figure 16. Wire basket before removal (left) and after removal of top levels (right).**

## Preparing and Setting the Root Ball

The root ball of your tree will need to be handled and prepared for planting in accordance with the way it was contained in the nursery.

Trees grown in **plastic or other hard-sided containers** can be removed from their containers and placed directly in the holes prepared for them. Cut any circling roots so that they will not strangle the tree later on. If a tree is pot-bound, use pruning shears or a serrated knife to make slices 1 to 2 inches deep going from the top of the root ball to the bottom. Make these slices in three or four places around the root ball (Figure 15). Pull the roots growing along the outside of the root ball away from the root ball. Recent studies show that although this kind of pruning does not increase root growth after planting, slicing root balls (whether pot bound or not) does enhance the distribution of regenerated roots in the surrounding landscape soil. Instead of occurring almost exclusively from the bottom of the root ball, root regeneration occurs along the slice from the top to the bottom of the root ball. Current research also indicates that root pruning container-grown trees at the time of planting has a negligible effect on shoot growth.

When preparing the hole for a **bare-root** tree, dig it wide enough so that roots can be spread out. (Do not cut or break roots or bend them in order to fit the hole.) Use a sharp pruning tool to cut or trim any roots that are obviously dead, injured or dried. (Pruning roots indiscriminately at planting will not stimulate root regeneration and is not recommended.) Spread the roots out and position the topmost root just under the soil surface. Shallow roots either may be parallel with the soil surface or angled slightly downwards. Some people spread the roots over a mound of firm soil in the planting hole and carefully place soil between groups of roots; others wash soil between the roots.

Natural or synthetic burlap is used on trees that are **balled-in-burlap**. To determine which type has been used, hold a match to a small portion of the burlap. As a rule, natural burlap will burn, synthetic will melt.

Synthetic burlap will not decompose in the soil and can cause roots to girdle the tree. This could ultimately strangle the tree. Remove synthetic burlap entirely. When a wire basket is holding synthetic burlap in place (see next paragraph), cut away the basket in order to remove the synthetic burlap or, if the lower portion of the basket

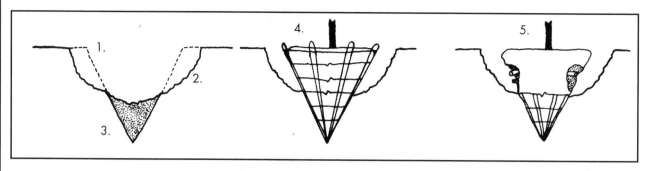

**Figure 17. Using a tree spade to plant a tree previously placed in a wire basket: 1) dig a hole with the spade, 2) widen the hole near the top, 3) remove extra soil from bottom of hole, 4) set tree in hole, and 5) remove top portion of wire basket.**

must be left intact, cut an X in the burlap in each section of the basket. Natural burlap is biodegradable and can be left along the sides and bottom of the root ball but should always be removed from the top of the root ball where it is subject to drying out. Dry burlap repels water, making it difficult to rewet the root ball.

**Wire baskets** and **wire wrapping** are frequently used to help hold a balled-in-burlap root ball intact during shipping and handling. Trees that are stored after being dug with a tree spade are also placed in wire baskets. This is an effective means of keeping roots in contact with soil until planting. Although there are no documented reports of wire baskets strangling trees in Florida, it might be safer to remove the top layer or two of wire from the basket at the time of planting (Figure 16). The top portion of the basket can be removed as shown in Figure 17 if the hole was dug with a tree spade.

When removing burlap, wire baskets or wire wrapping, remember not to leave any straps, ties, string or wire secured around the root ball. These materials will not decompose.

In Florida, trees grown in **fabric containers** are almost always transferred to plastic containers before being marketed to the general public. However, if you are handling

trees in their fabric containers, be aware that their root balls are very fragile and must be handled with great care. Soil inside the ball can become loose with just a moderate disturbance, and trees will go into shock if they are dropped. The fabric container must be completely removed before planting. To remove, make a slit in the fabric from the bottom of the root ball to the top and gently pull the fabric from the ball. Trees planted from fabric containers require more frequent irrigation than other trees.

Some fabric container designs allow only small roots to develop outside the fabric, in which case the fabric will be fairly easy to remove without disturbing the root ball. Other fabrics allow large roots to develop so that fabric removal is more challenging. Using a hand pruner, cut roots from the inner side of the fabric. Some nursery operators have special tools that quickly remove fabric containers.

## Filling the Planting Hole

The soil used to fill in around the root ball of the newly planted tree is called backfill. Unless your site analysis reveals that the site's soil is unsuited for root growth, your best backfill will be the loosened original soil dug from the planting hole. (When soil is contaminated or otherwise unusable, the recommended practice is to replace it with good quality soil.) The best additive to the soil is water. According to the best information now available, other additives or amendments of any kind, be they gels, polymers, liquids, dusts, powders, fertilizers or organic matter, generally provide no benefit when incorporated only into the planting hole. In most instances, roots grow so fast regardless of amendments that they soon leave the backfill soil and grow into the surrounding undisturbed soil. There is one research report where amendments in sandy soil confined roots to the planting hole for a period of time after planting.

Loosen and break up any clods of soil before backfilling. Clods in the backfill soil will create undesirable air pockets around the root ball and could hinder root growth and establishment. Next, backfill the bottom half of the space around the root ball. Tamp the soil lightly with your foot, but do not tamp so heavily as to compact the soil. Finish filling the hole with loose, unamended soil, and gently tamp again. Settle the soil by pushing a hose with running water in and out of the backfill soil all around the hole. Finally, form a three inch high water ring around the perimeter of the root ball. This will help hold irrigation water. Remember that initially the root ball will need to be watered directly as roots haven't yet spread into the surrounding soil.

## Pruning at Planting

Little if any pruning should be necessary at the time of transplant. Do not prune a field-grown tree to compensate for root loss. The latest research indicates that pruning does not help overcome transplant shock unless the plant is receiving insufficient irrigation. If you must prune because you can't provide sufficient irrigation, you purchased stock too big for your site (see *How to Select a Tree*). When compelled to prune, thin the canopy by drop crotching; do not head back or top the tree. (See *Pruning Trees and Shrubs*.)

Branches that are injured, diseased or dead may be pruned but are also an indication of a poor quality tree. You are better off exchanging it for a healthy one.

Trees with poor structure should be pruned at planting to correct the problem, especially if no further pruning is planned for the next year or two. Poor form should not be permitted to develop as it will become increasingly more difficult to correct. On trees with adequate form, begin pruning for structural development a year or two after planting.

## Time of Year for Planting

In Florida, container-grown or hardened off balled-in-burlap trees may be planted year round. Many nursery operators refrain from digging trees balled-in-burlap, especially live oak, in the fall when roots regenerate poorly unless the trees have been root pruned at least once. Roots on live oak regenerate best during the summer months when shoots are not growing. Some nurseries now dig live oaks in summer, others dig their oaks when the buds begin to swell in spring, and some dig in the dormant season.

Many nurseries and landscape contractors prefer not to dig trees while shoots are actively elongating. They wait until leaves have fully expanded.

— *Edward F. Gilman*

# CARE DURING
# the Establishment Period

Even the healthiest trees planted in the most ideal circumstances need a substantial amount of time, care and, particularly, proper irrigation to become established in the landscape (Table 6). During the establishment period, roots are expanding out into the landscape soil, and shoots and trunk grow more slowly than they did before transplanting (Figure 18). Once shoot and trunk growth rates match the rates before planting, the tree is considered established. An established tree has developed a root system substantial enough to keep it alive without supplemental irrigation.

Establishment occurs more rapidly in warm climates and when irrigation is supplied in correct quantity and frequency. Irrigation is especially important in Florida. Trees transplanted from containers take longer to establish and therefore require supplemental irrigation for a longer period than do field-grown trees. Research indicates that establishment time for container-grown trees can be an additional 1 to 2 months **per inch of trunk diameter**. If supplemental irrigation is halted too soon, the mortality rate for container grown trees will be higher than for hardened off field-grown trees.

In addition to requiring special attention to irrigation, trees in the establishment period need mulching and may require staking. Pruning and fertilization are also handled in specific ways during the establishment period.

## Irrigation

When trees die, blame is often placed on pests, disease, the method by which they were produced or the plants themselves. The truth is that many trees die from too little or too much water during the first few months after planting. Trees are likely to get too little water in well-drained soil and too much in soil that is poorly drained.

Determine when and how much to water by becoming familiar with the characteristics of the planting site and then striving to maintain constant moisture in (but not saturation of) the root ball. The variables shown in Table 7 will affect the irrigation schedule at a given site. Remember that the proper frequency and duration of irrigation is rarely the same from one site to the next, so the moisture level in the root ball is the final determinant of whether irrigation is being correctly supplied.

The practice of intense irrigation management can save resources in the long term. While less frequent irrigation over a long

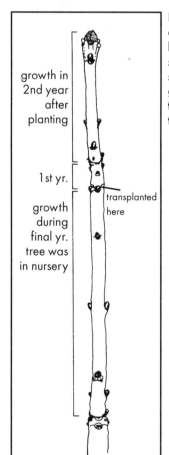

**Figure 18. Twig from a tree not yet established in the landscape. Growth in the second year was greater than in the first year after transplant.**

growth in 2nd year after planting

1st yr.

transplanted here

growth during final yr. tree was in nursery

**TABLE 6. Length of tree establishment period with optimum irrigation**[*]

| Trunk diameter of nursery stock | ESTABLISHMENT PERIOD (in months) | | |
|---|---|---|---|
| | North Florida | Central Florida | South Fla. |
| less than 2" | 4 - 8 | 3 - 6 | 2 - 4 |
| 2" to 4" | 8 - 15 | 6 - 12 | 5 - 9 |
| over 4"** | 15+ | 12+ | 10+ |

[*]See Table 8 for optimum irrigation schedule.

**For each additional inch of trunk diameter, trees in north Florida require about 4 more months for establishment. Trees in central Florida require 3 months and in south Florida 2 months per additional inch.

**TABLE 7. Factors affecting irrigation requirements after planting**

| | Factors that **increase** irrigation requirements after planting | Factors that **decrease** irrigation requirements after planting |
|---|---|---|
| **Landscape Characteristics** | | |
| *soil quality* | well-drained soil | poorly-drained soil |
| *slope/grade* | sloping ground | flat ground |
| **Weather** | | |
| *humidity* | dry weather | rainy weather |
| *sun* | sunny days | cloudy days |
| *wind* | windy days | calm days |
| *temperature* | warm weather | cool weather |
| *season* | warm season planting | cool season planting |
| **Stock Character** | | |
| *root ball* | sandy textured root ball | clayey textured root ball |
| *size* | large nursery stock | small nursery stock |
| *production method* | container-grown stock | hardened-off field-grown stock |

period of time spreads out the cost of irrigation, the dollar amount spent will be about the same as for intensively irrigating trees for a short period of time. Intensive irrigation results in trees that establish more rapidly and thus become more quickly resistant to drought, pests and disease. The concentrated up-front costs of intensive irrigation are thus offset by lower mortality and healthier trees.

## Irrigation Systems

Problems may arise if newly planted trees are irrigated by systems designed to water turf, flower beds or established plants. In **well-drained soil**, such systems cannot supply enough water to the new trees without overwatering everything else and wasting water. These trees must be watered by hand with a hose or with a temporary micro-irrigation system designed specifically for them. Once trees are established and their roots spread out, the usual irrigation system will be adequate, and the temporary system can be removed.

In **poorly-drained sites**, trees planted in or near regularly irrigated turf are especially susceptible to over-watering. Irrigation water and rainfall run over the soil surface and collect in the looser soil of the planting hole, drowning the tree's roots. For this reason, trees are best located away from the turf and its irrigation system, in their own specially irrigated beds. If this is not possible, adjust the turf irrigation system so that the root balls of the newly planted trees do not become saturated. This solution may, however, result in under-watered turf. A third and highly recommended solution is to plant trees slightly higher than surrounding soil (see Figure 14c and 14d in the chapter *Planting a Tree*). This keeps the top portion of the root ball out of the standing water in the planting hole.

## Frequency of Irrigation

In order to maintain rapid growth, trees transplanted into **well-drained soil** require daily irrigation for at least the first month (Table 8). Frequent irrigation benefits the

**Table 8. Irrigation schedule for quickly establishing trees in well-drained sites during the growing season.** **

| Trunk diameter of tree | North Florida | Central/South Florida |
|---|---|---|
| Under 2" | Daily for 1 month, then 3 times a week for 2 months, then weekly until established. | Daily for 1 month, then 3 times a week for 3 months, then weekly until established. |
| 2" to 4" | Daily for 1 - 2 months, then 3 times a week for 3 months, then weekly until established. | Daily for 2 months, then 3 times a week for 4 months, then weekly until established. |
| Over 4" | Daily for 2 months, then 3 times a week for 4 months, then weekly until established. | Daily for 2 - 3 months, then 3 times a week for 5 months, then weekly until established. |

*Frequency of irrigation may be slightly reduced for hardened-off field-grown trees. Frequency may also be reduced when planting in the cooler months or in poorly-drained soils. See Table 7 for other factors affecting frequency of irrigation. Apply 1-2 gallons per inch of trunk diameter at each irrigation. Trees often survive without the daily irrigation but will grow slower. See Table 6 for establishment times.

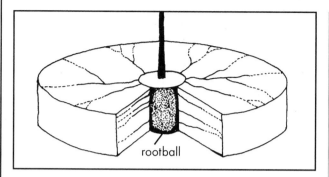

**Figure 19. Solid lines indicate root growth under less than optimum soil moisture conditions. Dotted lines show the root growth possible with frequent and regular irrigation.**

transplanted tree more than large volumes of water infrequently applied. In well-drained soil in Florida's climate, apply water to the root ball every day during the first few weeks after planting. Irrigation conducted according to the schedule in Table 8 will provide for the most rapid establishment. At this stage, all of the tree's roots are still located in the root ball. However, you may wet surrounding soil if it is dry.

In **poorly-drained soil**, a set irrigation schedule may be impractical. Instead, monitor the site for changes in moisture levels caused by rainfall or, possibly, run-off from adjacent irrigation. Essentially, the root balls of newly planted trees must not be allowed to dry out nor must they be saturated. It is easy to kill trees that have been planted into poorly drained sites. See *How to Select a Tree* and *Planting a Tree* for information on methods of dealing with this problem.

Maintaining adequate moisture in the root ball and surrounding soil allows for faster and more extensive root growth (Figure 19). The more rapid the root growth, the faster the rate of establishment and the sooner the tree develops a resistance to drought. Root growth is slow on trees that are not irrigated regularly after planting. Such trees will normally stay alive until a drought occurs

but can die back during the drought. Regular irrigation in loose soil promotes the extensive root system that is a tree's best defense against drought.

Trees without adequate irrigation during the establishment period may also develop a weak, multi-trunk habit (Figure 20). This can happen in response to dry weather-induced tip die-back on the main trunk and branches. When wet weather returns, several new shoots often emerge from the living tissue

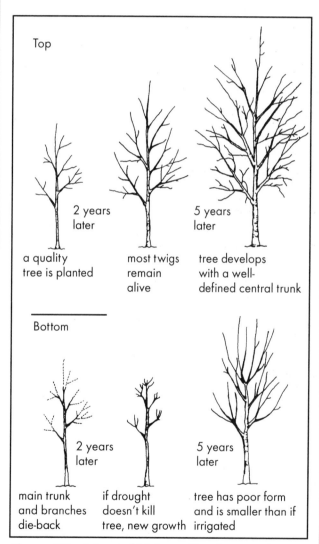

**Figure 20. A tree of high quality that receives adequate irrigation during establishment (T) develops good structure, while trees that are insufficiently irrigated (B) die back (as indicated by dotted lines) and can develop multiple trunks or other types of poor form.**

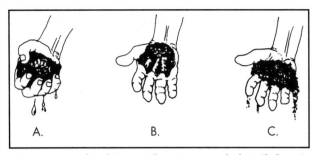

**Figure 21. Checking soil moisture. (A) Soil that is too wet. (B) Soil with the right amount of moisture. (C) Soil that is too dry.**

back of the dead tips. These shoots can become equally dominant with the trunk, resulting in several trunks and an inferior, poorly structured tree.

In the first few months after planting, do not skip an irrigation because of rainfall, unless it measures over an inch. Rain water should not be counted on to provide any benefit in the first few months after transplanting. Later, normal rainfall should provide enough soil moisture in most years to allow for adequate tree root growth into the soil surrounding the root ball. If the site has no irrigation system or if there is a drought, occasionally water the soil surrounding the root ball. If this soil becomes too dry, root growth will be slow. Gradually increase the irrigation area around the tree to accommodate root growth. During the first few years after planting, roots grow 1 to 2 inches per week in Florida.

## Amount of Irrigation

The best way to determine how much irrigation to apply to **container-grown trees** in the first several weeks after planting into well-drained soil is to ask the nursery operator how much was applied in the nursery just prior to purchase. Apply this amount or slightly more directly to the root ball. There is no need to wet the surrounding soil at this time because it will be wetted by water

draining from the container root ball and by rainfall. Container grown trees planted into poorly drained soil may need a smaller volume of irrigation than they received in the nursery.

As a rule of thumb for **field-grown trees**, 1 1/2 to 3 gallons of water **per inch of trunk diameter** applied each time the tree is irrigated during the growing season should be enough to maintain adequate root growth. For example, a tree with a 2-inch trunk diameter needs about 3 to 6 gallons each time it is irrigated. Trees planted during the cooler months may need less water, depending on the weather and soil drainage. Those planted in compacted or poorly drained soil with a portion of the root ball above the surrounding soil may need more water due to the drying effect of the mounded planting. Trees mistakenly planted too deeply in poorly drained soil should not be irrigated until they are raised and replanted (Figure 14 in the chapter *Planting a Tree*).

To determine whether the amount of water being supplied is adequate for the site conditions, conduct the following tests. Within the first week after planting, gently dig a small hole in the loosened backfill soil just outside the root ball and half its depth. Do this several hours after watering. Squeeze soil taken from the bottom of the hole in the palm of your hand. If water drips out between your fingers, you are watering too much (Figure 21a); if soil crumbles and falls out of your hand as you open your fingers, you are watering too little (Figure 21c.) If soil stays together as you open your fingers (Figure 21b), moisture in the backfill soil is just right, but the root ball might be bone dry. Poke a finger into the root ball to check the moisture there. If it feels dry, increase the amount of daily irrigation. If the soil smells sour or you can squeeze water from it, it is too wet. With practice, these techniques become quick and easy ways to evaluate soil moisture.

Some people use a soil probe to judge soil moisture. If the probe is easy to push into the root ball, soil moisture may be fine; if penetration is difficult, you may need to increase irrigation. Soil moisture sensors with various types of gauges are designed to help schedule irrigation for established landscapes. There is no evidence of their usefulness in judging when newly planted trees need watering.

## Managing with Less Water

If proper irrigation cannot be provided following planting, consider planting smaller trees which establish more quickly or extend the irrigation period following planting to conform to Table 8.

## Staking and Wood Supports

There are two types of staking, each used for a different purpose. **Anchor staking** prevents a newly planted tree from tilting in the planting hole when the wind blows. Such tilting will cause root ball movement and can break roots and slow plant establishment. **Support staking** holds a weak trunk in an upright position. Many trees do not require staking after planting; don't stake a tree unnecessarily.

Until their root systems are well established, trees with large canopies and those planted in areas open to the wind, such as parking lots and parks, are more likely to require **anchor stakes and guy wires** than trees planted in protected areas near buildings or among existing trees. Use two or three anchor stakes for trees with trunk diameters under 2 inches, three stakes for trunks 2 to 3

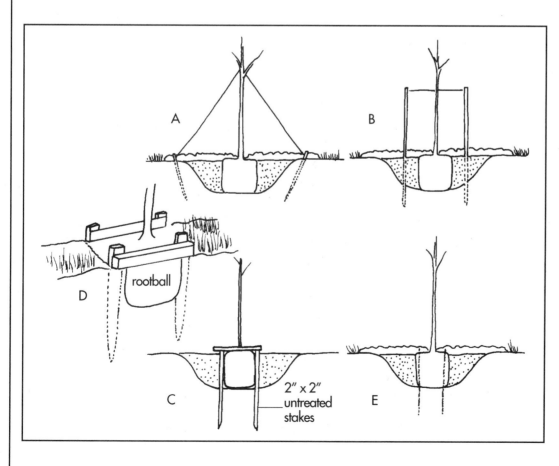

A

B

D

rootball

C

2" x 2" untreated stakes

E

**Figure 22. Methods of staking. (A and B) Anchoring with above-ground stakes and wires. (C, D and E) Below-ground anchoring.**

inches in diameter and three or four stakes for larger trees (Figures 22a and 22b). Stakes should be driven at least 24 inches into the ground. Often wire threaded through a short piece of garden hose is used to secure the tree to the stake. However, this system can damage the trunk as it moves in the wind and rubs against the hose. You need to use a wide, smooth material such as one of the rubber-like products now becoming available for this purpose. Wrap this material around the trunk above the base of a lower branch, pull it firmly so there is no slack, and attach to the stake. Guy wires and stakes should be removed within a year after planting. If anchor stakes are required for more than a year, there is a problem with the tree.

The anchoring systems shown in Figures 22c, 22d, and 22e stabilize trees without using above-ground wires or supports. For the techniques shown in Figures 22c and 22d, you will need 2" x 2" stakes (made of untreated lumber) that measure twice the depth of the root ball. Drive these stakes almost all the way into the ground just **outside** the perimeter of the root ball (Figure 22c). Position the stakes so they are nearly opposite each other. Connect them with a crosspiece nailed into their sides (Figure 22d); if the crosspiece is nailed into the tops of the stakes, it can work loose. Use two stakes and one crosspiece for small trees (i.e. with a root ball smaller than 30 gallons) and four stakes and two crosspieces for trees that are larger. On container-grown trees, drive 3/4" diameter dowels that are two times the depth of the root ball all the way into the ground just **inside** the perimeter of the root ball (Figure 22e).

Poor nursery practices often yield trees with thin, weak trunks that require **support staking** to keep them upright. If you must plant such a tree, the staking must not only provide support but also enable the tree to develop trunk strength. Taking care to avoid major roots, drive the stake approximately 24 inches into the ground immediately next to the trunk. The support stake should be secured to the trunk at the lowest position which will hold the trunk erect. To find this point, hold the tree upright and slide your hand from the top of the trunk down to the spot where the top of the tree begins to bend over. Using a wide, smooth material (as mentioned earlier), attach the stake 6 inches above this point. Trim the stake just above the point of attachment so that it does not injure the trunk. Six months after staking and when the foliage is wet, remove the stake to see if the tree can stand erect. If not, repeat the process every two months until sufficient strength is developed. If the tree requires staking for more than 1 year, it may never develop the strength to support itself. Leaving small branches along the lower trunk will also help the trunk increase in diameter and strength. These branches can be removed once the tree can support itself.

For information on support for palms, see "Support" in *Selecting and Planting Palms*.

## Protecting the Trunk
### Trunk Wrap
Trunk wrap may provide some protection during shipping but should be removed, along with any accompanying string or twine, before the tree is planted. Inspect the trunk for damage and other irregularities when the wrap is removed.

During the winter in some parts of the country, professionals wrap the trunks of young, thin-barked trees. This is thought to prevent the trunks from cracking when direct sun shines on them in cold weather. However, no research exists to support this practice.

Trunk wrap probably does no harm to the tree provided it remains intact and is removed along with any string or twine the following spring. Insect and disease problems are encouraged when wrap is left on too long. If parts of the wrap fall off, substantial temperature fluctuations in the trunk tissue may occur and cause cracks to develop. Some protection from the winter sun can be provided by leaving the lower short and temporary branches in place until the upper branches are able to shade the trunk.

To wrap a trunk, begin at the ground and spiral the wrapping material around the trunk and up to the first major branches. Overlap each layer by half a width.

### Protection from Rodents and Lawn Equipment

Polypropylene protection tubes will safeguard newly planted trees from rodents and deer, which chew bark. Small trees can be enclosed in wire or mesh screening, and saplings (under 4 feet tall) can be protected from rodent damage by tree shelters (plastic tubes that slip around the lower trunks). Such shelters can also increase growth rates, though root growth rate may be slightly reduced. Some horticulturists slit plastic drain pipe with a hand shear and slip it around the lower trunk, and others use white plastic trunk wrap spiraled around the trunk and lower branches. Trees fitted with these devices may be more prone to nest building by fire ants.

Thick plastic drain pipe around the base of the trunk will also shield the tree from damage caused by lawn mowers, line trimmers and other equipment. Even greater protection is provided when three or four stakes are driven into the ground several feet from the trunk. These stakes are not attached to the tree and can remain in place

indefinitely. Mowers will bump into the stakes, not the tree.

## Mulching

Before applying mulch, remove any soil that may have been placed over the root ball. As discussed in earlier chapters, excess soil over the root ball prevents water from reaching the roots and can cause a tree to die from drought even when surrounding soil is moist.

Apply mulch 2 to 3 inches deep in a circle at least 2 feet in diameter **for each inch** of trunk diameter (Table 9). Increase the size of the circle of mulch as the tree grows until the tree is fully established (Table 6). This technique will help a tree establish quickly by reducing competition from other plants, especially turf. A mulched soil also encourages root growth in and under the mulch. Keep mulch 2 to 3 inches away from tree trunks to prevent moisture from initiating bark decay and to discourage rodents.

**Table 9. Minimum diameter of mulch circles for establishing trees.***

| Trunk diameter (in inches) | Mulch circle diameter (in feet) |
|:---:|:---:|
| 1 | 2 |
| 2 | 4 |
| 3 | 6 |
| 4 | 8 |

* A larger mulch area will help even more. Keep mulch free of weeds.

## Fertilization

Results from the soil samples collected during your site analysis will indicate if any elements are lacking in the soil. Adding potassium and phosphorus to the soil will not give a growth response unless the soil is lacking these. Nitrogen is the only element that occasionally gives a slight growth benefit on trees. Although a number of products are sold as transplant aids, there is no scientific evidence that either natural or synthetic fertilizers, gels, vitamins, powders or emulsions help trees become established. Proper irrigation will be the best promoter of growth.

Research indicates that **field-grown** trees transplanted to the landscape benefit little or not at all from fertilizing the root ball at the time of planting. In no case has research shown that chances of survival are enhanced by the application of fertilizer at planting. Healthy field-grown trees are well fertilized in the nursery and will need no further applications for 4 to 6 weeks. Concentrate your resources on correct irrigation management. If, however, you will be unable to fertilize 4 to 6 weeks after planting, go ahead and make a light application of fertilizer to the top of the root ball and the backfill soil at the time of planting. A controlled release fertilizer is preferable to a soluble one.

There is little research on the results of fertilizing **container-grown** trees at planting. If trees will be irrigated regularly, slow-release fertilizer spread on and around the root ball soon after planting may enhance tree growth. Since regularly irrigated container-grown trees suffer little transplant shock, they might respond sooner than field-grown trees to an early application of fertilizer. This is only speculation and has not been tested.

If not applied at planting, 4 to 6 weeks after planting, give trees a small application of slow-release fertilizer on the surface of the root ball and the backfill soil. (Although a few horticulturists mix a small amount of fertilizer in the backfill soil at the time of planting, achieving a thorough mixture of soil and fertilizer is time consuming and is not a better method than surface application unless fertilizer will run off during rain or irrigation.) Use the amount recommended by the manufacturer but not more. Excess fertilizer can burn roots and stress the tree.

## Pruning During and After Establishment

While pruning at the time of planting appears to have little if any positive impact on post-transplant survival and growth, many trees that mature at heights greater than 40 feet will need regular pruning in the first 25 years after planting in order to establish or maintain good structure (see *Pruning Trees and Shrubs*). If a tree possesses good structure at the time of planting, pruning should not be required for several years after planting. Trees with minor structural problems such as a double leader in the top half can be pruned at planting to correct the problem. If poor quality trees were planted, the costs of pruning to develop good structure during the establishment period may outstrip the cost of purchasing and planting trees of good quality.

Pruning care in the first 25 years after planting is of such great consequence that if you cannot arrange for such care, consider planting fewer trees and using the savings on caring for them. Another option is to plant those trees whose inherent structures and growth habits require less regular pruning.

—*Edward F. Gilman*

# SELECTING
# and Planting Palms

Palms are easier to transplant than similarly sized broad-leaved trees. The common sight of tractor trailers loaded with palms 20 or more feet tall is a testimonial to this fact. Nonetheless, transplant failure is not unknown, and replacement percentages can rise up to and beyond 30% on an installation. Such failures can be greatly minimized by paying closer care to palms in the first critical months after installation.

## Transplanting

### Age of a Palm
### and Transplant Success

Until visible trunk development has taken place, a palm is not very tolerant of the extreme root disturbance that accompanies digging. This fact is especially critical for species that characteristically complete a great deal of stem development deeply below ground (for example, *Bismarckia nobilis*, *Latania* spp., *Sabal* spp.). Even if the palms are not killed by premature transplanting, growth setbacks and less than optimum trunk development may occur. Young palms (i.e. without visible trunk development) are best transplanted from containers only.

### Time of Year to Transplant

Palms establish most quickly if transplanted during the spring and early summer when soil temperatures are on the increase. The higher rainfall normally experienced in Florida at this time provides the further advantage of reducing the need for supplemental irrigation during the first critical months of establishment. In south Florida, time of year is not as critical from the perspective of temperature, though mid-winter planting should be avoided if possible.

## Root Ball Size

For single-stemmed palms less than 15 feet tall, a root ball that measures approximately 8 to 10 inches from any point at the base of the trunk is a common nursery industry average for size (Plate 1) and should provide for adequate root survival. For clustering palms or larger solitary specimens, an incrementally larger root ball may be advisable to ensure successful establishment when site conditions may be less than ideal.

## Root Pruning

With the exception of the Bismarck palm (*Bismarckia nobilis*), root pruning generally has not been considered necessary for palms. Nevertheless, most palms would benefit from root pruning 6 to 12 weeks before digging from the harvest site to encourage new root initiation. If the species is a particularly high value palm for which replacement costs would be expensive, the extra labor and cost may be worthwhile. To root prune a valuable specimen palm in the home landscape prior to re-locating it, a sharp tree spade with a blade at least 1 foot long should be used. The spade is inserted vertically as far as it will penetrate in a circle 8 to 10 inches from the trunk. If two root prunings will be performed before moving the palm, each should complete only 1/2 of the circle around the palm. The first pruning should be performed 12 weeks before moving the palm, the second at 6 weeks. When the palm is finally dug, allowances should be made so that the root ball is several inches wider than the root pruning circle. This helps ensure that branch roots stimulated by the pruning are not damaged. The decline of a few leaves after root-pruning is not unusual. If extensive root pruning is performed before transplanting, removal of a third of the palm's leaves may be advisable.

## Digging the Palm

Prior to digging, the soil around the root system should be thoroughly wetted to help keep the root ball together. Palms grown on sandy soils will usually need to have their roots balled-in-burlap after digging. Palms grown on soils with greater structural integrity may not require burlapping.

If the dug palms will be held in storage in the field for some time before shipment, burlapping may also be necessary, regardless of the soil type. In such a situation, the root ball as well as the trunk and foliage should be periodically moistened to keep them from drying out.

## Preparation for Transport

When being moved from the field, a specimen-sized palm should be well supported to prevent injury to the tender growing point or "palm heart" located within the stem between the youngest and oldest emerged leaves. Some palms (for example, King Alexander, *Archontophoenix alexandrae*) are much more sensitive than others to heart injury due to rough handling and will require extra care in transport. For certain species with slender trunks (for example, Senegal date, *Phoenix reclinata*; Paurotis palm, *Acoelorrhaphe wrightii*), a supporting splint should be tied to each trunk and extended into the foliage to protect the bud. Palms with very heavy crowns (for example, Canary Island date palm, *Phoenix canariensis*) should be braced similarly to prevent the

weight of the crown from snapping the bud. Stems of clustering palms should also be tied together for additional support.

A tree crane is usually required to lift large palms out of the field. The palm trunks should be protected with burlap or other material wherever ropes, cables, chains or straps will be attached.

## Leaf Removal

The greatest loss of water in newly dug palms occurs from transpiration through the leaves. To minimize such loss, half or more of the older leaves should be removed at the time of digging. The remaining leaves should be tied with biodegradable twine in a bundle around the bud. Complete leaf removal at the time of digging appears to be the best method for transplanting sabal palms (*Sabal palmetto*), which lose all their roots in the transplant operation (see "Special Cases" section later in this chapter).

## Site Preparation

Newly dug specimen palms are best transplanted immediately to minimize stress and possible loss of the palm. If delivered palms cannot be planted immediately upon arrival at the installation site, they should be placed out of direct sun and the trunk, root ball and canopy kept moist. Temporarily "heeling in" the root balls under a layer of mulch is advisable, especially if no other means of keeping the roots from drying out is available.

Conditions at the installation site also determine the establishment success of transplanted palms. A well-drained location is essential; standing water should not appear at the bottom of the planting hole. If drainage is a problem at the site, a berm should be constructed to raise the root ball above the level of water. (See the section "Compacted Low Oxygen Soils" in *The Planting Site*.) Though some palm species may adjust to less than optimal drainage after establishment, standing water around a newly dug root ball will have an adverse effect on establishment.

The planting hole should be wide enough to easily accept the root ball and provide at least several inches of room for new growth from the ball. The hole should only be deep enough to situate the palm at the same depth at which it previously grew.

The amending of backfill soil from the planting hole is not recommended. If the backfill soil differs greatly in structure and texture from the surrounding site soil, new roots will have a tendency to remain within the backfill. If amending the backfill soil is demanded, the volume of amendment should not exceed 25% of the soil removed from the hole.

## Planting and Support

### Planting Depth

Palms must not be transplanted any deeper than they were originally grown. Planting too deeply will cause root suffocation, nutritional deficiencies, root rot disease and perhaps even loss of the palm. The decline of palms planted too deeply may take several years to become apparent, especially in very well drained soils, and can only be reversed by removing the backfill from the suffocated root initiation zone or by replanting the palm.

All air pockets should be tamped out of the backfill as the planting hole is filled. A water ring should be mounded up at the periphery of the root ball to retain water during irrigation. The initial irrigation should be deep and thorough; filling the planting hole with water up to the water ring two or three times will be necessary to fully wet and settle the soil at the time of planting.

## Support

Large transplanted palms usually require anchorage for 6 to 8 months after transplant. Support can be supplied either with guy wires or, more commonly, with wood supports. Wrap three or four boards about 4 feet long in several layers of burlap. Fasten these to the trunk of the palm with metal straps, then nail support posts to the padded boards, being careful that nails do not pierce the trunk (Plate 2). Never nail supports directly into the trunk as such damage is permanent and provides an entryway for pathogens and possibly insect pests as well.

## Establishment Care

The root ball and surrounding backfill should remain evenly moist but never saturated during the first 4 to 6 months after installation. Supplemental irrigation is necessary unless adequate rainfall is received during this time period. Newly transplanted specimen-sized palms should not be expected to produce a great deal of new top growth during the first year after transplanting; much of the palm's energy reserves will (and should) be channeled into root growth. Drenching the root zone 2 to 4 times during the first few months with a fungicide labelled for landscape use on soil-borne root fungal pathogens is recommended for high value palms. A light (i.e. one third of recommended rate) surface application of a partially slow-release "palm special" granular fertilizer can be banded at the margins of the root ball 3 to 4 months after transplanting. A foliar spray of soluble micronutrients may be beneficial during this period, since root absorption activity is limited. Macronutrients (nitrogen, phosphorus, potassium, magnesium) are negligibly absorbed through the leaves and should not be applied as a foliar fertilizer. When the appearance of new leaves indicates that establishment has been successful, a regular fertilization program at an optimum of 3 to 4 times per year can begin. (See *Palm Nutrition Guide*.)

## Special Cases
### Cabbage or Sabal Palms

Sabal or cabbage palms (*Sabal palmetto*) are the most widely planted of all palms in the southeastern United States. Virtually all are dug as mature specimens from natural stands because their slow growth rate makes nursery production uneconomical. Survival rates for transplanted sabal palms are often low. In sabal palms, virtually no cut roots of any length survive, so there is no functional root system for the 6 to 8 months after transplanting.

Complete removal of leaves at the time of digging from the field appears to be the best method for transplanting sabal palms. However, the standard procedure has been to remove the lower two-thirds of the leaves before transport and tie the remaining leaves into a tight bundle around the bud to reduce transpiration. Care should be taken not to injure the internal bud when the leaves are removed. Leaves left on the tree usually become desiccated and die within 1 to 2 months, and the palm may appear to be dead. If it survives, new green leaves will eventually emerge from within the canopy of dead foliage. Sabal palms with all leaves removed at digging typically establish faster and with fewer losses than those whose leaves were retained.

## Palmetto Weevil Infestation

Palmetto weevils (*Rynchophorus cruentatus*) are large beetles that are drawn to stressed palms. They most frequently attack cabbage palms (*Sabal palmetto*) and Canary Island date palms (*Phoenix canariensis*), but have been reported on Mexican fan palms (*Washingtonia robusta*), Bismarck palms (*Bismarckia nobilis*) and latan palms (*Latania* spp.). Adult females lay eggs in the leaf bases of the crown, and the large larvae quickly tunnel into the heart, destroying the palm. The palmetto weevil has no natural enemies.

All efforts should be made to reduce transplant stress on susceptible species. A recommended insecticide should be sprayed as a preventative at the time of installation and again several weeks later. Although preventative spraying is generally discouraged, in this instance, **for susceptible palm species**, it is the only effective control of the palmetto weevil. Once infestation has occurred, nothing can be done to get rid of this pest. (See *Pest and Other Problems of Palms*.)

— *Alan W. Meerow*

## PALM Nutrition Guide

Palms are among the most important ornamental plants in Florida landscapes and will suffer quickly and conspicuously from improper mineral nutrition. Compared to other ornamentals, palms may exhibit certain of their nutritional disorders in unique ways.

Some nutritional problems in palms are difficult to diagnose accurately because symptoms of several different mineral deficiencies may overlap. In this guide, nutritional disorders common to palms growing both in the landscape and in containers are discussed and illustrated. Fertilization recommendations are also provided.

## Nutritional Disorders in the Landscape

### Nitrogen

Nitrogen deficiency is fairly common in Florida palms, although deficiencies of elements such as potassium, magnesium and manganese are much more prevalent and serious. Symptoms of nitrogen deficiency include an overall light green color and decreased vigor of the palm (Plate 3). Correct by applying any nitrogen fertilizer to the soil.

### Potassium

Potassium deficiency is perhaps the most widespread and serious of all disorders in Florida palms. Symptoms occur first on the oldest leaves and appear on progressively newer leaves as the deficiency becomes more severe. Symptoms vary among palm species but typically begin as translucent yellow or orange spots on the leaflets (Plate 4). These may or may not be accompanied by necrotic spots, which are areas of dead tissue. Leaflets will typically have areas of necrosis along the margins (Plate 5). As the symptoms progress, the leaflet or entire leaves will become withered or frizzled in appearance (Plate 6). The midrib usually remains alive on potassium deficient leaves, although it may be orange in color instead of green in some species. In date palms (*Phoe-*

*nix* spp.), symptoms are slightly different in that older leaves show an orange-brown discoloration near the tip (Plate 7). Also, the leaflet tips, rather than the margins, become necrotic as the deficiency progresses. The color of the chlorotic (i.e. yellowing) region in *Phoenix* leaves is a dull orange or even tan (Plate 7) in comparison to the bright yellow of a magnesium deficiency (Plate 8).

Potassium is moved from older to new leaves as required by the palm. In severe deficiencies, the canopy will be greatly reduced in size due to the removal of potassium from all of the leaves. Once all potassium has been removed from older leaves, the palm will go into a state of decline, with reduced trunk diameter (pencil-pointing) and the emergence of small, frizzled or chlorotic new leaves. Without prompt treatment, the palm will usually die. Potassium deficiency affects all species of palms but is most severe in royal, queen, coconut, areca and spindle palms. Treatment requires soil applications of sulfur- or resin-coated potassium sulfate at rates of 2 to 5 lbs per tree four times per year plus half as much magnesium sulfate to prevent a potassium-magnesium imbalance and resulting magnesium deficiency. Symptomatic leaves on potassium deficient palms will never recover and must be replaced by new, healthy leaves. In severely deficient palms, this means replacement of the entire canopy which may take 2 years or longer. Foliar sprays with potassium fertilizers are ineffective in correcting the problem since the amount of potassium supplied by a foliar spray is insignificant compared to the amount needed to correct the problem.

### Magnesium

Magnesium deficiency is also quite common in Florida palms, but especially in *Phoenix* species. As with a potassium deficiency, symptoms occur first on the oldest leaves and progress up through the canopy. Typical symptoms are a broad light yellow band along the margin of the older leaves with the center of the leaf remaining distinctively green (Plate 8). In severe cases, leaflet tips may become necrotic, but a magnesium deficiency is rarely, if ever, fatal to palms.

Magnesium deficiency is best treated preventatively since treatment of deficient palms takes considerable time. As with a potassium deficiency, symptomatic leaves will never recover and must be replaced by new healthy leaves. Applications of magnesium sulfate at rates of 1 to 3 lbs per tree four times per year plus coated potassium sulfate at the same rate should correct the problem and prevent the occurrence of a potassium-magnesium imbalance.

## Manganese

Manganese deficiency or "frizzletop" is a common problem in palms growing in the alkaline soils that cover much of south Florida. Symptoms occur only on new leaves which emerge chlorotic, weak, reduced in size and with extensive necrotic streaking in the leaves (Plate 9). As the deficiency progresses, succeeding leaves will emerge completely withered, frizzled or scorched in appearance and greatly reduced in size (Plates 10 and 11). Later, only necrotic petiole stubs will emerge, and death of the bud quickly follows.

Manganese deficiency is primarily caused by the element's insolubility at high pHs. In some palms such as coconut, which are not normally affected by the problem, cold soil temperatures during the winter and spring months reduce root activity and thus the uptake of micronutrients (especially manganese). Coconut palms that are severely

deficient in manganese during the winter and spring will usually grow out of the problem without special treatment once soil temperatures warm up in late spring. Other palms such as queen, royal, paurotis and pygmy date palms are highly susceptible to manganese deficiency and must be treated with soil or foliar applications of manganese sulfate or they will likely die.

## Iron

Iron deficiency is relatively uncommon in landscape palms and is not usually caused by a lack of iron in the soil or even by high soil pH as is the case with many other plants. Iron deficiency usually appears in palms that are growing in poorly aerated soils or that have been planted too deeply. Waterlogged soils and deep planting effectively suffocate the roots. Symptoms appear first on the new leaves and in most palms consist of uniformly chlorotic new leaves (Plate 12). As the deficiency progresses, new leaves will show extensive necrosis and reduced leaf size. Early symptoms in queen palms include pea-sized green spots on otherwise yellowish new leaves (Plate 13).

Iron deficiency symptoms can sometimes be temporarily alleviated by regular foliar applications of iron sulfate or chelates, but long term correction will only occur when the poor soil aeration or improper planting depth that caused the deficiency is corrected.

Diagnosis of nutrient deficiencies by visual symptoms alone can be difficult since some of the symptoms overlap considerably in some species. For instance, manganese and later stage potassium deficiencies are easily confused on queen and royal palms. Potassium and magnesium deficiencies are very similar in pygmy date palms. Late stage potassium and iron deficiencies can be similar in royal palms. Correct diagnosis can only be assured if leaf nutrient analysis is performed on symptomatic palms.

## Nutritional Disorders in Container-grown Palms

Palms growing in containers are susceptible to the same deficiencies that landscape palms experience, but the relative importance of the various deficiencies, as well as the causes, are different. Container media generally are more acid and have greater nutrient holding capacities than Florida native soils. Leaching and insolubility of nutrients are therefore much less of a problem. Also, container-grown palms are often fertilized with more complete slow-release fertilizers or regular liquid fertilization which prevents most deficiencies from occurring.

In container-grown palms, nitrogen deficiency is the most common deficiency and is simply caused by insufficient nitrogen in the medium (Plate 3). Potassium deficiency can occur in containers if fertilizers having low potassium content are used, and magnesium deficiency will occur if the dolomite added to the medium is insufficient or low grade. Amendment of container media with dolomite is absolutely essential unless other sources of calcium and magnesium are used in the fertilization program.

Sulfur deficiency occasionally occurs in containers if sulfate fertilizers are not used. Symptoms are virtually identical to those of iron deficiency and can only be correctly diagnosed by leaf nutrient analysis. Manganese deficiency is much less common in containers since the growing medium is usually acid and manganese is much more soluble at lower pHs.

Iron deficiency is quite common in container-grown palms (Plate 12). Containers generally provide poor soil aeration at the bottom of the pot where palm roots typically are concentrated, and iron deficiency is usually the result. Planting palms more deeply than they were originally growing will have the same effect and is a major cause of chronic iron deficiency in container-grown palms. Although foliar sprays with iron sulfate or chelates may temporarily correct the problem, permanent correction can only be achieved by replanting the palms at the correct depth and in new, well-drained media. For this reason, it is important to use a container medium that will not quickly break down into finer particles and reduce aeration. Our studies have shown that dibbling of slow-release fertilizers (i.e. applying under the root ball when transplanting to a larger container) as opposed to surface application prevents the rapid breakdown of container media and greatly reduces nutritional problems associated with poor soil aeration.

Other essential elements such as phosphorus, calcium, copper, zinc, boron and chlorine are occasionally found to be deficient if one of these elements is omitted from the fertilizer program, but such deficiencies are generally quite rare in containers or landscapes.

## Landscape Palm Fertilization

Mature palms (i.e. with developed trunks) in the landscape should receive a complete granular fertilizer formulated for palms ("palm special") four times per year at a rate of 2 to 4 lbs each application. More frequent applications of smaller amounts of fertilizer are preferable to fewer, larger applications unless controlled-release fertilizers are used. For palms under 8 feet tall, 1 to 3 lbs of fertilizer per application should be adequate. Special palm fertilizers contain additional magnesium and a complete micronutrient amendment. Nitrogen and potassium rates in the formulation should be equivalent, and all or at least some of both elements should be available in slow release form. Fertilizers should be broadcast or banded under the canopy of the palm but should not be placed up against the trunk where newly emerging roots may be injured.

— *Timothy K. Broschat and Alan W. Meerow*

# LANDSCAPE
## Use and Pruning of Palms

A palm that is well established in the landscape requires little maintenance as long as it receives a regular program of fertilization and irrigation suited to its species as well as the particular conditions of its site. Overwatering palms that are adapted for dry conditions can be detrimental, leading to various disease problems. Failure to provide adequate water to a rain forest dwelling palm can result in poor growth and even loss of the plant. It is important to know the requirements of your palm in its native habitat and compare those needs to what you will be able to provide in your landscape.

Palms are best planted in a situation where turfgrass can be kept away from the trunk, if only by mulching a small area around the base of the palm. The main reason for this practice is to prevent trunk injuries from line trimmers, mowers and other lawn care equipment. The wounds this equipment can cause are permanent and allow entry of disease organisms such as the *Ganoderma* fungus and possibly some insect pests as well. Mulch should also be pulled 2 or 3 inches back from the palm trunk so that it cannot become an agent for disease transmission or a harbor for pests. Palms from arid regions are often not compatible with turf-oriented irrigation schedules, and such species are best not planted as lawn specimens if irrigation will be frequent and shallow. Turf will also compete with palms for water and nutrients, and growth may not be optimum compared to the what the same palm could achieve when planted in a large, mulched landscape bed.

Within a landscape bed, the palms used should be compatible with neighboring plants. Consider questions like these: *Will the massing of ground covers or annual flowers near the base of the palm create difficulty in properly fertilizing the palm? Will the water needs of the shrubs, ground covers or flowers in the bed prove detrimental to the palm?* Because of the high cost of replacing or moving specimen palms, it is wise to ask these questions before installation.

## Where to Use Palms in the Landscape

Palms can be used for a variety of purposes in the landscape. While few palms can really provide as much shade as a broad-leaved tree, tall growing cluster palms or group plantings of solitary palms can create a functional amount of shade for a small home or a quiet nook in the backyard.

The boldly defined appearance of many palms will draw attention to the area of the landscape they occupy. While most tall clustering palms are effective as single accent specimens, tall solitary palms make effective border or boundary plantings for lining a long driveway or boulevard. Such tall growing palms as the royal palm (*Roystonea* spp.) provide a strong vertical accent in the landscape but can overpower a small building and make it appear even smaller.

Palms can be planted in combination with each other as well as with other types of landscape plants. A well-designed bed of various palm species can be the focal point of a subtropical landscape. Growth rates, habit and eventual size must be considered carefully when combining species to avoid a helter skelter mix that fails aesthetically.

Small groves of the same species can create an attractive landscape accent. King Alexander (*Archontophoenix alexandrae*), queen palms (*Syagrus romanzoffiana*), various *Veitchia* species and many other slender or moderate trunked species can be grouped successfully in the landscape. Densely clustering species such as the lady palms (*Rhapis* spp.), some *Chamaedorea* species and areca (*Chrysalidocarpus lutescens*) can be used to create a screen.

Avoid planting tall growing palms directly under roof overhangs and eaves. A misplaced palm will one day have to be removed.

## Pruning Palms

Palms do not require the same kind of pruning as branching, broad-leaved trees. The only trimming any palm needs is removal of dead or badly damaged or diseased leaves. Some landscape maintenance workers have an unfortunate tendency to overtrim palms, removing perfectly good green leaves along with the dead or dying fronds. No doubt the reason for this practice is an attempt to lengthen the interval before trimming is once again necessary, but the removal of healthy leaves is a disservice to the palm, especially those species whose canopy consists of no more than eight to twelve leaves. Out of fear that palm fronds could become projectiles in a storm, removal of healthy lower leaves is sometimes carried out as a safety measure. However, by this logic, the limbs of broad-leaved trees also pose a threat and require removal. Such precautions are obviously too extreme. Overtrimming reduces the food manufacturing efficiency of the living palm and can result in sub-optimum development of the trunk diameter at the point in the crown where diameter increase is currently taking place. There is also some evidence that overtrimming makes the palm more susceptible to cold damage. Do not permit the use of climbing spikes on your palms as palms lack the ability to produce callus to cover wounds. Any holes in the trunk, including those caused by spikes, can lead to disease problems.

There is no evidence to indicate that a palm will grow better or worse if the boots (old leaf bases) are removed. The boots do provide protection and insulation from cold damage, fire and other natural calamities. Sometimes, too, trunk tissue can be stripped off when a boot is removed before it is ready. Care should be taken to avoid causing such damage. Growing ferns in the "pockets" created by boots, though aesthetically pleasing, can trap moisture close to the trunk and create a potential for fungus and vermin in the crown.

— *Alan W. Meerow*

# PESTS
# & Other Problems of Palms
## Insect and Mite Problems

We are fortunate indeed that, relative to most landscape plants, a well-grown palm remains fairly free of damaging insect pests. Nevertheless, certain insects will occasionally attack landscape palms in sufficient force to warrant control measures.

**Palm aphid** (*Cerataphis palmae*). This aphid is unusual in that the female does not move and forms a distinctive ring of white wax around its body (Plate 14). These aphids heavily infest young leaves and excrete honeydew upon which black sooty mold will grow. They are sometimes tended by ants. Lady beetles are an excellent biological control, and spraying should be avoided if these aphid predators are observed on the infested palm.

**Scales**, in great variety, do turn up on palm leaves from time to time and include thread scale, magnolia white scale, oyster scale, Florida red scale and others. The hard shell of many scales reduces the effectiveness of many chemicals. Scales are more frequently a nuisance than a menace to palms. On a landscape size specimen, the most effective control for an infestation on a single leaf is removal.

**Spider mites**. Spider mites are particularly troublesome on palms grown indoors or in greenhouses and also on many *Chamaedorea* species. The predatory mite species, *Phytoseiulus persimilis* has been used very successfully to control two-spotted mites (*Tetranychus urticae*) on palms in the greenhouse and other interior environments. Many chemical miticides work successfully, too.

**Coconut mite**. This tiny spider mite feeds on the husk of coconut fruits, causing mostly cosmetic damage (Plate 15) but sometimes premature fruit drop as well. There is no known control for the coconut mite.

**Banana moth** (*Opogona sacchari*). The larvae of this moth have been a destructive pest in tropical areas on palm species such as Chamaedorea, arecas and others. Though it is more commonly a palm production pest, infestations of landscape palms have occurred. Damage occurs when the caterpillar tunnels through the stems of the palms. Parasitic nematodes have been fairly effective in controlling infestations of this insect.

**Palm leaf skeletonizer** (*Homaledra sabalella*). The caterpillars of this small moth feed on the upper and lower leaf surfaces of many palms, producing large quantities of "frass" (brown fibrous excrement) that is often the first conspicuous sign of an infestation. The tissue between the veins or ribs is usually their preferred food (Plate 100), but they will also feed on the leaf stems, disrupting the vascular tissue and causing the death of the entire leaf.

**Royal palm bug** (*Xylastodoris luteolus*, Plate 16) is a troublesome pest of royal palms (*Roystonea* spp.) in Florida and the Caribbean. Infestations in south Florida tend to increase in the spring and summer following a particularly mild winter. This tiny bug feeds on the young leaves of the palms (Plate 17), often getting in between the folds of an emerging leaf. When the leaf unfolds it appears scorched and brown and usually fails to mature.

**Palmetto weevils** (*Rynchophorus cruentatus*) are large beetles that are drawn to stressed palms (Plate 18). They most frequently attack cabbage palms (*Sabal palmetto*) and Canary Island date palms (*Phoenix canariensis*), but have been reported on Mexican fan palms (*Washingtonia robusta*), Bismarck palms (*Bismarckia nobilis*) and latan palms (*Latania* spp.). Adult females lay eggs in the leaf bases of the crown, and the large larvae (Plate 19) quickly tunnel into the heart, destroying the palm (Plate 20). All efforts should be made to reduce transplant stress on susceptible species. A preventative spray of a recommended insecticide, applied at installation and again a few weeks later, has shown some success in keeping palms free of infestation. A related species of weevil, *R. palmarum*, occurs in Central and South America and the Caribbean and spreads a destructive nematode that causes red ring disease in coconuts and African oil palms.

**Rotten sugar cane borer** (*Metamasius hemipterus*) is a relatively new pest of palms in south Florida. It attacks royal palms (*Roystonea* spp.), majesty palm (*Ravenea rivularis*), spindle palm (*Hyophorbe verschaffeltii*), Mexican fan palm (*Washingtonia robusta*) and possibly others. The larvae of this weevil completely riddle the stems of the palms which then succumb to various secondary disease organisms.

Various caterpillars and some grasshoppers feed on the leaves of palms from time to time. Small infestations can be dealt with mechanically without recourse to pesticides. If, however, these insects are on palm foliage in force, they can very quickly do appreciable damage, completely defoliating a young palm in as little as 1 to 2 days.

## Disease Problems

**Leaf Spots**. A number of leaf spot fungi cause variously shaped lesions on the leaf surface of many palm species. High rainfall or frequent overhead irrigation are often instrumental in their spread. If only a single leaf is affected, removal and disposal of that leaf is a simple and effective control. Some leaf spot fungi move in as secondary prob-

lems on palm leaves that are deficient in nutrients or have received some sort of damage.

Leaf spot diseases caused by various *Bipolaris* and *Exserohilum* fungi (often called **Helminthosporium-complex leaf spots**) affect a broad range of palms. The results are characteristically round, dark brown lesions (Plate 21) that eventually merge and form large blighted areas. The disease is easily spread by overhead irrigation. *Cercospora* **leaf spot** is frequently a problem on Rhapis palms and **Cylindricladium** on kentia (*Howea forsterana*). Anthracnose caused by a **Colletotrichum** fungus can affect a large number of palms, especially where overhead irrigation is used. **Stigmina** (*Exosporium* fungus) **leaf spot** can be a particular problem on date palm (*Phoenix*) species. *Graphiola* **leaf spot** or "false smut" can become a significant problem on landscape palms during periods of high rainfall. The disease becomes conspicuous when the fungus produces its greyish-black fruiting bodies which rupture through both leaf surfaces (Plate 22). *Pestalotiopsis* **leaf spot** affects a number of species. It seems to be a particular problem on date palm (*Phoenix*) species on which lesions often first appear on the rachis tissue (the leaf stem between the leaflets). **Tar spot** (*Catacauma* **leaf spot**) causes elongated, diamond-shaped lesions on the leaf surface.

**Sooty Mold**. This superficial fungus, caused by *Capnodium* spp., is more a nuisance than a life-or-death problem on palms. When present, it is always associated with infestations of sucking insects such as palm aphid, scales, or mealybugs. These insects excrete "honeydew," a waste product high in sugars that the sooty mold fungus feeds upon. The fungus appears on the leaf surface (and sometimes the trunk) as a conspicuous black, sooty deposit (Plate 162). Heavy infestations will interfere with the food-manufacturing efficiency of the leaf. The best control is to keep the palm free of honeydew producing insects.

## Bud, Root or Trunk Rots and Wilts

***Phytophthora* bud rot** is one of the more common diseases encountered in palms in wet tropical climates. It is primarily a warm season disease. This soil-borne disease causes collapse or brown-out of the younger foliage and emerging leaf. If the bud is cut open, discoloration is evident (Plate 23), often accompanied by a foul smell. *Phytophthora* can also cause leaf spots. Over watering and planting too deeply aggravate incidences of *Phytophthora*. *Pythium* and *Rhizoctonia* root rots can also affect palms.

***Thielaviopsis* trunk or bud rot** is increasing in frequency on palms in Florida but is not yet terribly common. This soil-borne fungus generally enters the palm through wounds and causes the disintegration of the trunk or bud. It can also infect the leaves of young palms. A cross-section through the trunk will reveal blackened fruiting bodies. Affected palms will blow over easily.

***Ganoderma* butt rot** has become a serious and incurable disease of older landscape palms (usually 15 years or older). The disease progresses upward from the older leaves, which turn brown and droop from the trunk. Wounds on the lower portions of the trunk or roots favor entry of the fungus. The fruiting body of the fungus is a conspicuous bracket or "conch" found emerging from the lower portions of the trunk (Plate 24). These fruiting bodies should be destroyed as soon as they appear by either burning them or breaking them up and tossing the pieces into chlorine bleach. The disease spreads rapidly from plant to plant, and the fungus

can persist in the soil for many years. Affected palms must be completely removed and destroyed and the soil fumigated. Affected palm stems should not be chipped and used as mulch.

Poor air circulation around the base of the palm trunk or frequent wetting of the trunk by sprinklers may also increase susceptibility to *Ganoderma*. Avoid mounding mulch at the base of a palm, and pull mulch 2 or 3 inches back from the trunk. Make sure line trimmers and other lawn care equipment do not damage the trunks of palms planted in turf. If *Ganoderma* has been diagnosed in a landscape site, it may be best to replant with a broad-leaved tree as no palm species can yet be declared reliably resistant.

***Fusarium* bud rot and wilt**, more common a problem in California, may become a serious disease in Florida. The disease frequently causes an uneven decline in the canopy of an infected palm, with leaflets along only one side of a single leaf dying first. The water and food conducting tissue within the leaves is usually discolored. Canary Island and date palms have been the worst affected in California. Pruning tools are known to transfer the fungus from tree to tree and should be sterilized before using on a different tree. Dip tools into rubbing alcohol for 30 seconds before each re-use to kill this harmful fungus.

**Bacterial bud rot** causes a wet blight of the emerging spear leaf which can then spread downward to the irreplaceable bud. Affected spear leaves can often be easily pulled from the bud. A foul odor frequently accompanies the damage. Bacterial bud rot often follows hard on the heels of recent cold damage to a palm.

**Lethal yellowing (LY)** is an incurable disease of many palm species caused by a mycoplasma-like organism (a form of life sometimes described as intermediate between a virus and a bacterium) that is spread by a leaf hopper bug (*Myndus crudus*). Fortunately, the popular cabbage palm, Florida's state tree, has so far proven resistant to the disease. The disease organism is now known to reside in the Florida counties of Palm Beach, Broward, Dade, Monroe, Lee and Collier as well as in southern Texas, Mexico and parts of Africa. The disease often begins with the blackening of young flower stems on infected palms. On coconuts, developing fruits will suddenly drop off the stems. One by one, mature leaves may begin to yellow on the palm and finally all the leaves in the canopy wilt and die (Plate 25). On other species (and some varieties of coconut as well) the yellowing may not be conspicuous; instead, leaves collapse and the palm quickly dies. The only practical control is to avoid planting highly LY- susceptible palms (Table 10). The decline caused by the disease can be temporarily suspended (though not cured) with a program of injections of tetracycline antibiotics (but only on palms with a developed trunk). Contact your county Extension agent for further information. Injections can be maintained until a resistant replacement palm achieves acceptable size, after which the infected palm is allowed to die.

## Miscellaneous Palm Problems

Landscape palms occasionally experience other problems that are not necessarily the

**Table 10. List of relative susceptibility to Lethal Yellowing of some ornamental palms**

| SCIENTIFIC NAME | COMMON NAME | SUSCEPTIBILITY |
|---|---|---|
| *Allagoptera arenaria* | Seashore palm | SLIGHT |
| *Arenga engleri* | Sugar palm | HIGH |
| *Borassus flabellifer* | Palmyra palm | MODERATE |
| *Caryota mitis* | Clustering fishtail palm | MODERATE |
| *C. rumphiana* | Solitary fishtail palm | MODERATE |
| *C. urens* | Toddy fishtail palm | MODERATE |
| *Chrysalidocarpus cabadae* | Cabada palm | SLIGHT |
| *Cocos nucifera*\* | Coconut | HIGH |
| *Corypha elata* | Gebang palm | HIGH |
| *Dictyosperma album* | Princess palm | MODERATE |
| *Hyophorbe verschaffeltii* | Spindle palm | SLIGHT |
| *Latania* spp. | Latan palms | MODERATE |
| *Livistona chinensis* | Chinese fan palm | MODERATE |
| *Livistona rotundifolia* | Footstool palm | MODERATE |
| *Nannorrhops ritchiana* | Mazari palm | SLIGHT |
| *Neodypsis decaryi* | Triangle palm | SLIGHT |
| *Phoenix canariensis* | Canary Island date | MODERATE |
| *P. dactylifera* | Date palm | MODERATE |
| *P. reclinata* | Senegal date palm | SLIGHT |
| *Pritchardia* spp. | Pritchardia | HIGH |
| *Syagrus schizophylla* | Arikury palm | MODERATE |
| *Trachycarpus fortunei* | Windmill palm | MODERATE |
| *Veitchia arecina* | Arecina palm | SLIGHT |
| *V. merrillii* | Christmas palm | HIGH |
| *V. mcdanielsii* | Sunshine palm | SLIGHT |
| *V. montgomeryana* | Montgomery palm | SLIGHT |

\*resistant varieties available

consequences of pests, diseases or nutritional deficiency.

**Trunk splits or cracks.** Some palm species (e.g. hurricane palm, *Dictyosperma album*) characteristically develop vertical fissures on their trunks. When these appear on palms that normally do not express them, it is usually an indication of water problems. Too much or too little soil moisture can result in small cracks on the trunk as can overly deep planting. Large scale trunk splitting is often associated with an over-abundance of water (Plate 26). Trunk cracking can also occur as a consequence of cold damage.

**Trunk constrictions**. At the point in the palm heart (bud) where active growth is taking place, palm stems increase in diameter before elongating. The optimal trunk diameter that a palm species will achieve is partially determined by the intrinsic character of the species and partially by the quality of the growing conditions at that point in time. If nutrition or water supply is limiting or if some other type of environmental stress occurs (a freeze, for example), the palm stem may fail to achieve the same increase in diameter as occurred in past years. As conditions improve, the stem will once again reach optimum trunk diameter. The result over the long term will be a constriction in the trunk at the point where the stem was actively growing when the stresses occurred. In older palms, it is sometimes possible to "read" the past history of growing conditions by the patterns of constrictions that appear along the length of the trunk.

**Pencil-pointing**. This syndrome is often related to that of trunk constriction. "Pencil-pointing" refers to a sudden, unnatural narrowing of the stem towards the crown of the palm. It is often associated with acute nutrient deficiencies but can also be caused by continuous over-trimming of the canopy. If conditions improve, the palm will return to its normal growth in trunk diameter, and a trunk constriction will develop at the point where pencil-pointing was observed.

**Lightning strike** (Plate 27). A direct lightning hit on a palm is usually fatal. Sudden collapse of the crown, trunk splitting and/or bleeding and dark streaks on the trunk are all possible symptoms of lightning damage.

**Power line decline**. Tall palms that have grown close to high voltage power lines have been observed to have yellowed or necrotic leaves despite regular fertilization and no evidence of pests or disease. This suggests that the electromagnetic fields around these lines may injure palms.

**Herbicide toxicity**. Many herbicides can cause damage to palms. Signs of herbicide injury include distorted and under-sized new growth and patches of dead tissue on the leaves. Damage from some herbicides may take months to become apparent. Consequently, special care should be taken when using weed-killing chemicals around landscape palms. Avoid any contact of the chemical with new roots or any green tissue on the palm. Only herbicides labelled for use around palms should be applied.

**After-flower decline**. Certain palms species (e.g. fishtail palms, *Caryota* spp.) flower and fruit once and then die. On clustering species with this habit, new stems are produced that continue the growth of the palm, but solitary palms will have to be replaced.

**Salt injury**. Leaf burn on the seaward side of palms planted near the shore is often indicative of salt injury. Such injury usually follows a period of high winds. A sudden intrusion of salt water into the root zone of palms can cause an overall decline and death of the plant. The best way to deal with this problem is to plant only those palms with high salt tolerance in exposed coastal locations.

— *Alan W. Meerow*

# TREATING Cold Damaged Palms

Cold weather slows down the growth of palms, reduces the activity of the roots and often weakens the plant to the point where a disease can become active and kill the palm. Severe cold damage from frost or freezing temperatures destroys plant tissues and may severely reduce water conduction in the trunk for years afterwards. Often the only above-ground portion of a cold-damaged palm that remains alive is the protected bud. As warmer weather returns, primary or secondary plant pathogens often attack weakened plants and may eventually kill the bud and the palm.

## Possible Preventative Action

Bacteria that are present at low levels on healthy palm tissue can become a problem when freeze damage occurs. In most cases, these are the secondary plant pathogens that cause the death of the bud soon after damage occurs. For this reason, there may be value in applying a preventative spray of fungicidal copper **before** freezing temperatures are reached in order to reduce bacteria populations to the lowest levels possible. (This strategy has not been tested under controlled conditions.)

It is evident that palm tissue deficient in one or more essential plant nutrients is less tolerant of exposure to freezing temperatures. To ensure that foliar nutrient levels are near optimum as winter approaches, be sure that palms receive a balanced fertilization in late summer or early fall.

# Protecting the Damaged Palm
## While Waiting for Warm Weather

Take these steps to avoid attacks by primary or secondary plant pathogens and protect the healthy bud until active growth resumes:

1. Remove cold-damaged **portions** of leaves; however, do not remove any green parts, even if they are spotted from the cold. Intact green portions are important to assure adequate photosynthesis during the recovery stage.

2. Immediately after pruning, spray the palms with a fungicide containing copper at the recommended rate. Include a spreader sticker, which is a product that helps other materials spread and stick to the leaves.

3. Repeat the copper spray 10 days after the first treatment or use another broad spectrum fungicide. (Contact your county agent for current fungicide recommendations.) In all cases, these sprays must cover the damaged tissue and healthy bud thoroughly. **Copper sprays should not be used more than twice a year because of the possibility of copper phytotoxicity.**

4. Palms growing in containers may benefit from a soil drench of fungicides that suppress root diseases. Contact your county agent for current recommendations of available fungicide formulations.

5. Occasionally, cold damage is so severe or disease has already progressed so far that the spear leaf (new

developing leaf) becomes loose and pulls out easily. With such a palm, there is still a chance of recovery if the meristem (growth point) is alive. To treat, remove as much dead and decaying material from around the bud as possible so it can dry out. The hollow collar of overlapping leaf bases that is left when the spear leaf pulls out should be pierced just above the solid tissue to allow water to drain from it. Drench the bud with a copper fungicide using the force of the sprayer to clean out the bud as much as possible. Repeat 10 days later.

6. Warmer weather promotes rapid growth, and this helps the palms recover. After the two initial sprays of copper fungicide, a monthly application of soluble nutrients should be applied to the leaves. A formulation of 1/4 to 1/2 tsp/gal S.T.E.M.™ (Peter's Soluble Trace Element Mix) mixed with a spreader sticker has been tested by the Institute of Food and Agricultural Sciences. Other products containing similar nutrients should work equally well.

## Delayed Cold Damage

Palms that were severely damaged during the winter should be watched carefully during the subsequent spring and summer seasons. Damage to embryonic leaves within the bud may not show up until those leaves emerge (as much as 6 months to a year after the freeze) at which time, they may appear deformed, partially browned or otherwise abnormal. In most cases, the palm will grow out of such problems later in the season. (Leaving the old boots on the palm provides a natural cold protection barrier.)

Freeze damage to conducting tissue in the trunk may limit the ability of the palm to supply water to its canopy of leaves. Unlike typical broadleaved trees, palms have no ability to regenerate conducting tissue in the trunk. A sudden collapse of some (or even all) of the leaves in the crown during the first periods of high temperature in the spring or summer after a winter freeze may indicate that this type of trunk damage has occurred. Unfortunately, nothing can be done to remedy this, and loss of the palm is inevitable.

## Conclusion

The above recommendations will help reduce loss from cold damage and speed up recovery. Continue nutrient sprays into the summer if the plants are young or newly established in the landscape. Older palms will benefit from a granular palm fertilizer applied to the soil in the spring and repeated every 3 to 4 months.

— *Alan W. Meerow*

# SHRUB SELECTION, Planting and Establishment

To fully appreciate the role shrubs can play in your landscape, imagine them as part of an outdoor living area. In this scheme of things, trees provide the framework and overhead cover, turfgrass and other ground covers are the flooring, and shrubs form the walls, internal dividers and decoration. To take maximum advantage of both the usefulness and beauty of the wide variety of shrubs available to the Florida gardener, you will need to be able to select a healthy plant that is the right size and species for its place in the landscape and harmonizes with neighboring plants and buildings. You will also need to see that the shrub is properly planted and established, so that it is a healthy and beautiful addition to your landscape.

## Selecting Quality Shrubs

### Climatic Considerations

Shrubs used in landscape plantings should be adapted to the environment in which they are to be grown to obtain the most satisfactory landscape effects. In general, the northern areas of Florida are subject to frequent heavy frosts, while the central area is less frequently so. South Florida rarely experiences frosts. Because of such differences in minimum winter temperatures throughout the state, comparatively few shrubs are adapted for statewide use, though some species can be grown in more than one of the areas.

There are no clear cut lines of demarcation between the three major climatic zones. Furthermore, a given location may be warmer or cooler than the rest of its zone because of its proximity to a lake or coast, its elevation or its air drainage. (Air drainage refers to the phenomenon of cold air moving down a slope to settle in the lowest area in the landscape.) As a consequence of such variables, an affected location may accommodate plants that are more tender or more hardy than those used elsewhere in the zone.

On the basis of response to low temperatures, shrubs may be classified as tender, semi-hardy or hardy in each of the three climatic sections of the state listed above (i.e. a plant that is considered hardy in south Florida might be considered tender in north Florida). Adapted hardy plants can be grown throughout the northern Florida area. Some semi-hardy plants grown in central Florida can be successfully grown in warmer parts of northern peninsular Florida. The tender plants are confined largely to southern Florida, but a few species are adapted to the warmest parts of the central area. Semi-hardy and tender plants will normally survive lower temperatures when mature, or if they have been previously conditioned by several weeks of cool or cold temperatures prior to a freeze. At the other extreme, some shrubs require specified periods of cool or cold temperatures to induce dormancy required for proper growth and flowering.

### Environmental Considerations

Before heading to a nursery, study the environmental conditions in your landscape. The time you spend doing this now will pay dividends in lower maintenance costs and fewer plant replacements in the future. Plants have different requirements, and the success of a planting depends on how well you select plants that match the light level, soil and other characteristics of the site (see *The Planting Site*). Site characteristics can differ greatly within the same landscape.

Light levels in various parts of a landscape can range from full sun exposure to dense shade. Soil can vary from well-drained sand to poorly drained clay.

Most shrubs selected for Florida are well adapted to a wide range of soil types, soil moisture conditions and pH ranges, but most grow best in slightly acid soils (pH of 5.5 to 6.5). Although a few shrubs will tolerate dry sandy soils and some will tolerate poorly drained soils, most grow best in moist, well-drained soils. Most shrubs adapted to well-drained soils do not grow well in poorly drained soils, and shrubs adapted to moist soils usually grow poorly in dry sandy locations. Better plant growth results from using shrubs adapted to the existing soil conditions unless high maintenance costs are acceptable.

## Determine Plant Sizes and Numbers

Choose the appropriate plant size for the site. Don't think that just because a shrub looks small in the nursery, it will not rapidly outgrow its allotted area after a few years. Decide plant size to buy by considering its final height and spread as well as how long it will take to reach that size. Often, dwarf varieties of shrubs are good choices. You don't need to prune these cultivars frequently and, because they stay small, you won't have to replace them for becoming too big.

Base the number of plants you need on the mature spread of the plant, the space to be planted and the planting density you desire. In areas where a mass effect is desired, plants should be planted close together. In other instances, space plants far enough apart to allow each plant to develop its natural form or shape.

## Examine the Plants at the Nursery

After deciding the kind and number of plants you need, you are ready to shop for reasonably priced, good quality plants. Healthy plants establish faster and have fewer problems than plants in poor health. That is why it is so important that you examine plants very closely and look for healthy, vigorous ones. Avoid plants that are infested with aphids, lacebugs, spider mites, whiteflies or scales (Plates 28, 29 and 30). These pests suck juices from leaves and stems and can seriously damage a plant. Some of these pests are very small and are only visible through a magnifying lens. You can easily detect their damage to plant foliage, which often manifests itself as flecking or spotting on the upper sides of leaves. (Spotted leaves also can be a symptom of a leaf-spot disease. Although this disease is not usually serious, you are better off to buy plants without any diseases.)

### Inspect for Mechanical Injury

Inspect plants closely, and don't purchase any with scars or open wounds along their stems (Plate 31). Large pruning wounds are unsightly and expose the shrub to a higher incidence of decay.

Don't buy shrubs with many broken branches or leaves. A plant with a few small, broken branches is acceptable, if they can be removed without destroying the plant's shape. Removal of large branches creates large holes in the plant's canopy, and it will take years for the plant to regain its natural shape.

Examine grafted plants to determine if the graft union has healed properly. The union should be smooth and clean. There should be no suckers on the stem below the graft union.

## Check for Cold Injury

Plant stems and roots unprotected from frost or freezing temperatures may be damaged. Obvious cold injury symptoms are brown leaves, bark splitting and dead branches. Some plants may not express cold injury symptoms until they are stressed by warmer weather in the spring. Therefore, if you are buying plants after a hard winter, you should closely inspect their roots and stems in the spring for signs of root injury or split bark.

## Study Condition and Shape of Canopy

After you find the species of plants you want to buy, select specimens with uniform canopies densely filled with healthy, vigorous leaves of normal size, shape, color and texture. Avoid plants with abnormally sized or excessively yellowed leaves. These symptoms indicate health problems.

High-quality plants have stems that are well-formed and sturdy with plenty of uniformly distributed branches forming a well-balanced plant. Uneven branches on the main stem usually result in weak or leggy plants that you should avoid.

## Examine the Root System

Don't look only at the above-ground parts of a plant because the ultimate survival of a plant depends on the health of its root system. For this reason, buy your plants from a nursery that allows customers to examine plant roots. This is not easy because you usually have to remove pots or other coverings from around root balls or roots.

You can purchase shrubs from nurseries either in containers or balled-in-burlap. Inspect the roots of a container-grown plant by laying it down and sliding the container off the root ball (Plate 32). If you find it difficult to remove the container, the plant may be pot-bound. Pot-bound plants have a mass of roots circling near the outside surface of the root ball (Plate 33). This root mass can stop roots from penetrating the soil after planting. The circling roots can also girdle and kill the plant as it grows. On the other hand, if the root ball disintegrates when you remove it, it may have just been "stepped up" to a larger container (Plate 34). You could be buying a large container of potting media with very few roots. Examine the roots on the surface of the root ball. Don't buy a plant with black roots (Plate 35). These roots were probably killed by heat stress, freezing temperatures or over watering.

If you try to pick up a container plant and find it is fastened to the ground by escaping roots, move to another plant (Plate 36). Roots should be distributed throughout the container medium. They should not protrude outside the container or penetrate the ground. The root ball should be free of weeds, which will slow the establishment rate of a plant and may spread into the surrounding landscape (Plate 37).

The root balls of plants balled-in-burlap should be moist with the soil firmly held around the roots by burlap that has been tightly secured with pins, twine or wire. The stem of the plant should be sturdy in the root ball. A loose or droopy root ball indicates that the plant was roughly treated and may result in poor plant establishment and growth in the landscape.

# Planting Shrubs
## When to Plant

Shrubs can be planted throughout the year in Florida. However, in north and central

Florida, fall and winter planting are ideal. Planting during this period allows plants time to develop new roots and become established before they resume top growth in the spring. In southern Florida, where temperatures are often high enough to allow top growth year-round, planting just before the May rainy season is recommended.

## Handling and Preparing Root Balls for Planting

If shrubs are to survive and become established in a landscape, they have to be installed correctly. The procedures for planting container-grown and balled-in-burlap plants are essentially the same. However, handling and preparing the root balls for planting is quite different. Root balls in containers are more resistant to rough handling than those that have been balled-in-burlap. The root ball of a balled-in-burlap plant should be handled very carefully to prevent the soil within the root ball from shifting, which will cause cracks in the root ball and root breakage. A cracked root ball dries out quickly.

Prepare a container-grown plant for planting by slipping the container from the root ball. The root ball should stay together but be somewhat pliable when the container is removed. If the root ball has many roots circling around the outside, it is pot-bound. Use pruning shears or a serrated knife to make slices in three or four places around the root ball. These slices should be 1 to 2 inches deep and go from the top to the bottom of the root ball, much in the way you would slice a cake. Pull the roots growing along the outside of the root ball away from the root ball.

Begin the preparation of a balled-in-burlap plant for planting by determining whether the root ball has been wrapped in natural or synthetic burlap. To determine which type has been used, hold a match to a small portion of the burlap. As a rule, natural burlap will burn, synthetic will melt. Because it does not decompose in the soil and can girdle roots as they expand through the material, remove synthetic burlap entirely after setting the plant in the hole. After pulling the burlap away from the sides of the root ball, tip the root ball to one side and push the burlap underneath it as far as possible. Then tip the root ball to the other side, and slide the burlap out from under. The tipping should be performed by handling the root ball; pushing on the trunk of the tree could crack the root ball. Natural burlap decomposes readily in the soil and can be left along the sides and bottom of the root ball but should always be removed from the top of the root ball where it is subject to drying out. Dry burlap repels water, making it difficult to rewet the root ball. **Always remove nylon twine used to hold burlap around the plant stem. Nylon twine does not rot and will eventually girdle the stem if left in place.**

## Digging and Filling the Planting Hole

Begin planting by digging the planting hole two to three times the diameter of the root ball (Figure 23). The planting hole should never be dug any deeper than the height of the root ball. Disturbing the soil beneath the plant may cause it to settle too deeply in the soil. Gently place the plant straight into the hole, making sure again that the top of the root ball is not deeper than the existing landscape soil surface. In areas of compacted or poorly drained soils, the top quarter to third of the root ball should be positioned slightly above the soil surface and soil mounded around it to provide an

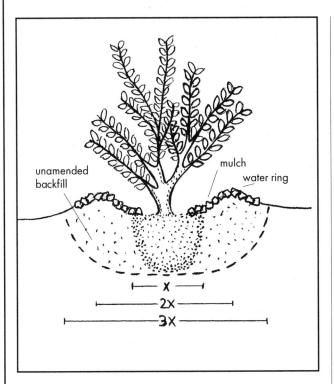

Figure 23. **Planting a shrub in well-drained soil.**

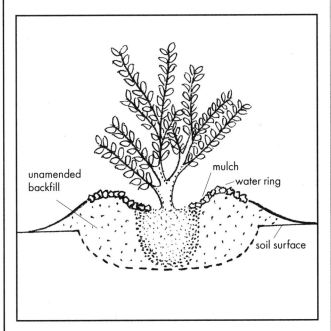

Figure 24. **Planting a shrub in compacted or poorly drained soil.**

adequate volume of well-drained soil for root development (Figure 24).

After placing the root ball into the planting hole, backfill the bottom half of the space around the root ball with existing soil. Mixing amendments such as organic matter into the backfill soil provides no benefit. Tamp the soil to settle it around the root ball, but not so heavily as to compact the soil. Finish filling the hole with loose, unamended soil and gently tamp again. Settle the soil by pushing a hose with running water in and out of the backfill soil all around the hole.

Construct a 3-inch-high water ring around the edge of the root ball to hold irrigation water (Figures 23 and 24). Water rings should be removed by the end of the second growing season.

## Planting Shrubs in Beds

If no trees or mature shrubs are in the vicinity, prepare beds for planting groups of shrubs by spading or tilling the entire bed to a depth of 8 to 12 inches. If shrubs are already present, keep spading or tilling activities outside their drip lines. Around trees, do not spade or till, simply dig a hole for each shrub. There may be some benefit to amending the soil in the entire planting bed with peat, compost or other soil amendments. If soil amendments are used, mix 2 to 3 inches of organic matter into the top 6 to 12 inches of soil before planting. Then dig holes for each shrub and backfill with the amended bed soil.

## Mulching

Mulch newly planted shrubs with a 2 to 3 inch layer of organic or inorganic material. Mulches reduce soil temperature fluctuations, prevent packing and crusting, conserve moisture, help control weeds and add to the beauty of the landscape by providing a cover of uniform color and interesting texture to the surface.

Mulch entire shrub beds with a layer of mulching material. When mulching individual shrubs in lawns, cover an area at least two times larger than the planting hole. Mulching in this manner will establish a shrub quickly by eliminating competition from turfgrass.

Pull mulch 2 to 3 inches away from the stems of shrubs. The high moisture environment created by mulch placed against the stem increases the chances of stem rot which can result in plant death.

## Watering and Fertilizing

Shrubs require months to develop roots into surrounding soil; therefore, they should be watered as frequently as when they were in containers. Strive to maintain constant moisture in the root ball, but avoid keeping it saturated. The first few weeks after planting, water the root ball every day. Gradually decrease the frequency of irrigation to every other day and then to every third day. Once the plants are well established, they do not need to be watered as often, but they should not be allowed to suffer from lack of water. Shrubs will benefit from a small amount of slow-release fertilizer applied to the top of the root ball 4 to 6 weeks after planting.

—*Robert J. Black*

# VINES

Vines are plants that grow horizontally over the ground or climb by twining or attaching appendages to a support. They may be annual or perennial, woody or herbaceous, evergreen or deciduous. Vines are often grown for their flowers since many have longer and more frequent blooming cycles than other plant forms. Other vines are grown primarily for their fruit or foliage.

Florida's mild climate is favorable for the culture of a wide variety of vines. There are vines in bloom every month of the year in different sections of the state. Many of these vines are evergreen, making them functional and beautiful year-round. Others are deciduous with desirable characteristics that may also be worked into landscape designs. Many vines which can be grown in Florida have unusual and striking foliage and flowers, but because people rarely try to grow them, they are seldom seen in the landscape. Where they can be adapted, these vines can offer interest and function to a landscape.

## Landscape Uses

Vines can be used in a variety of ways in the landscape. Undesirable trees, posts and poles can be transformed by using vines to alter their form, texture and color. Some species of vines cling or climb on wood, stone, brick or stucco, adding character to uninteresting walls or fences. Closely clinging vines can also be used to accentuate elements of a building's architecture, while larger, branching vines can soften harsh or unattractive lines. Certain species can be trained to cover a trellis or arbor to provide shade and privacy or screen unsightly views. Vines can also be used as ground covers in areas where turf is not desired or will not grow.

# How Vines Climb

Vines need some type of support when grown upright in the landscape. To choose the proper support for a particular species of vine, it is important to understand how the vine is going to climb. Vines can be separated into three basic types of climbers: clingers, twiners and winders.

**Clingers** are vines which grasp rough surfaces by means of rootlets or adhesive disks. Examples of these are English ivy (*Hedera helix*), climbing fig (*Ficus pumila*), heartleaf philodendron (*Philodendron scandens*) and split-leaf philodendron (*Monstera deliciosa*). This type of vine is often used to cover a solid upright surface like a tree, fence or wall. Vines should not be grown on wooden walls because they prevent the wood surface from drying and thus increase the chance of decay. Clinging vines may also loosen mortar between bricks or concrete blocks in masonry walls and can be hard to remove from some walls. These potential problems should be considered before planting vines to cover walls.

**Twining** vines climb by encircling upright vertical supports. They are often used on poles, vertical wires or lattice structures. Most of these vines will spiral in the one direction characteristic of the species. If an attempt is made to train them to spiral in the opposite direction, most will not cooperate, and the vine may be damaged. Twining vines include mandevilla (*Mandevilla splendens*), Confederate jasmine (*Trachelospermum jasminoides*), allamanda (*Allamanda cathartica*) and bougainvillea (*Bougainvillea* spp.).

The **winders** climb by means of tendrils. Tendrils come in many forms and sizes. They wind themselves around some kind of support in response to friction. These vines can be used to cover lattice, wire mesh or other supports which spread horizontally. Examples of vines that climb by tendrils include painted trumpet (*Clytostoma callistegioides*), cat's claw (*Macfadyena unguis-cati*), purple granadilla (*Passiflora edulis*) and Virginia creeper (*Parthenocissus quinquefolia*).

If your support is already determined, choose a vine that is adapted to climb it. When choosing the vine first, be sure to select the appropriate support for it.

# Selection
## Climatic Considerations

Florida is usually divided by differences in normal prevailing temperatures into three regions: north, central and south. Based on their climatic adaptation, plants are specified to be grown in one or more of these regions. The limits of each region for a given plant cannot be exactly defined. Local conditions such as elevation, bodies of water, proximity to the coast and other factors influence temperature. Yearly fluctuations in temperature should also be considered. Categorizing plants into these regions can, however, act as a guide.

To ensure their vigor and health in the landscape, vines need to be adapted to the region in which they are grown. If adapted to the cooler northern areas of Florida, a vine may not be suitable to warmer regions. Many of the tropical or subtropical vines grown in southern Florida are not hardy enough to survive the winter of north Florida. However, some of these vines may be planted in cooler areas of the state. In central Florida, they may be killed back to the ground during the winter but sprout back from the roots the following spring. These same vines will usually stay evergreen in the warmer regions of the state.

The location of a plant can help protect it from cold injury. Tender species of vines can be planted on the south and east sides of buildings where they are more protected from the cold northwesterly winds. Vines planted beside buildings or under overhangs or trees get more protection from cold than the same vines planted in exposed locations. Plants in locations that are shaded early in the morning may also suffer less cold damage.

## Environmental Considerations

Planting site characteristics such as amount of sun or shade, salt spray, soil moisture and soil type should also dictate the type of vine that can be grown and its placement within the landscape. Vines require different amounts of sunlight, but most vines grow and flower best in full sunlight to partial shade.

The tolerance of vines to salt water and salt spray is of particular concern to home gardeners living in Florida's coastal areas. Some vines are well-adapted to the soils and exposures of coastal areas.

Poor soil drainage can cause the roots of some vines to decay while others are adapted to wet areas. However, if vines recommended for wet areas are produced in a well-drained nursery soil, they may not be able to withstand a rapid transition. The best solution is to correct drainage problems by altering drainage patterns with tiles or landforms.

Most vines grow best in a slightly acid (pH 5.5 to 6.5), loose, well-drained soil. However, these soil conditions seldom exist at most planting sites. It is advisable to select vines which are adapted to the existing soil type rather than amending or changing soil conditions to suit a particular type of vine.

The procedure for selecting quality vines from a nursery is the same for selecting quality shrubs (see *Shrub Selection, Planting and Establishment*). The only difference is that, unlike shrubs whose branches are self supportive, vines have long branches called runners which must be staked or trellised to remain upright.

## Planting and Care

Vines are planted in the same manner as shrubs and require the same care. See *Shrub Selection, Planting and Establishment.*

## Pruning

Ornamental vines usually require little pruning except to keep them in bounds. Vines growing up walls should be kept off the roof to avoid damaging shingles. Some of the more vigorous vines may need occasional pruning to keep them on their support and looking attractive.

Vines grown for their attractive flowers should be pruned shortly after the blooming period. Later pruning may damage next year's buds, and earlier pruning could remove the current season's flowers.

—*Robert J. Black*

# GROUND COVERS

Often used in areas where grass is not desired or will not grow, ground covers are low-growing plants that can be cultivated to enhance the beauty and usefulness of a landscape. They can be arranged to create interesting contrasts in texture and color and are often the most unifying element in a total planting. The ideal ground cover is evergreen and provides a permanent covering.

By substituting ground covers for turfgrasses, you can realize an immediate savings in the time and energy spent maintaining top quality lawns which must be frequently mowed, fertilized and watered. Turfgrasses are difficult and/or dangerous to mow on slopes, near traffic and in out-of-the-way corners. Furthermore, they grow poorly in dense shade and in extremely wet or dry areas. Many ground covers are more adaptable than turf to these problem areas. However, the uses to which you put outdoor living space should be considered before replacing turfgrasses with ground covers. Turfgrass is still the best choice for recreational areas or locations with heavy foot traffic.

In addition to saving time and energy, ground covers can help provide a cooler, more comfortable environment in hot weather. In contrast, paved surfaces around the home contribute substantially to summertime heat loads because they absorb the sun's heat or reflect it back into the immediate environment. Paved areas also store heat during the day, keeping temperatures high around the home even after the sun has set. Temperatures over ground cover vegetation can be 15° to 25°F lower than those over asphalt or concrete, a significant difference when it comes to human comfort.

## Selecting Ground Covers
### Types of Ground Covers

The type of ground cover you select should satisfy the aesthetic and practical requirements of your overall landscape design. Plants used for ground covers vary widely. Like dichondra and lippia, they may have characteristics and maintenance requirements similar to grasses, or they may be shrubs that take a low growing, spreading form (e.g. shore juniper and dwarf forms of yaupon holly, firethorn and carissa). Such shrubs are particularly helpful in areas where foot traffic is a problem. Mass plantings of such perennial flowers as daylilies make effective ground covers and provide color at certain times of the year. Native plants such as gopher apple, partridge berry and beach morning glory have great potential as ground covers and should be encouraged where possible.

### Environmental Conditions

Determine the environmental conditions at the site before choosing a ground cover. Light intensity, soil conditions, exposure to salt water and salt spray and location in the state will have a marked influence on which plants can be selected. Some ground covers such as pothos, liriope, mondo grass and English ivy grow well in shade while juniper, lantana, beach morning glory and society garlic grow best in full sun. Others, such as dwarf confederate jasmine and coontie, grow equally well in full sun or shade.

There are ground covers for a wide variety of soil conditions. Ground covers such as lippia and selaginella tolerate wet soils while junipers and lantana grow best in dry, sandy soils.

Home gardeners living in coastal areas should, of course, select ground covers which are tolerant to salt water and salt spray. Beach sunflower, golden creeper, beach morning glory and sea oats are native ground covers which are well adapted to sandy coastal areas.

Relatively few ground covers are adapted throughout Florida due to differences in winter temperatures from north to south. Though mild winters do occur throughout the state, tender plants such as creeping charlie and peperomia are not recommended outside of south Florida because a freeze would kill them. By the same token, winter creeper and various other woody plants are restricted to northern Florida because they require chilling temperatures.

## Maintenance Requirements

Because one of the objectives of using a ground cover is to reduce maintenance in the landscape, don't forget that some ground covers can themselves become problems when allowed to overgrow their desired boundaries. In particular, dichondra, creeping charlie and varieties of wandering jew may spread and become weed pests. These plants should only be used in isolated areas where they may be kept in bounds by sidewalks or other natural barriers. Otherwise, they need to be watched carefully and contained by hand.

Ground cover plantings may suffer from weed problems, particularly when planted under or near trees that reproduce readily from seed. A ground cover is not recommended under cherry laurel, camphor tree or golden-rain tree.

## Uses of Ground Covers in the Landscape

Because ground covers are not isolated features in the landscape, you need to consider their effect on surrounding plantings as well as on the whole. Like trees and shrubs, ground cover plants vary in growth habit, texture and color. Their placement into the landscape requires care.

Though many interesting patterns may be created with ground covers, elaborate designs usually increase maintenance requirements. Thus ground cover areas should be kept as simple as possible in most home landscapes. This does not mean that the overall effect has to be dull or that some artistry cannot be expressed, but unnecessary curves and tight corners that are difficult to maintain should be avoided.

Ground covers can be used as transition elements between dissimilar features. Low growing woody plants, such as weeping lantana and shore juniper, can be used between the lawn and a row of larger shrubs. Vining plants, such as confederate jasmine and creeping fig, can be grown along the ground and then allowed to continue up a wall or over an embankment to cover harsh lines of structural features.

Color contrasts can be added to the landscape through the use of ground covers. The dark green color of Carolina yellow jessamine, liriope and mondo grass combined with the light green color of a lawn creates a pleasing color contrast. Other ground covers vary from the dull green of common winter creeper to the glossy green of dwarf confederate jasmine. A number of ground cover plants flower at certain times of the year and some, among them wedelia and daylily, are highly prized for their flowers.

## Planting Ground Covers

Preparation for planting begins with spading or tilling the area where a ground cover is desired. This loosens the soil and removes other plants as well as buried debris. The site should be examined for possible problems. If any problems are discovered, they should be corrected before planting. Otherwise, select a ground cover which will tolerate existing conditions. A soil test to determine soil's pH (acidity or alkalinity) and fertility level may be useful especially if grass or other plants have not grown well in the area. However, soil tests will not reveal the presence of insects, diseases, nematodes or improper drainage.

It is a good practice to add organic matter (e.g. peat, compost) to the soil. Spread a 2 to 3-inch layer of organic matter over the soil, and mix it in to a depth of 6 to 10 inches.

To keep down the weeds that will quickly sprout between ground cover plants, space plants to cover the area as soon as possible. Plant spacing also depends on the species selected. Small plants such as ajuga and creeping charlie may be planted as close as 3 to 4 inches from each other while larger woody plants may be spaced as far as 4 feet apart. Table 11 shows the amount of area that 100 plants cover when set at a given spacing.

Individual planting holes should be dug two to three times the diameter of the root ball and as deep as the root ball is tall. Plants should be set in holes at the same level they were growing in their containers and amended soil placed around the root balls. Immediately after planting, a thorough watering is essential. Newly set plants with poor root systems will require shading for a few days until they become established. A mulch will be helpful in reducing weed problems and retaining moisture, especially if a slow growing ground cover is selected.

Steep banks or sloping areas usually require special preparation. Instead of tilling the planting area, which may increase the chances of soil erosion, dig individual planting holes. On very steep banks where soil erosion is almost a certainty, cover the entire planting area with a plastic netting material. Applying a mulch which clings together well (e.g. pine needles) will also help to hold soil in place until the ground cover can become well established. Because sloping areas are often dry, use a plant such as juniper that can tolerate this condition.

## Ground Cover Maintenance

It may take up to 2 years to establish a ground cover area. Fertilizing, watering and weeding will probably be required during this period. Once established, most ground covers require only an occasional weeding and trimming to maintain them in bounds.

Determine the amount of fertilizer to apply based on how fast you want full coverage to occur. Begin fertilizing 4 to 6 weeks after

**Table 11. Area covered by 100 plants at a given spacing***

| Planting distance in inches | Square feet covered by 100 plants |
|---|---|
| 4 | 11 |
| 6 | 25 |
| 8 | 44 |
| 10 | 70 |
| 12 | 100 |
| 15 | 156 |
| 18 | 225 |
| 24 | 400 |
| 36 | 900 |
| 48 | 1600 |

*Spacing calculated from the center of one plant to the center of the next plant.

planting, then make one application around February (south Florida) or March (north Florida), another during May or early summer and a third application in September (north) or October (south). If rapid coverage is desired, make a fourth application during the summer months.

A complete fertilizer such 12-4-8 or 16-4-8 or a similar analysis applied at the rate of 1 pound of nitrogen per 1000 square feet is adequate for ground covers. This rate is easy to calculate from the information given on the fertilizer bag. Simply divide the nitrogen percentage (the first number of the analysis) into 100.

For example, if you have purchased a 16-4-8 fertilizer, divide 16 into 100. The resulting 6.25 pounds of 16-4-8 will supply one pound of nitrogen per 1000 square feet of ground cover area. To determine the amount to distribute over 100 square feet, simply move the decimal point one place to the left so that 6.25 pounds becomes .625 pounds.

Fertilizers that contain "slow-release" or "controlled release" nitrogen, such as IBDU or ureaformaldehyde, have extended release periods compared to fertilizers that are readily water soluble. Thirty to fifty percent of the nitrogen should be water insoluble or slow-release. This is beneficial because plant roots can absorb the nitrogen over a long period of time.

Water requirements vary with different plants. Carolina yellow jessamine, for example, requires a fairly moist soil, while the fig marigold tolerates dry sandy soils with only occasional waterings to supplement natural rainfall. Watering on an as needed basis is recommended; ground cover plants should not be allowed to wilt.

Weed control in ground covers is somewhat difficult. Preemergence herbicides (applied before weed seeds germinate) can offer some control if the correct herbicide is applied at the proper time and rate. (Read herbicide labels carefully to be sure they are appropriate for the plants.) Mulching along with hand weeding will usually control weeds until the ground cover has become established. Once well established, ground covers usually out compete undesirable plants.

— *Robert J. Black*

# SOIL pH and Landscape Plants

The degree of acidity or alkalinity of a soil is called soil pH and can be measured and expressed as a number on a scale of 0 to 14 (Figure 25). Soil pH is determined by the materials that make up the soil. For instance, the clayey soils of north Florida are more acid while south Florida's calcareous soils are more alkaline. Soil pH influences the chemical form of many elements in the soil as well as soil microbial processes. Because some of the elements in soil that are influenced by pH are essential nutrients for plants, soil pH affects plant nutrition. Certain other elements are toxic when present in excessive amounts, and soil pH helps to determine how much of one of these elements is in solution at any one time.

While keeping in mind the importance of soil pH, it should be noted that concern about its impact in typical landscape situations is often exaggerated. The purpose of this chapter is to put landscape soil pH into proper perspective and help you manage soil pH for better plant performance.

## The Desirable pH Range for Plants

There are plenty of charts and tables around that list the "desirable pH range" for just about any plant you might wish to grow. Sometimes the term "optimum pH range" is used. While these guides are helpful in a general sense, they present problems in many Florida situations. First, the ranges given are usually narrow. Landscape plants are more tolerant of variation in pH than is implied in the desirable pH range commonly given. Second, desirable pH ranges are generally biased toward fine-textured min-

eral soils such as silt loams and clays. In Florida, we have more coarse-textured soils (sands) than fine-textured ones. Fine-textured soils have greater potential for aluminum toxicity but less potential for micronutrient deficiencies.

Consider correcting soil pH only when it is appreciably higher or lower than the ideal for the kind of plants you are growing. You can determine this by having your soil tested by a responsible lab. If the soil pH is within 0.4 of a pH unit of the ideal range, adjusting the pH will probably not improve plant performance.

## How to Raise Soil pH

First, have a soil pH test run on your soil. Such a test measures a soil's buffering capacity and, if there is a need to increase soil pH, determines how much lime you will need to apply. Many Florida soils already contain excess lime and typically have pHs between 7.0 and 8.2, so don't just assume that lime is needed. If testing indicates that soil pH needs to be raised, apply the prescribed amount of agricultural limestone.

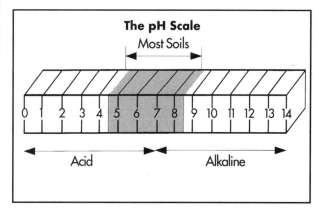

**Figure 25. The pH Scale. Soil pH generally falls near the middle of the pH scale.**

## Lowering Soil pH

When soil pH is high because of naturally-occurring lime (like limestone, marl or sea shells) or where excessive waste concrete or mortar has fallen during construction, there is no practical way of lowering the soil pH. There simply is too much lime present to neutralize. Under these circumstances, the obvious solution is to select plants which are tolerant of high pH conditions. This will help avoid continuing plant nutritional problems.

If you are prepared to engage in a never-ending, uphill battle, you can lower soil pH somewhat. Elemental sulfur added to soil will result in a lower soil pH. That's because soil bacteria will transform elemental sulfur to sulfuric acid which in turn neutralizes any alkalinity with which it comes in contact. However, as soon as the sulfur is used up, soil pH will return to its original value. The cycle of pH dropping and then rising again to its original high level can be as short as a couple of weeks, depending on the rate and method of sulfur application. If you try to get around this cycle by putting on high rates of sulfur or if you make the applications too frequently, you run the risk of damaging your plants.

Never apply more than 5 to 10 pounds of sulfur per 1,000 square feet in a single application. For small specimen trees or shrubs, it is sometimes successful to acidify only a small zone of soil near the dripline of the plant. To do this, dig a small hole about 1 foot deep and 8 to 10 inches in diameter, mix 2 to 3 tablespoons of sulfur into the soil taken from the hole, and return this amended soil to the hole. Repeated annually, that volume of acidified soil is frequently sufficient to prevent micronutrient deficiencies commonly associated with high soil pH. Observe plant performances carefully when embarking on any program of sulfur addition.

Please note that sulfate sulfur does not affect soil pH. There is much misunderstanding on this point because some sulfate compounds (e.g. ammonium sulfate, aluminum sulfate, iron sulfate) have soil-acidifying properties. However, there are many other sulfate compounds which increase sulfur level but do not acidify soil. Examples include calcium sulfate (gypsum), magnesium sulfate (Epsom salt) and potassium sulfate. Heavy applications of organic matter such as manure, composted leaves and peat help some landscape plants overcome the adverse effects of alkaline soil pH. Since these materials decompose with time, annual or semi-annual applications are usually required.

## The Effect of Acid-Forming Fertilizer on Soil pH

The so-called acid-forming fertilizers have relatively little effect on soil pH at the rates normally used in the landscape. They do lower the pH of already acidic soil, but are ineffective in lowering the pH of soil containing free carbonates such as shells or limestone.

## Managing with the Landscape's Soil pH

The best advice is don't try too hard for any predetermined pH. And definitely don't shoot first and ask questions later when it comes to applying lime or sulfur to adjust soil pH. There's probably as much damage done to plants by lime and sulfur applied where they aren't needed as there is damage done by not applying them where they are needed. Soil pH doesn't need to be tampered with in the vast majority of Florida landscape situations, especially when pH is considered in selecting landscape plants. Let's look at some of the reasons.

- Popular lawn grasses such as St. Augustine, bahia, centipede and bermuda are quite tolerant of acidic soil. As a matter of fact, bahia and centipede do a lot better in Florida at pH 5.0 than at pH 7.0. So if you have acidic soil, don't create a problem by liming. If you have an alkaline soil (pH over 7.0), you won't be able to change the pH appreciably with applications of acid-forming materials, especially when they can't be worked into the soil. Instead of trying to lower the pH, plant grasses which tolerate high-pH soil.

- Many popular woody plants such as pittosporum, ligustrum, hibiscus, oleander and pyracantha do as well at a soil pH of 5.0 as at 7.0. Others, like azalea, holly, blueberry and ixora, actually prefer more acidic soil conditions, so you certainly don't want to lime such species. By planting species tolerant of existing soil pH conditions, you will avoid continuing pH-associated problems.

- Trees such as oaks, pines and palms do well over a wide range of soil pHs. Their root systems explore large volumes of soil, frequently consisting of several pH levels.

## Summary

- Don't add lime or sulfur to your soil until you've had a pH and lime requirement test run by a reliable lab.

- Remember that many widely-published "desirable or optimum pH ranges," including those from some well-respected sources, are higher than necessary for Florida soil conditions.

- It's hard to grow acid-loving plants in soil which has a native pH over 7.0. Instead, grow plants that can tolerate such alkaline conditions.

- Relax. The vast majority of landscape plants are tolerant of a wide range of soil pHs, and you really don't have to adjust the pH.

*—Gerald Kidder, Robert J. Black and Kathleen C. Ruppert*

# PLANT NUTRIENTS and Fertilizers
## Why Fertilize?

For centuries plants grew without any help from human beings, and they are still doing so today. Obviously plants can grow by themselves, especially in environments to which they are adapted. However, as humans began cultivating plants, we learned that the addition of certain materials to the soil will sometimes cause plants to respond with characteristics which are considered desirable, for example by bearing more fruit, growing faster or exhibiting better color or more attractive flowers. Early in recorded history we find accounts of applications of animal manures, wood ashes and lime to enhance plant performance. Thus was born the practice of fertilization and soil amendment.

We should note here that the plant responses obtained from applying fertilizer and other soil amendments are not inherently good or bad. These are subjective terms which reflect personal judgment as to what is desirable. For example, a greater quantity of fruit which is too small for market is not the characteristic preferred by a peach farmer. Faster growth is usually not a desired effect for someone growing bonsai plants. Rank vegetative growth is not wanted in an already-lush lawn nor are profusely-blooming squash plants that are not setting fruit. Thus, a good response to fertilization under one set of circumstances may be a bad response under another set.

So, why do we apply fertilizer to the soil? We want our plants to do better and, as we set out to fertilize our plants, we should keep in mind **how** we want them to do better. Is the desired response faster growth, better flower or fruit production, greener leaves? We need to know if fertilization will contribute to that improvement.

The societal cost of fertilizer use is an issue which is receiving increasing attention. There is growing awareness that resource depletion and the potential for surface and groundwater pollution are possible consequences of excessive fertilizer use. The manufacture of nitrogen fertilizer requires considerable quantities of energy and also uses natural gas as a source of hydrogen. Phosphate reserves in the United States are estimated at only 80 years, given current rates of consumption. Most of the potassium fertilizer used in the United States today is imported from Canada. To use non-renewable fertilizer resources in situations where there is no likely response to the nutrients is a long-term societal cost which must be considered.

Water pollution by fertilizers is not a serious problem if the materials are properly used. However, excessive lawn fertilization has polluted the water in nearby lakes and ponds, creating algae blooms. This happens because runoff water carries fertilizer into

surface waters where aquatic plants subsequently "respond" to the fertilization. The resultant overgrowth may lead to the death of fish and other organisms. The effects of excessive landscape fertilization on groundwater aquifers is much more difficult to evaluate, and also much more expensive and difficult to correct. Apply only those nutrients that are needed and only in the amounts that are needed to avoid waste and pollution.

## When Should Fertilizer be Applied?

Stated simply, you need to fertilize whenever you want a specific plant response that a given fertilizer is known to elicit. The difficulty, however, is when you try to predict what a plant needs. Out of fear of growing plants under nutrient-deficient conditions, many people apply fertilizer as insurance against nutrient deficiencies. As a result, over-fertilization in the United States is now a problem as prevalent as under-fertilization.

The following steps are a suggested approach to fertilization.

· Identify the desired plant response.

· Determine from observation or consultation if fertilizer application is likely to promote that response.

· Apply fertilizer only if your desired response is likely.

· Apply only the amount of fertilizer necessary to give the desired response.

## What Nutrients Do My Plants Need?

There are 16 nutrient elements that have been proven to be essential for the growth and reproduction of all higher plants (Table 12). Plants obtain the three most abundant — carbon, hydrogen and oxygen — from water and the air, and 94% or more of their dry tissue is composed of these three elements. The other elements combined represent less than 6% of a typical plant's dry matter. Yet, growth is frequently reduced or limited by a deficiency of one or more of these essential elements, which may be supplied in fertilizers.

The elements are often divided into three groups, although this grouping is losing favor among plant nutrition professionals. The primary group of nutrients is composed of nitrogen (N), phosphorus (P) and potassium (K). In the secondary group are the nutrients sulfur (S), calcium (Ca) and magnesium (Mg). The primary and secondary nutrients are often collectively referred to as macronutrients. The essential elements in the third group are called micronutrients because they are required in small (micro) amounts by plants. (Although these elements are frequently referred to as minor or trace elements, the term micronutrient is preferred.) Manganese (Mn), iron (Fe), boron (B), zinc (Zn), copper (Cu), molybdenum (Mo) and chlorine (Cl) are all micronutrients. In addition, cobalt (Co) is essential for symbiotic N fixation in legumes; sodium (Na) is essential for plants with the $C_4$ photosynthetic pathway; and nickel (Ni) is essential for grain viability in barley. The following discussion of some essential elements is intentionally detailed for those readers who want an in-depth understanding of the chemical properties of the elements and their effects on plants. By understanding how these elements work, one has a better chance of making a good choice among the many fertilizers and their claims.

**Table 12. Essential elements required by plants.**

| ELEMENT | CHEMICAL SYMBOL |
|---|---|
| **Nutrients from Water and Air** | |
| Hydrogen | H |
| Oxygen | O |
| Carbon | C |
| **Nutrients from Soil and Fertilizers** | |
| *Macronutrients* | |
| **Primary Nutrients (a fertilizer term)** | |
| Nitrogen | N |
| Phosphorus | P |
| Potassium | K |
| **Secondary Nutrients (a fertilizer term)** | |
| Sulfur | S |
| Magnesium | Mg |
| Calcium | Ca |
| *Micronutrients* | |
| Iron | Fe |
| Manganese | Mn |
| Copper | Cu |
| Zinc | Zn |
| Boron | B |
| Chlorine | Cl |
| Molybdenum | Mo |

## Nitrogen

Nitrogen is probably the nutrient whose deficiency most often limits plant growth. This is also the element which gives the visual green-up response most often associated with landscape fertilization. Plants use large quantities of nitrogen, and most mineral soils simply can't supply enough to give satisfactory plant performance. (The bulk of soil nitrogen is found within 2 feet of the surface.) Soil nitrogen is present in three major forms: organic, inorganic and elemental.

**Organic nitrogen** makes up about 5% of the soil's organic matter (humus) by weight and about 98% of the total soil nitrogen. Although organic nitrogen is not available to plants, soil organisms convert a portion of it each year to inorganic forms (ammonium and nitrate) that are readily used by plants. Organic nitrogen fertilizers (e.g. manures or biosolids) are popular for lawns and gardens because of their slow release and long-lasting properties.

Nitrogen in fertilizers for agricultural crops is largely **inorganic nitrogen** consisting of three types: ammonium ($NH_4^+$), nitrate ($NO_3^-$), and urea ($CO(NH_2)_2$). Although urea is an organic nitrogen fertilizer, it is rapidly converted to the ammonium form within a short time after exposure to moist, aerated soil. Therefore, under most conditions urea acts more like inorganic, ammonium fertilizers than like natural organic fertilizers.

In warm, moist soils with a pH above 5.0, the majority of ammonium nitrogen is converted to nitrate nitrogen by soil organisms rather quickly (within days). Therefore, most nitrogen taken up by plants is in the nitrate form, although ammonium is taken up when present in the soil solution. The nitrate ion ($NO_3^-$) carries a negative charge which prevents its retention by the negatively-charged soil colloids. Since it is soluble and mobile, the nitrate ion is readily and easily available to plants.

Nitrate moves in the soil solution (i.e. the water that is in the spaces between the soil solids) and can be leached below the plant root zone when water in the soil is excessive. The loss of nitrate by leaching is a common problem on coarse-textured, sandy soils of Florida. Leaching losses of fertilizer nitrogen are minimal when rates of application conform to recommendations consistent with the yield potential for the crop and soil in question. Nitrate nitrogen is also subject to denitrification, a process in which the nitrate ion ($NO_3^-$) is reduced through several intermediate steps to a gaseous nitrogen oxide or to elemental nitrogen.

**Elemental nitrogen**, found in a gaseous form ($N_2$) in the soil atmosphere, cannot be used by plants. It is of direct significance to plants only as it may be involved in bacterial nitrogen fixation. (For example, *Rhizobium* bacteria live in nodules on legume plant roots and convert $N_2$ into other nitrogen compounds which can be utilized by plants.)

Nitrogen is a constituent of all living cells and is a necessary part of all proteins, enzymes and metabolic processes involved in the synthesis and transfer of energy. Nitrogen is a structural part of chlorophyll, the green pigment of the plant that is responsible for photosynthesis. The energy of light is combined with water and carbon dioxide through the process of photosynthesis to form simple carbohydrates essential for plant growth. Other functions of nitrogen include stimulating plants into rapid, vigorous growth, increasing seed and fruit yield and improving the quality of leaf and forage crops. Proper use of nitrogen fertilizer in the landscape is vital for proper plant performance and as a way of reducing environmental pollution.

## Phosphorus

Like nitrogen, phosphorus (P) is an essential part of the process of photosynthesis. Plants use the energy of sunlight, and phosphorus must be present in the active portions of the plant for this energy transfer to be made and for photosynthesis to occur.

The immediate source of phosphorus for plants is that which is dissolved in the soil solution. Plants absorb phosphorus primarily as the $H_2PO_4^-$ and $HPO_4^=$ ions. A few tenths of a part per million of phosphate ions in soil solution are usually adequate for plant growth. Concentrations of phosphate ions in the soil solution may be as low as 0.001 parts per million. Phosphate ions are absorbed from the soil solution and used by plants; the soil solution is replenished from soil minerals, soil organic matter decomposition or applied fertilizers.

In young plants, phosphorus is most abundant in tissue at the growing point. It is readily translocated (moved about) from older tissue to younger tissue, and as plants mature, most of the element moves into the seeds and/or fruits. Phosphorus is responsible for such characteristics of plant growth as utilization of starch and sugar, cell nucleus formation, cell division and multiplication, fat and albumen formation, cell organization and transfer of heredity.

## Potassium

Potassium (K), one of the big three macronutrients, is absorbed by plants in larger amounts than any other mineral element except nitrogen and, in some cases, calcium (Ca). Potassium is supplied to plants by soil minerals, organic materials and inorganic fertilizer. Due to the exposure to the elements endured by Florida soils, their potassium supplying power is quite low in most cases. Potassium occurs in the soil solution as a monovalent cation ($K^+$). The cation exchange capacity (CEC) of the soil controls the retention of $K^+$ and in very sandy soils (low cation exchange capacity) under high rainfall, potassium is subject to leaching losses. (A cation is the positively charged form of an element such as potassium. Soil cation exchange capacity is the ability of the soil to hold cations in a way that they can be easily replaced or exchanged by other cations.)

Unlike nitrogen and phosphorus, potassium is not found in organic combination with plant tissues. Potassium plays an essential role in the metabolic processes of plants and is required in adequate amounts in several enzymatic reactions, particularly those involving the adenosine phosphates (ATP and ADP), which are the energy carriers in the metabolic processes of both plants

and animals. Potassium is also essential in carbohydrate metabolism, a process by which energy is obtained from sugar. There is evidence that potassium plays a role in photosynthesis and protein synthesis as well.

## Calcium

Calcium (Ca) occurs in the soil solution as a divalent cation ($Ca^{++}$) and is supplied to plants by soil minerals, organic materials, fertilizers and liming materials. There is a strong preference for $Ca^{++}$ on the cation exchange sites of most soils and it is the predominant cation in most soils that have a pH of 6.0 or higher.

An essential part of the wall structure of plant cells, calcium provides for normal transport and retention of other elements as well as strength in the plant. It is also thought to counteract the effect of alkali salts and organic acids within a plant. Calcium is absorbed as the cation $Ca^{++}$ and exists in a delicate balance with magnesium and potassium in the plant. Too much of any one of these elements may cause insufficiencies of the other two.

## Magnesium

Soil minerals, organic material, fertilizers and dolomitic limestone are sources of magnesium (Mg) for plants. Magnesium occurs as a divalent cation ($Mg^{++}$) and is held on the exchange sites, as are calcium ($Ca^{++}$) and potassium ($K^+$).

Magnesium is part of the chlorophyll in all green plants and thus is essential for photosynthesis. It also helps activate many plant enzymes needed for growth. A relatively mobile element in the plant, magnesium is absorbed as the cation $Mg^{++}$ and can be readily translocated from older to younger plant parts in the event of a deficiency.

## Sulfur

In most soils, sulfur (S) is present primarily in the organic matter (e.g. humus and plant residues) which becomes available upon their decomposition. Much like the nitrate ($NO_3^-$) ion, the available sulfate ($SO_4^=$) ion remains in soil solution until it is taken up by the plant. In this form it is subject to leaching as well as microbial immobilization. In water-logged soils, it may be reduced to elemental sulfur or other unavailable forms. Sulfur may be supplied to the soil from the atmosphere in rainwater. It is also added in some fertilizers as an impurity, especially the lower grade fertilizers. The use of gypsum ($CaSO_4$) also increases soil sulfur levels.

Sulfur is taken up by plants primarily in the form of sulfate ($SO_4^=$) ions and reduced and assembled into organic compounds. It is a constituent of the amino acids cystine, cysteine and methionine and, hence, proteins that contain these amino acids. It is found in vitamins, enzymes and coenzymes. Sulfur is also present in glycosides which give the characteristic odors and flavors in mustard, onion and garlic plants. It is required for nodulation and nitrogen fixation of legumes. As the sulfate ion, it may be responsible for activating some enzymes.

## Micronutrients

Of the 16 elements known to be essential for growth of all higher plants, seven are required in such small quantities that they are referred to as micronutrients. These are iron, manganese, zinc, copper, boron, molybdenum and chlorine. Micronutrients have become of more widespread concern during the past 30 or so years than was the case earlier.

Deficiencies in micronutrients are most likely to limit crop growth under the following conditions: 1) highly leached acid sandy soil; 2) muck soils; 3) soils high in pH or lime content; and 4) soils that have been intensively cropped and heavily fertilized with macronutrients. Four of the micronutrients occur predominantly as cations in the soil solution. They are iron ($Fe^{+++}$), copper ($Cu^{++}$), manganese ($Mn^{++}$) and zinc ($Zn^{++}$). Two occur predominantly as anions. These are molybdenum ($MoO_4^=$) and chlorine ($Cl^-$). Boron occurs as the neutral species $H_3BO_3$.

## Manganese

Manganese (Mn) is mainly absorbed by plants in the ionic form $Mn^{++}$. Although we believe it activates many enzymes, only one manganoprotein, manganin, has been isolated from higher plants. Manganese may substitute for magnesium by activating certain phosphate-transferring enzymes, which in turn affect many metabolic processes. High manganese concentration may induce iron deficiency in plants.

Manganese availability is closely related to the degree of soil acidity. Deficient plants are usually found on slightly acid or alkaline soils. Liming Florida soils to pH above 6.5 frequently causes manganese deficiency.

## Iron

Iron (Fe) is a constituent of many organic compounds in plants. It is essential for the synthesis of chlorophyll, which gives rise to the green pigment of plants. Iron deficiency can be induced by high levels of manganese. High iron can also cause manganese deficiency.

## Copper

Copper (Cu) is essential for growth and activates many enzymes. A deficiency interferes with protein synthesis and causes a buildup of soluble nitrogen compounds. Excess quantities of copper may also induce iron deficiency.

## Zinc

Zinc (Zn) is essential for plant growth because it controls the synthesis of indoleacetic acid, which dramatically regulates plant growth. Zinc is also active in many enzymatic reactions.

## Boron

Boron (B) primarily regulates the metabolism of carbohydrates in plants. The need varies greatly with different plant species. Rates required for responsive crops may cause serious damage to boron-sensitive crops. Boron deficiency may occur on both alkaline and acid soils but is more prevalent on the calcareous, alkaline soils.

## Molybdenum

Molybdenum (Mo) functions largely in the enzyme systems of nitrogen fixation and nitrate reduction. Plants which can neither fix nitrogen nor incorporate nitrate into their metabolic system because of inadequate molybdenum become nitrogen deficient. Molybdenum is required in minute amounts.

## Chlorine

Chlorine (Cl) is an enzyme activator for one or more reactions in which water is split for photosynthesis. Chlorine deficiency is not likely to be a problem in Florida since the salt air from the ocean or gulf will usually provide in rainwater the trace of chlorine necessary to plant growth. The general use of muriate of potash in fertilizers is another common source of chlorine.

## Commonly Applied Nutrients

The most commonly applied nutrients are nitrogen (N), phosphorus (P) and potassium (K). Responses to all three elements were fairly widespread in the past, and it became customary to apply the three together. As a result of habit, all three are still applied even though there are now many situations, especially in home landscapes, where plants don't respond to phosphorus and potassium fertilization.

Other plant-essential nutrients used in fairly large quantities are calcium, magnesium and sulfur. However, fertilization with these nutrients is not usually necessary because the calcium and magnesium contents of soil are generally sufficient. Also, large quantities of calcium and magnesium are supplied when acidic soil is limed with dolomite. Sulfur is usually present in sufficient quantities from the slow decomposition of soil organic matter, an important reason for not throwing out grass clippings and leaves.

Micronutrients are often used to sell fertilizers. While there are instances of deficiencies of one or more micronutrients in specific plant-growth settings, most micronutrients in fertilizer are included as a preventative measure and do not give a plant response. Buy and apply only those nutrients which you have reason to believe will be needed by your plants. If one of your plant species has a micronutrient deficiency, apply the recommended rate of the deficient nutrient. Recycling organic matter by leaving grass clippings on the lawn and by mulching with tree leaves is an excellent means of providing micronutrients (as well as macronutrients) to growing plants.

## Organic Matter as a Source of Nutrients

Organic matter (such as grass clippings, tree leaves, shrubbery and tree trimmings) are excellent sources of plant nutrients. The plants which produced that organic material accumulated all the essential nutrients for their own growth needs. Upon decomposition, those nutrients in the organic material become available for reuse. When you recycle "homegrown" organic matter such as grass clippings, leaves and shrubbery trimmings, you are practicing an excellent way of fertilizing your landscape (see *Mulches for the Landscape* and *A Guide to Composting*). You are keeping these valuable materials on-site and are also greatly reducing the municipal solid wastes placed at curb-side. Other organic materials, such as animal manures, biosolids (sewage sludge) or various composted materials, are also alternative sources of plant nutrients.

## How Do I Shop for Fertilizer?

There is no magical way of knowing which nutrient may be in limited supply in the soil. Soil testing helps predict deficiencies of some of the nutrients, but testing is only one of the tools in plant nutrient management. If you recycle organic matter such as grass clippings (don't use a bag on your mower) and leaves, you will be returning to the soil the nutrients those plants had taken up. It's the easiest, least expensive, and most environmentally sound way to fertilize. You may still have to supplement, but you'll need fewer nutrients and a lot less fertilizer. Plants need all of the elements listed above for proper growth and reproduction. However, under many conditions, they will obtain enough of these elements from the soil, water, and air. It is only in certain environments and growing conditions that one or

more of the nutrients are deficient. The best way of knowing what your plants need is by observing plant performance and understanding the multiple factors affecting such performance (e.g. light, water, temperature, pests, nutrition). If observations indicate that supplemental fertilizer is necessary, follow these guidelines in selecting the best fertilizer for the job.

- Know what nutrients are needed.
- Be informed when reading fertilizer advertisements.
- Read the fertilizer label before buying.
- Consider all costs.

Buy nutrients, not "fertilizer." Many fertilizers contain a number of plant nutrients even though only one or two may be needed. Buying such mixtures results in your paying for nutrients which are not really needed. Know what nutrients are needed and buy only those.

## Fertilizer Terms

Certain terms are in common use in fertilizer circles. They are found in technical and commercial literature and in state fertilizer laws. Many have been abused over time and have multiple meanings. Several continue to be used even though their use reflects antiquated concepts about plant nutrients and fertilizer materials. It is important to remember that although the terms can make a product sound right, it may or may not be, depending on what your particular plants need.

**Fertilizer grade or analysis.** The grade (popularly referred to as the analysis) is the percent nitrogen, phosphorus and potassium guaranteed by the manufacturer to be in the fertilizer. For historical reasons, the nitrogen is expressed as N, the phosphorus as $P_2O_5$ and the potassium as $K_2O$. The percent sign is not used, but instead the numbers are separated by dashes, and the order is always N, $P_2O_5$ and $K_2O$ (e.g. 16-4-8). It is a convenient way of expressing the N, P, and K content of a fertilizer.

**Complete fertilizer.** A fertilizer is called complete when it contains nitrogen, phosphorus and potassium. If your plants need only one of these nutrients, a complete fertilizer is not called for. "Complete" fertilizer is a term with false implications for plant nutrition. This term should be avoided; the term "NPK fertilizer" is preferred.

**Fertilizer ratio.** The ratio describes the relative proportions of N, $P_2O_5$ and $K_2O$ in a fertilizer. Fertilizer ratio is an outdated concept, and use of this term should be discontinued. The ratio of 16-4-8 fertilizer is 4:1:2 or 4 parts N to 1 part $P_2O_5$ to 2 parts $K_2O$.

**Balanced fertilizer.** A fertilizer is called "balanced" only because it contains equal amounts of N, $P_2O_5$ and $K_2O$. A 6-6-6 or 10-10-10 fertilizer is a so-called balanced fertilizer. This is another term which is flawed in its plant nutrition implications and should thus be avoided.

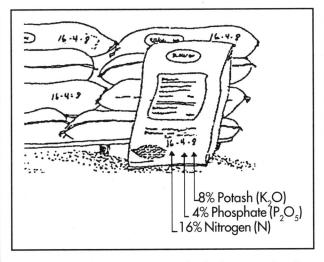

**Figure 26. The first thing to look for on a fertilizer bag is the Grade or Analysis.**

---

Florida Registration No.

**BRAND NAME**
1.) **Name and Address of Registrant**
**Net Weight**
2.) Nitrogen: __% Organic (__% synthetic, __% natural)

**GUARANTEED ANALYSIS**
3.) Total Nitrogen ......................... %
4.) Nitrate Nitrogen .................... %
5.) Ammoniacal Nitrogen .............. %
6.) Water Soluble Organic Nitrogen ........ %
    And/or Urea Nitrogen ................ %
7.) Water Insoluble Nitrogen ........... %
8.) Available Phosphoric Acid .......... %
9.) Soluble Potash ........................ %
10.) Chlorine, not more than ................. %
11.) **Derived from:**
    (Actual source materials for primary plant nutrients)

12.) **Statement of Secondary Plant Nutrients**
    Total Magnesium as Mg ................... %
    Water Soluble Magnesium as Mg ........... %
    Manganese as Mn ..................... %
    Copper as Cu ........................ %
    Sulfur (combined) as S ................. %
    Sulfur (free) as S ...................... %
13.) **Derived from:**
    (Actual materials and forms used in the fertilizer mixture, e.g., manganese oxide, copper sulfate)

**Figure 27. The Florida Fertilizer Label.**

## How to Read a Fertilizer Bag

Marketing in the consumer sector generally depends on selling in large volume. Advertisers may seek to increase sales by emphasizing low prices per bag or such extras as micronutrients or organic forms of the nutrients. Learning how to read a fertilizer bag (Figure 26) is the key to shopping for fertilizers without becoming a victim of creative marketing. The first thing to look for is the Analysis or Grade of the fertilizer. This appears on the bag or tag as three numbers separated by dashes. For example: a 40 lb bag marked 16-4-8 contains 6.4 lbs of N, 1.6 lbs of $P_2O_5$ and 3.2 lbs of $K_2O$. That is because 16% of 40 lbs = 6.4 lbs N; 4% of 40 lbs = 1.6 lbs $P_2O_5$; and 8% of 40 lbs = 3.2 lbs of $K_2O$.

Fertilizer manufacturers are required by Florida law to supply a tag (Figure 27) from which a wealth of information can be derived. Let's analyze a sample tag line by line beginning at 1, Net Weight.

1. The actual weight present in the bag or package. Check it out. For example, what sometimes appears to be a 40 pound bag is actually 35 pounds.

2. When the term organic is used in the label, it usually refers only to the nitrogen content, and it must be qualified as to what percent is synthetic and what percent is natural. Synthetic organic seems like a contradiction in terms, doesn't it? Organic nitrogen in fertilizer causes considerable confusion because people usually associate organic with slow release and no-burn properties. However, claims of 100% organic nitrogen in a fertilizer usually mean that the nitrogen source is urea, a synthetically-produced, water-soluble, organic material. Urea is a common and perfectly good nitrogen fertilizer, it just isn't a slow-release nitrogen source unless it has been treated with sulfur to produce a product called sulfur coated urea. To avoid being misled by the organic nitrogen advertising, read the label to determine where the organic nitrogen is coming from. If it's from urea, it will be listed as synthetic organic nitrogen in the Guaranteed Analysis section, and urea will be listed in the Derived From section. If it's from biosolids (sewage sludge), it will be listed as natural organic nitrogen in the Guaranteed Analysis, and biosolids or sewage sludge will be listed in the Derived From section. Changes in the Florida Administrative Code are expected in late 1998 which should eliminate this confusing labeling situation.

3,8,9. The percentages of nitrogen (N), phosphorus expressed as $P_2O_5$ and potassium expressed as $K_2O$ which are guaranteed by the manufacturer.

4-7. A breakdown of the chemical forms of nitrogen which make up the total nitrogen. This will be discussed in detail further on in this chapter.

10. Chlorine must be stated as "Not more than" because it may reduce the quality of some plants (e.g. the burning quality of tobacco or the cooking quality of potatoes). However it has been proposed that Cl content no longer be required on "specialty fertilizer," defined in the Florida Administrative Code as fertilizer packaged, marketed, and distributed for home and garden use in packages of less than 50 pounds.

11. "Derived From" is a statement of the materials supplying the plant nutrients.

12. The "Statement of Secondary Plant Nutrients" will list all the nutrients other than N, P, and K contained in the fertilizer mixture.

## What Else?

You will notice that in a 100 lb bag of 16-4-8 fertilizer, the 16 lbs of N, 4 lbs of $P_2O_5$ and 8 lbs of $K_2O$ add up to only 28 lbs of the actual net weight of the fertilizer. In large part, the remaining weight is made up of the other elements (e.g. O, H, Ca, Cl) which are part of the chemical molecules containing the nutrient elements.

Some fertilizers also contain conditioners and fillers. **Conditioners** keep the fertilizer in a granular, easily spread form. **Fillers** are used to dilute concentrated fertilizer materials (e.g. 46-0-0, 18-46-0, and 0-0-60) to make low analysis fertilizers (e.g. 6-6-6, 16-4-8). Dolomite, sand or rock phosphate are often used as fillers. Home gardeners frequently complain that the fertilizer stays on the soil months after they have applied it. What they are actually seeing are the fillers which are very slow to dissolve. Some fertilizers also contain an insecticide or weed killer but, if so, they must have a yellow label with lettering in a conspicuous, contrasting color.

## Nitrogen Sources

Now, we turn to the nitrogen sources. It's important to single out nitrogen for more discussion because it is usually the most expensive component in a fertilizer bag, and the various nitrogen sources that are used behave very differently once applied.

For example, nitrate nitrogen dissolves readily in water and moves freely in the soil with the movement of water. The nitrate form is readily absorbed by plants and will give quick growth results. However, under heavy rainfall or irrigation it can leach through the soil rapidly and be lost from the plant root zone.

Ammoniacal nitrogen also dissolves readily in water but does not leach from the soil as rapidly as nitrate nitrogen. Soil bacteria usually convert it to the nitrate form in a few days or weeks. Ammoniacal nitrogen has an acidifying effect as it converts to nitrate and is, therefore, almost always found in acid-forming fertilizers such as Azalea-Camellia Special fertilizer.

Water-soluble organic nitrogen is supplied mainly from urea. As explained earlier in this chapter, urea fertilizer is an organic compound that is synthetically produced. In soil, it changes to ammoniacal nitrogen within a few days of application. Urea is a comparatively inexpensive form of nitrogen.

Water-insoluble nitrogen originally meant natural organic materials such as manure or dried blood. Natural materials such as these break down very slowly and yield their nitrogen over a long period of time. Today, however, many forms of water-insoluble

nitrogen have been developed such as IBDU (isobutylidene diurea) and sulfur coated urea. These materials are manufactured so as to release nitrogen slowly so are also included under water-insoluble nitrogen. This form of nitrogen is the most expensive of the four discussed, but it will provide a continued release of nitrogen over an extended period of time.

The anticipated changes in Florida fertilizer labeling requirements which should become effective in late 1998 will eliminate the "organic" distinction. The simple distinction of water-soluble N and water-insoluble N should remove much of the confusion caused by the current label requirement.

## What's a Good Fertilizer Buy?

When you shop for a good fertilizer buy, look for a few key things:

**The nitrogen sources**. If you want quick results, look for fertilizers that contain the majority of the nitrogen in the nitrate, ammoniacal and/or urea forms. If you want long-lasting results, shop for a high percentage of water-insoluble nitrogen which will be more expensive than the readily soluble forms. The best buy for routine lawn and garden maintenance is a combination of fast and slow release nitrogen.

**Get the most for your money**. Once you've decided on your nitrogen sources, check for other plant nutrients and buy the fertilizer which offers these extras if they are necessary. Micronutrients often are used as an incentive to buy one fertilizer instead of another. Fear of micronutrient deficiencies and the feeling that somehow micronutrients make the fertilizer better are motives exploited in fertilizer sales promotions. However, as a rule, lawns and gardens exposed to reasonable recycling of organic matter seldom need the small amounts of micronutrients contained in general fertilizer mixes. If a serious micronutrient deficiency does exist, the small quantities of micronutrients applied in popular fertilizer mixes would usually not be sufficient to correct the problem.

If you find two or more fertilizers that fit your needs, but the prices vary, **calculate the actual cost per pound of plant nutrients.** Price per bag can be deceptive because bag weights differ (a 35-lb bag contains 12% less material than a 40-lb bag), and the concentration of nutrients in a bag can also be very different. One way of comparison-shopping for fertilizer is to compare the cost per pound of primary nutrients in the various products. Add the nitrogen, phosphorus, and potassium percentages; multiply by the net weight of the package to approximate the pounds of nutrients contained. Then divide the cost of the package by the pounds of $N + P_2O_5 + K_2O$ in the package to obtain the per pound cost. For example, a 40 lb bag of 20-3-7 fertilizer would contain 12 pounds of nutrients (i.e. 20% $N$ + 3% $P_2O_5$ + 7% $K_2O$ multiplied by 40 pounds). If the bag of fertilizer costs $6.00, the average cost of the nutrients would be $0.50 per pound ($6 ÷ 15 lb). While this method has shortcomings (e.g. nutrients have different values, nitrogen costing about twice what potassium does, and nutrients other than nitrogen, phosphorus, and potassium aren't considered), it allows quick comparisons between products. Remember that a higher analysis fertilizer (e.g. 16-4-8) will probably cost more but will cover more area than a lower analysis (e.g. 6-6-6) material.

**Just because a fertilizer is labeled as a lawn fertilizer** (or tomato or citrus or whatever) doesn't mean it can't be used on everything in your yard if it meets the nutritional requirements of the other plants. The exception of course is if a fertilizer also contains a weed killer or insecticide which might be injurious to certain plants. Don't buy six different fertilizers if one would fit the bill.

All these shopping tips depend on your ability to read and understand the fertilizer label. You'll know this chapter has been helpful if you find yourself at the local garden center flipping fertilizer bags over, debating the pros and cons of various tags and doing calculations on your pocket calculator.

## What Fertilizers are Found in Stores?

There are literally hundreds of fertilizers on the market. Some fertilizers contain only one nutrient, whereas others contain several nutrients. Most of the multi-nutrient fertilizers are made by simply mixing single-nutrient fertilizers together in the proportions needed to give a desired nutrient analysis.

The chemical form of some materials automatically means that they contain more than one nutrient. For example, magnesium sulfate ($MgSO_4$) contains both magnesium and sulfur. Other materials, such as ammonium nitrate ($NH_4NO_3$), contain only a single fertilizer nutrient, nitrogen. A mixture of magnesium sulfate and ammonium nitrate would contain the three nutrients nitrogen, magnesium, and sulfur.

Some common fertilizer materials are listed in Table 13. These materials are sold separately or are mixed in an almost infinite number of combinations to produce the fertilizers available on the market.

The other elements of the chemical compounds used as fertilizers make up much of the weight of the materials shown in the table. For example, the hydrogen (H) and oxygen (O) atoms in a molecule of ammonium nitrate ($NH_4NO_3$) contribute 67% to the weight of the molecule, while the nitrogen contributes the remaining 33%.

Non-fertilizer materials (fillers) are added to dilute the nutrient content in many mixed fertilizers. The amount can be large, especially in low-analysis fertilizers such as 6-6-6. For example, 100 pounds of a 6-6-6 fertilizer made with diammonium phosphate (18-46-0), ammonium nitrate (33-0-0), and muriate of potash (0-0-60), would contain 13.1 pounds of 18-46-0, 10.9 pounds of 33-0-0, 10.0 pounds of 0-0-60, and 66 pounds of filler. A 17-17-17 fertilizer made using the same three materials would contain only 4 pounds of filler. Fillers often remain visible on the soil surface long after the fertilizer has dissolved and moved into the soil.

Conditioners are sometimes added to keep the fertilizer in good physical condition for handling. Their content seldom exceeds 5% of the total weight.

## Why to Use Low-Analysis Fertilizers

It's harder to overdose with dilute materials than with concentrated ones. High analysis fertilizers must be applied at considerably lower rates than many people are accustomed to using. Also, many advisors prefer to recommend the more dilute fertilizer

materials in order to minimize plant damage caused by overzealous fertilizer applicators. It takes only one-fourth as much 33-0-0 as it does 8-8-8 to give the same dose of nitrogen! Hint: if you'd rather use your head than your back, calibrate your spreader carefully and then use high-analysis fertilizers.

## Where to Find High-Analysis Fertilizers

Any good lawn and garden center will stock a full range of fertilizers. However, often only the most popular materials are prominently displayed. If you can't find what you want, ask store personnel for the desired material.

## What About Fertilizer Costs?

The dollar value of fertilizer was addressed earlier when we showed how to get an approximate cost per pound of nutrient. Since it is nutrients that you are buying in fertilizer, that approach is the most straightforward means for approximating the cost. It gets you around the chrome trim and mudflaps of the fertilizer trade. In all fertilizer purchases, the goal of the responsible person is to buy only the nutrients the plants actually need. The societal cost of fertilizer use was discussed at the opening of this chapter.

**Table 13. Some common fertilizer materials.**

| MATERIAL | USUAL GRADE | PERCENT COMPOSITION | | |
|---|---|---|---|---|
| | | N | $P_2O_5$ | $K_2O$ |
| Ammonium nitrate | 33-0-0 | 33 | 0 | 0 |
| Urea | 46-0-0 | 46 | 0 | 0 |
| Ammonium sulfate | 20-0-0 | 20 | 0 | 0 |
| Diammonium phosphate | 18-46-0 | 18 | 46 | 0 |
| Concentrated superphosphate | 0-46-0 | 0 | 46 | 0 |
| Ordinary superphosphate | 0-20-0 | 0 | 20 | 0 |
| Potassium chloride (muriate of potash) | 0-0-60 | 0 | 0 | 60 |
| Potassium sulfate | 0-0-50 | 0 | 0 | 50 |
| Potassium magnesium sulfate | 0-0-22 | 0 | 0 | 22 |

# Summary

- Plants respond to individual nutrients.

- Observe plant responses and use only those nutrients which are giving you the response you desire.

- Buy nutrients, not fertilizer.

- Study the fertilizer label before making your purchase.

- Get wise about fertilizers and fertilizer advertising.

- Consider the societal costs of fertilizer use.

- Responsible fertilizer use produces desired plant responses and does not waste resources or pollute the environment.

—*Gerald Kidder and Sydney Park Brown*

# FERTILIZATION
# Recommendations for Trees and Shrubs
## Deciding if Fertilization Is Needed

Fertilization of plants usually results in additional growth and production of leaves, stems, branches and roots. This growth often only means additional maintenance costs and more yard trimmings to be disposed of, so it is important to determine if growth is the result we want with our trees and shrubs.

Fertilization is usually desirable when we are trying to get newly planted trees and shrubs established. We normally want the new plants to get off to a quick start and grow rapidly so they fill the planted area. When this is the case, fertilize about 4 to 6 weeks after planting and then two to three times per year for the following 3 years or so. Two of the annual applications are normally scheduled around February and October for south Florida, March and September for north Florida. A third application can be made during the summer. (For palms, see "Establishment Care" in *Selecting and Planting Palms* and "Landscape Palm Fertilization" in *Palm Nutrition Guide*.)

Once trees are established (3 to 5 years after transplanting), they will not need additional fertilizer if they are growing in a landscape where turf and shrubs are fertilized. (In this case, beware of weed-and-feed products. Read labels carefully, and see "What Fertilizer to Use" further on in this chapter.) The trees' root systems extend past the driplines of their canopies and throughout the landscape, taking up nutrients (and water) from fertilized areas. Such trees seldom benefit from their own separate fertilization. Many large shrubs can be treated like trees in this respect. However, smaller shrubs and ground covers may benefit from continued fertilization.

## Soil Testing

Soil testing provides some information about the nutritional status of soil and may aid in the detection of potential nutritional problems. Soil tests routinely measure soil pH and give an index of the available phosphorus and potassium. (If you are prepared to modify your fertilization practices to fit specific fertilization recommendations based on a soil test, the following instructions on conducting soil sampling will be useful. However, if you plan on simply using one of the commonly recommended fertilizers such as 12-4-8 or 16-4-8, there is no logical reason to go to the trouble of testing. Skip to the section on how much fertilizer to use.)

Test the soil area to be fertilized prior to purchasing fertilizer. Collect the sample(s) and send them to the lab a couple of months before you anticipate needing to fertilize. This allows ample time for the lab to get results back to you.

Obtain a composite soil sample by removing subsamples from 10 to 15 small holes dug throughout the sample area (e.g. the front yard of your home). To obtain the subsamples, carefully pull back mulch, grass or ground covers to expose bare soil. With a hand trowel or shovel, dig small holes 6 inches deep, then remove a 1-inch thick by 6-inch deep slice of soil from the side of each hole. Combine and mix the subsamples in a clean plastic bucket. The soil sample will amount to about a pint. When various areas in the landscape have different soil types, receive different cultural practices or contain plants that have distinctly different fertilization requirements, obtain separate composite samples. Often a 1/4 to 1-acre lot will have two or three areas that require separate sampling. Soil samples need to be sent immediately to a commercial laboratory, or check with your local county Extension office.

## How Much Fertilizer to Use

Once you have decided to fertilize, use Table 14 to determine the amount of fertilizer to apply to individual trees and shrubs. In most instances, roots will ultimately extend quite a bit beyond the dripline, so the fertilized zone should be one and a half times the distance from the base of the plant to the edge of its branches.

The amount of fertilizer to apply to shrubs and/or trees in a bed can be determined by calculating the area of the bed and then applying fertilizer at the rate of 1 pound of nitrogen per 1000 square feet of bed area. To find the area of a shrub and/or tree bed, simply multiply the length of the bed by its width. For example: if the length of your bed is 20 feet and its width is 10 feet, then

**Table 14. Amounts of various commonly available fertilizers needed to fertilize shrubs and young trees.[1,2]**

| | Diameter of plant canopy in feet | | | | | | | | | | | |
| | 2 | | 4 | | 6 | | 8 | | 10 | | 12 | |
| | Diameter of area to be fertilized in feet[3] | | | | | | | | | | | |
| | 3 | | 6 | | 9 | | 12 | | 15 | | 18 | |
| Fertilizer | lbs | tbs[4] | lbs | tbs | lbs | tbs | lbs | cups[5] | lbs | cups | lbs | cups |
|---|---|---|---|---|---|---|---|---|---|---|---|---|
| 12-4-8 | 0.059 | 1.9 | 0.24 | 7.5 | 0.53 | 17.0 | 0.94 | 1.9 | 1.5 | 3.0 | 2.1 | 4.2 |
| 15-5-15 | 0.047 | 1.5 | 0.19 | 6.0 | 0.42 | 13.6 | 0.75 | 1.5 | 1.2 | 2.4 | 1.7 | 3.4 |
| 16-4-8 | 0.044 | 1.4 | 0.18 | 5.6 | 0.40 | 12.7 | 0.71 | 1.4 | 1.1 | 2.2 | 1.6 | 3.2 |
| 23-6-12 | 0.031 | 1.0 | 0.12 | 3.9 | 0.28 | 8.8 | 0.49 | 1.0 | 0.77 | 1.5 | 1.11 | 2.2 |
| 34-0-0 | 0.020 | 0.7 | 0.08 | 2.6 | 0.19 | 6.0 | 0.33 | 0.7 | 0.52 | 1.0 | 0.75 | 1.5 |

[1] The amounts of fertilizer indicated in this table were calculated on the rate of applying one pound of nitrogen per 1000 square feet.
[2] Spread this amount of fertilizer in a circle with a diameter that is 1.5 times the diameter of the plant canopy.
[3] Diameter of plant canopy times 1.5.
[4] Approximate number of tablespoons of fertilizer for a given weight (lbs) of fertilizer.
[5] Approximate number of cups of fertilizer for a given weight (lbs) of fertilizer.

the area of the bed is 20 feet x 10 feet which equals 200 square feet. Because fertilizer recommendations are given on a 1000 square feet basis, divide the area of the bed (200) by 1000, then multiply this number by the pounds of fertilizer, such as 16-4-8, to supply one pound of nitrogen over 1000 square feet of bed area.

The pounds of 16-4-8 fertilizer needed to supply 1 pound of nitrogen over 1000 square feet can be calculated by dividing the nitrogen percentage (the first number of the analysis) into 100. Your calculations then would be:

200 square feet ÷ 1000 square feet = 0.2

100 ÷ 16 = 6.25 pounds

0.2 x 6.25 pounds = 1.25 pounds of 16-4-8

Therefore, 1.25 pounds of 16-4-8 spread evenly over the bed will supply the amount of fertilizer needed for the shrubs and/or trees in the bed.

## What Fertilizer to Use

A complete fertilizer with a ratio of approximately 3:1:2 or 3:1:3 (e.g. 12-4-8 or 15-5-15) of nitrogen (N), phosphorus as $P_2O_5$ and potassium as $K_2O$ is generally recommended unless the soil test reveals that phosphorus and potassium are adequate. Similar analysis fertilizers such as 16-4-8 (4:1:2) can also be used.

Many fertilizers are formulated for use on lawn grasses. Some of these, known as weed-and-feed fertilizers, may contain an herbicide that can damage ground covers, vines, shrubs and trees. Read labels and carefully follow the directions.

Fertilizers that are slow-release, controlled release, sulfur coated or with nitrogen as IBDU or ureaformaldehyde have extended release periods compared to fertilizers that

are readily water soluble. Thirty to fifty percent of the nitrogen should be water insoluble or slow-release so that plant roots can absorb the nitrogen over a long period of time.

A fertilizer containing 30 to 50% slow-release potassium should be used in south Florida or where soil potassium is frequently inadequate. A fertilizer containing magnesium may be needed if plants often exhibit magnesium deficiency symptoms and for soils with inadequate magnesium.

Water-soluble fertilizers are less expensive than products that provide extended release, but the components of a water-soluble fertilizer may leach quickly through the soil. In sandy, well-drained soils, the soluble fertilizer may move past the root system after only a few inches of rainfall or irrigation. In finer-textured marl, clay or muck soils, leaching will be slower, but runoff may be greater.

Micronutrient deficiencies can be corrected with foliar sprays if deficiencies are not severe; however, correction is usually temporary. Persistent deficiencies may be prevented by applying a fertilizer with micronutrient supplements to the soil. Because of the danger of applying excessive amounts, a single micronutrient should be applied to the soil only in the case of severe deficiency.

## Where and How to Apply Fertilizer

Fertilizer placement in relation to the plant root zone is very important. Because of the naturally high oxygen concentrations near the soil surface, a plant's principal feeding roots are usually within the top 10 to 14 inches of soil. Several tree species have more than half of their roots extending beyond their driplines by as much as three times the canopy diameter. Many roots of mulched plants are located just beneath the mulch on the soil surface. Consequently, for maximum utilization, fertilizer should be applied to the surface of the soil or mulch. Since most feeder roots on trees and shrubs are shallow, there is no need to inject or place fertilizer deep in the soil. However, shallow soil injections in compacted soil or on mounds, berms and slopes will reduce the amount of fertilizer runoff due to irrigation or rain.

A large, aesthetically pleasing mulched area should be maintained around trees and shrubs. A general rule is to maintain a mulched area 2 feet in diameter for each inch of trunk diameter on newly planted trees. This means that a tree with a 2-inch diameter trunk would grow best in a mulched area 4 feet in diameter. The size of the mulched area can be increased as plant size increases. This mulched area promotes faster tree establishment by eliminating competition from grass roots for water and nutrients. Ground covers that are not as competitive as grass for water and nutrients can be planted near trees. The maintenance of turf areas adjacent to plant trunks is further discouraged because it is difficult to trim the turf without damaging tree trunks.

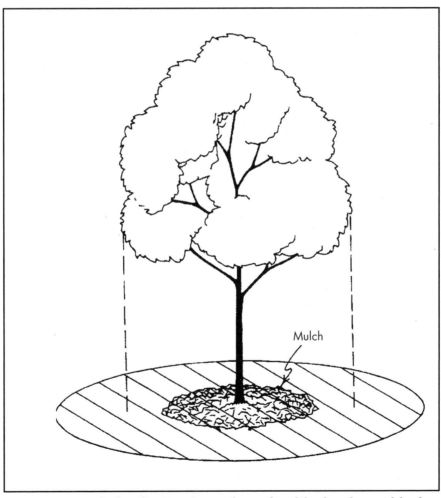

Mulch

**Figure 28. Apply fertilizer to the surface of mulched and unmulched areas extending out from the tree's trunk no more than one and a half to two times the canopy's diameter.**

Fertilizer should be applied to the surface of the mulched and unmulched areas around a tree out to a distance no more than one and a half to two times the canopy diameter (Figure 28). If the turf was fertilized within the two preceding weeks, do not apply additional fertilizer to the turf area around the tree. Fertilize only the mulched area around the tree, calculating the amount of fertilizer to apply based on the radius of the mulched area. Fertilizer nutrients will rapidly move with water through the mulch.

There are a few situations where trunk injection of fertilizer is warranted. A good candidate for trunk injection would be a tree with a micronutrient deficiency that did not respond to soil applications of fertilizer. Each situation is different, and the merits of injection should be judged by a professional tree specialist. Remember that trees are permanently damaged by trunk injections, so the potential benefits must outweigh this damage.

## Palm Fertilization

Palm fertilization recommendations are provided in the chapter, *Palm Nutrition Guide*.

## Other Considerations

Too much nitrogen promotes excessive growth which increases maintenance. Disposing of excess growth as yard waste is an additional problem and expense. Application of too much soluble nitrogen causes environmental concerns, as when nitrogen leaches into water supplies or the surface waters of lakes, rivers, bays and retention ponds. Additionally, nitrogen is not utilized efficiently by unthrifty plants. Diseased or damaged roots, improper soil pH, water-

logged sites and plantings that are too deep can result in inefficient nutrient absorption and nutrient deficiency symptoms.

*— Robert J. Black, Edward F. Gilman and Gerald Kidder*

# NUTRITIONAL Deficiencies in the Basic Plant Groups

The majority of the plant world is comprised of seed-bearing plants that belong to one of two classes: gymnosperms or angiosperms. **Gymnosperms** do not produce fruit and their naked seed is borne on scales which together form a cone. They are represented by three principal groups, conifers (e.g. pines, cedars, junipers, yews), cycads (e.g. sago palms, coontie) and ginkgo. **Angiosperms** are flowering plants and have their seeds enclosed within a fruit. The angiosperms form two large, complex groups that are named and based on the number of their embryonic seed-leaves (cotyledons).

**Dicotyledonae** (dicots) have two embryonic leaves in the seed. They can be recognized by a vein structure in their leaves which is usually net-like but may also be either pinnate or palmate. The flower parts (such as sepals, petals, stamens and carpels) of dicots generally come in fours or fives or in multiples of four or five. Some dicots like willows and poplars have catkins, which are composed of many small petal-less flowers that hang in long upside-down clusters. Others, like the rose and the southern magnolia, have flowers with separate petals and sepals. Still others have flowers in which petals or sepals or both are fused to form a trumpet shaped flower. Honeysuckle and allamanda are examples of this type of dicot.

**Monocotyledonae** (monocots) are plants that have one cotyledon in the seed. Their leaves generally have parallel veins, and their flower parts come in threes or multiples of three (but never fours or fives). A few of the monocots such as bamboos and palms are tree-like, but the majority are herbaceous plants such as grasses, cattails, lilies, irises, orchids, bananas and bromeliads.

In many cases, nutritional deficiencies manifest themselves differently in monocots and dicots. However, it is useful to note that in both monocots and dicots, nutrients that move around in the plant are called **mobile** and will travel to the new growth. Because mobile nutrients are available first to new growth, deficiencies in these nutrients make their initial appearance in old growth. Conversely, deficiencies in **non-mobile** nutrients are first apparent in new growth. In the two sections that follow, specific nutritional deficiencies first of monocots and gymnosperms and then of dicots are discussed in detail.

# Nutritional Deficiencies of Monocots and Gymnosperms

Please see the introduction to this chapter for general descriptions of monocots, gymnosperms, mobile and non-mobile nutrients.

## Boron

New leaves of boron deficient palms emerge crumpled and greatly reduced in size. Leaf edges may have extensive necrosis, often giving the leaf a singed appearance. Fruits and flowers of coconut palms usually abort

prior to the appearance of foliar symptoms. Boron deficiency may be locally common on palms growing in the highly leached (nutrient poor) sand soils of south Florida.

## Iron

Iron deficiency appears as a general or interveinal chlorosis on the newest leaves which, in severe cases, become totally yellow (Plate 12). As the deficiency progresses, new leaves or leaflets may have necrotic tips with reduced size. New leaves of queen and rhapis palms are uniformly chlorotic with extensive green spots (Plate 13). In species that do not exhibit this spotting or interveinal chlorosis, symptoms are virtually indistinguishable from those of sulfur deficiency. Iron deficiency symptoms are fairly common on monocots in Florida, especially when planted too deeply or grown in poorly aerated soil.

## Magnesium (mobile)

Magnesium deficiency of monocots and cycads usually appears as broad yellow bands along the margins (edges) of the oldest leaves. Central portions of these leaves remain distinctly green. Later, leaf blades or leaflets become completely yellow with tip necrosis. Magnesium deficiency is quite common on some species of palms in Florida (Plate 8). *Podocarpus nagi* will have a yellow band across older leaves (Plate 38).

## Manganese

Manganese deficient plants usually exhibit varying degrees of interveinal chlorosis, accompanied by interveinal necrotic streaking on the newest leaves or leaflets. As the deficiency progresses, the necrosis becomes more extensive and new leaves may emerge frizzled or reduced in size (Plates 10 and 11). Leaves do not become totally yellow, which differentiates a manganese deficiency from iron deficiency. Death of the plant usually follows quickly if not treated. Manganese deficiency is very common for many species of palms and cycads in Florida, especially when plants are grown in alkaline soils (Plate 39).

## Nitrogen (mobile)

Nitrogen-deficient plants typically exhibit a uniform loss of green color (chlorosis) beginning on older foliage and eventually encompassing the entire plant (Plate 3). The leaves may be thin and reduced in size. Eventually the entire plant becomes stunted and retains few leaves. Nitrogen deficiency is very common in containerized or recently transplanted plants but is less common in well-established plants.

## Potassium (mobile)

Potassium deficient monocots such as palms or pandanus typically exhibit orange, yellow, or brown spots on the oldest leaves (Plate 4). The spots may appear translucent if held up to the light. Dead tissue on the sides of the leaflets or leaves (marginal necrosis) is also typically present (Plate 5). The necrosis often causes the lower leaves to become totally withered or frizzled (Plate 6). As the deficiency progresses, all leaves within the canopy eventually display the symptoms. This is followed by stunting and chlorosis of new growth, a reduction in stem diameter and, finally, death of the plant. Potassium deficiency of *Phoenix* spp. is similar to that of magnesium deficiency except the leaflets of potassium deficient *Phoenix* spp. have orange-brown rather than bright yellow

leaflet tips (Plate 7). Potassium deficiency is very common in south Florida.

## Sulfur

New growth of sulfur deficient plants will be uniformly chlorotic. Newly emerging leaves will achieve near-normal size but in severe cases will often have extensive tip necrosis (Plate 40). Sulfur deficiency symptoms are virtually identical to those of iron deficiency for some species of monocots. Sulfur deficiency is rather uncommon in Florida landscapes.

— *Timothy K. Broschat*

# NUTRITIONAL
# Deficiencies of Dicots

*Please see the introduction to this chapter for a general description of dicots and of mobile and non-mobile nutrients.*

## Boron

In boron deficient plants, raised corky areas on the main veins on the underside of young leaves usually occur before other symptoms. Leaves appear leathery and are small and possibly cupped, wrinkled or thickened (Plate 41). Leaf chlorosis and yellowing may be evident in some species. Other affected parts may become stiff, brittle, cracked and shortened. Growing points stop cell division causing tip dieback. Lateral buds develop into 1 to 2 inch shoots with dwarfed and twisted leaves. Flower petals lose color and fail to form fruit and seeds.

## Calcium

In cases of calcium deficiency, growth stops and roots are often clubbed (swollen). Upper leaves do not expand and are usually thick and brittle, chlorotic and frequently curled up (Plate 42). The plant is generally stunted with a gummy secretion oozing from the leaves. Death of the terminal shoot (tip) occurs in advanced stages, although shoot tip die-back can occur without chlorotic foliage as a main symptom.

## Copper

Young leaves of copper deficient plants are often reduced in size and cupped, and the length between nodes is reduced (Plate 43). Other symptoms may include burning or dieback of the leaf margin or tip, weak multiple buds or a tendency for the plant to wilt easily.

## Iron

Many iron deficient plants have interveinal chlorosis of their young leaves. Veins appear as fine green lines on a pale ivory colored surface (Plates 44 and 45). In advanced stages the leaves are entirely cream colored and dwarfed. Tip and marginal leaf burn is possible. Iron deficiency is common for plants grown in alkaline or poorly aerated soil.

## Magnesium (mobile)

Magnesium deficiency is exhibited as bronze or chlorotic areas on older leaves (Plate 46). These areas are irregular in outline and occur in irregular blotches between the midrib and the main green lateral veins toward the leaf's middle. Chlorotic areas advance to leave an inverted green V at the base of the leaf, but this pattern differs with leaf structure.

## Manganese

Young leaves of manganese deficient plants exhibit interveinal chlorosis with a relatively wide area of green associated with the veins (Plates 47 and 48). Leaves do not, however, become cream colored. Leaves, shoots, fruits or stems may be contorted, and plant parts may be reduced in size or have necrotic spots that are tan or gray. Interveinal necrosis or necrotic spotting is also typical of manganese deficiency in some species. Manganese deficiency is very common for plants grown in alkaline soils.

## Molybdenum

Young leaves of molybdenum deficient plants are thick, roughened and often elongated to form a strap appearance (Plate 49). Leaves have prominent venation with margins that are irregularly wrinkled and may have interveinal chlorosis. Flower numbers and sizes are reduced. In severe cases, the petals of flowers are fused together.

## Nitrogen (mobile)

One of the first symptoms of nitrogen deficiency is the uniform loss of green leaf color (chlorosis) on older foliage (Plate 50). In advanced stages, leaf color fades to almost ivory (often with a pink or reddish cast), and the leaves become thick, brittle, reduced in size and fewer in number. Eventually, the entire plant is stunted, chlorotic and sparsely foliated. Growth slows dramatically.

## Phosphorus (mobile)

Phosphorus deficiency is not very common and may not be recognized because plant stunting is often the only visible symptom. Older leaves are usually not chlorotic but may exhibit a reddish color or have reddish veins on the undersides of dark green leaves.

## Potassium (mobile)

Chlorosis of older foliage is initially interveinal for many potassium deficient plants. As the deficiency becomes more severe, chlorosis extends to new growth. Interveinal speckling or browning, marginal yellowing and leaf scorch develop (Plates 51 and 52). Irregular dead spots on the leaves may occur.

## Sulfur

When sulfur is deficient, growth at the tip or branch end or the young leaves become light green then entirely yellow. Stunted plants with reduced leaf size and tip necrosis may be prevalent if sulfur deficiency is severe.

## Zinc

With zinc deficiency, young leaves are reduced in size, a condition sometimes referred to as little leaf (Plate 53). In severe cases, size reduction can go up to 95%. Young leaves may exhibit interveinal chlorosis. Internodes may remain very short and cause what is known as a rosetting effect. (Tufts of abnormally small leaves or shoots are called rosettes.) Chlorosis of young leaves may not be the main symptom. Leaves are often narrow with wavy margins, or one side of the leaf may expand faster than the other side resulting in a puckered leaf.

— *Thomas H. Yeager*

# PRUNING
# Trees and Shrubs

Pruning is an important task in the maintenance of a landscape. Through the selective removal of shoots and branches, pruning a plant can improve its health, control its growth and enhance fruiting, flowering or appearance. Pruning should be a part of your gardening routine and not delayed until the landscape is overgrown. An unpruned plant can end up tall and leggy with little foliage close to the ground. In this condition, it cannot be pruned to a desirable size or shape in a single pruning without causing severe damage. Instead, it must be pruned back gradually over a period of several years.

Proper plant selection can eliminate many pruning requirements. Too often plants are selected for the landscape based on their current size and shape rather than those which the plant is likely to attain at maturity five or more years later. The homeowner or landscape manager soon finds it necessary to clip or prune plants frequently to keep them within bounds. It is less time consuming and less costly to select and install the right-sized plant for the location at the outset. Consult books, CD-ROMs, nursery operators or your county Extension agent for growth rate and size of the plant species you are considering for your landscape. If a plant needs to be pruned several times each year to control size, it is quite likely the wrong species for that location.

## Reasons for Pruning

Although we tend to think of pruning as a measure for controlling the form of a plant, plants may be pruned for a number of other reasons. Before pruning, determine which of the following benefits you hope to achieve through your efforts.

## Health and Improved Vigor

The weekly inspection of your landscape is necessary to detect plants threatened by disease or infestation. Often insect, pest and disease problems can be nipped in the bud by the removal of dead, dying, damaged or infected plant parts. For example, if several branch tips are infested with aphids or scale, pruning and discarding the affected shoots can be an effective alternative to spraying with insecticides if the infestation is small and localized. Pruning to remove diseased or infested plant parts can also help stop a problem from spreading to neighboring plants.

## Plant Size and Form

A common objective of pruning is to maintain or develop a desired size or form. As mentioned earlier, this reason for pruning can be largely eliminated by installing the proper species. Compact and dwarf shrubs are now widely available and are a good choice where small or low growing plants are desired. Avoid over-fertilizing and over-watering, which can cause plants to grow more rapidly than desired.

Pruning young trees can dramatically influence their long-term health, function and survival. Branch spacing and arrangement as well as the ultimate structural strength and safety of a tree can be controlled by selectively removing branches on a young sapling (Figure 29). Always work with the natural form of a plant. On trees, encourage a single central trunk to develop by removing competing upright trunks or branches. Begin this process within the first 2 to 3 years after the tree is propagated. Tree training continues for 10 or more years on large maturing species. Frequent light prunings several times each year encourage faster growth and prevent undesirable

**Figure 29. Desirable form and branching pattern. Major limbs are spaced along the trunk, not clustered at the same point.**

sprouting. Several light prunings are preferable to one heavy pruning each year. As a rule, do not attempt to dramatically alter the natural form of a plant; instead, choose a species which has a natural tendency to grow into the form desired. Study the sizes and forms various plants have attained in existing landscapes.

For special effect, plants can be pruned into geometric shapes or to look like animal figures. This practice is known as **topiary** and has become popular in recent years. Topiary plants are attention-getters and should be used sparingly in most landscapes. Small-leaved plants like boxwood, surinam cherry, natal plum, dwarf yaupon holly and pyracantha can be trained to achieve specific forms. Another approach to topiary involves tightly packing a wire mesh frame with sphagnum moss. Plants such as begonias, ivy and creeping fig can be planted in the sphagnum and will form a fully grown topiary in several months to 2 years.

An **espaliered** plant is one which has been trained to grow more or less flat against a wall. This technique requires frequent pinching and pruning, and not all plants are adaptable to these measures. Pyracantha, sea grape, fatshedera, magnolia, yaupon holly, podocarpus and loquat make excellent espalier plants.

Plants considered by many to be large shrubs (e.g. photinia, wax myrtle and pittosporum) can be trained into small trees by gradually removing all the foliage and small branches from the lower portion of one or more stems. The removal process should take 1 to 3 years to complete and should not start before a plant is 8 feet tall. By allowing the plant to reach this height, the main trunk has time to develop properly. During this time, small branches left along the lower trunk will build trunk caliper and create a sturdier tree. The longer the small branches remain on the trunk, the thicker and stronger the trunk becomes.

## Flowering and Fruit Production

Light pruning helps to maintain annual flowering and fruiting on fruit trees. Larger fruit can be produced by the selective removal of flowers or developing fruit. Severe pruning of the current season's growth on flowering plants such as crape myrtle will generally stimulate vegetative growth and produce fewer but larger flower clusters. On species which flower at the tips of the branches (e.g. azalea, cassia, hibiscus, crape myrtle), pinching new vegetative growth during the growing season will stimulate growth of lateral shoots and will increase the number of blossoms produced. Removing the developing seed heads on crape myrtle will promote a second and perhaps even a third flower display.

## Safety

The manner in which branches are attached to each other and to the trunk influences the structural strength of the tree. When branches meet in narrow "V" shaped crotches, one of them should be removed (Figure 30A and 30B). This formation cre-

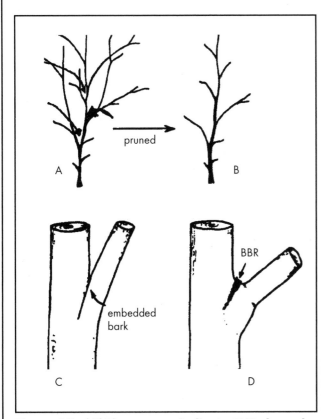

**Figure 30. (A) The arrows indicate "V" shaped crotches where embedded bark could develop. (B) Correct pruning to remove problem limbs. Best done when the tree is young. (C) "V" shaped crotch with embedded bark. (D) "U" shaped crotch with raised branch bark ridge at the union of the stems.**

ates a condition known as embedded (or included) bark in which the bark is literally pinched or squeezed in on itself and looks like a long crease running downwards from the point of the V (Figure 30C). Embedded bark is often difficult to spot at a glance but is apparent on close inspection. Limbs with embedded bark are poorly attached and can split from the tree as they grow older. The wider angled "U" shaped crotches are a healthy formation (Figure 30D). In this type of crotch, there is often a ridge of bark that is usually darker and rougher than the surrounding bark. This is called the branch bark ridge (BBR) and, unlike embedded bark, is a healthy formation.

Large tree limbs that are decayed, broken or poorly attached should be identified and promptly removed by a professional before they fall. Dead branches and branch stubs or their incorrect removal can also lead to serious trunk decay. When a dead branch is removed, take care not to cut into the swollen collar growing around the branch (Figure 31). This collar is composed of trunk tissue, and injuries will affect the trunk. Periodic tree inspection by a professionally trained tree specialist (certified arborist) is a good idea. (Also see "Removing Large Tree Branches" later in this chapter.)

## Rejuvenation of Old Plants

Sometimes a shrub which is not growing well despite receiving adequate light, water and nutrients can be invigorated or shocked into growing by a severe pruning. Typically, the plant either dies or begins flourishing in response to this drastic treatment. (See "Rejuvenation of Shrubs" later in this chapter.)

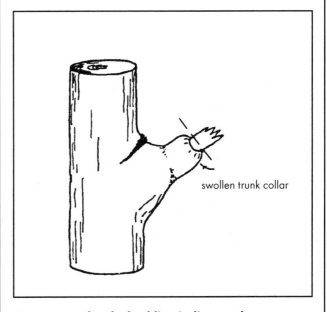

**Figure 31. The dashed line indicates the correct place to cut when removing a dead branch.**

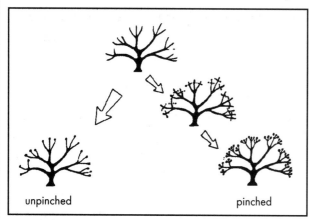

**Figure 32. Pinching encourages lateral shoot development and more flower buds.**

## Pruning at Transplanting

The pruning of shoots in order to compensate for the root loss caused by transplanting is not recommended (see "Pruning at Planting" in the chapter *Planting a Tree*). Prune only to remove branches that are dead, diseased, crossed, rubbing or broken. About 1 year after transplanting, begin pruning to develop appropriate form and structure.

## When to Prune

Trees and shrubs can be lightly pruned anytime. Early pruning on young shrubs encourages branching and fullness, which are frequently desirable characteristics of landscape plants. Some plants set their flower buds on the previous season's growth, and buds winter over on this older growth (Table 15). For example, dogwoods and azaleas form flower buds in July for the following year's flower display. Therefore, prune spring-flowering plants such as azaleas, spireas and dogwoods in late spring before the flower buds set for the next season. Additional pruning or pinching during the interval between the end of the flower display and early summer will not reduce the number of flower buds set.

Pinching back the new shoots on azaleas anytime from several weeks after they begin elongating through the month of May will encourage them to branch laterally. Each of these lateral branches is likely to develop a flower bud. For this reason, a pinched plant will produce many more flowers the following year than will an unpinched plant (Figure 32). Pruning between July and the beginning of the flower display will remove flower buds and reduce the flower display but should not affect the health of the plant.

Plants that produce flowers on the current season's new growth (e.g. abelia, hibiscus, rose) are usually pruned while dormant or just before the spring growth flush (Table 16). Developing shoots can be pinched to encourage lateral branching which will in turn enhance the flower display. Moderate to severe pruning may encourage production of fewer but larger blossoms or blossom clusters.

It is best to prune trees late in the dormant season or several weeks following a growth flush. Pruning at other times frequently promotes undesirable sprouting and tree damage. Trees sprout excessively and are easily damaged when pruned during active shoot elongation. The worst times to prune are when leaves are forming. Do not prune trees which are under stress.

Closure (callusing) of pruning wounds on most trees and shrubs should be most rapid if pruning is conducted just before or immediately following the spring growth flush. A closed wound is not only more aesthetically pleasing, but it also discourages insects, diseases and decay organisms from entering the plant.

Some trees such as birch, maple, dogwood, elm and walnut ooze sap from pruning wounds if they are pruned during late winter or early spring. This bleeding is not usually

**Table 15. Winter and spring flowering plants that can be pruned after flowering but before flower buds form for next year's bloom.***

SHRUBS

| | |
|---|---|
| azaleas | spireas |
| some hydrangea | Indian hawthorn |
| banana shrub | wisteria |
| camellia | star and saucer magnolia |

TREES

| | |
|---|---|
| dogwoods | redbud |
| fringe tree | magnolias |
| African tulip-tree | |

* The only effect from pruning at other times is a reduction in the number of flower buds.

**Table 16. Plants that can be pruned during the dormant season. (Flowers are produced on current season's growth.) ***

SHRUBS

| | |
|---|---|
| allamanda | plumbago |
| abelia | thryallis |
| hibiscus | golden dew-drop |
| oleander | bougainvillea |
| rose | princess-flower |

TREES

| | |
|---|---|
| frangipani | acacia |
| bottle brush | golden rain tree |
| cassia | vitex |
| royal poinciana | crape myrtle |
| jacaranda | |

* Structural pruning can be done at any time.

harmful to the tree, but the dripping sap is often objectionable. Trees which show this tendency should be pruned in late fall or early winter.

Most evergreens, such as podocarpus, holly, boxwood, ligustrum, juniper and wax myrtle, can be pruned anytime. To encourage rapid shoot development and the greatest overall plant growth, prune just prior to bud swell in the spring. To retard growth for maximum dwarfing effect, prune just after each growth flush, when leaves have expanded fully. Late summer pruning may stimulate an additional flush of shoot growth on species which flush several times each year. These shoots could be damaged by an early frost.

Pines can be pruned by removing approximately one-half of the new shoot in the spring just prior to needle expansion (Figure 33). This encourages new bud formation at the pinch, slows growth on the pinched branch and creates a more compact plant. Never pinch a pine at other times of the year since new buds will not form.

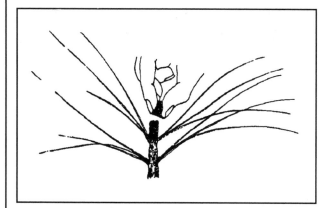

**Figure 33. Prune pine shoots in the spring before the needles elongate.**

Cold injury can be reduced if pruning is conducted close to the spring bud break. Late fall and early winter pruning can stimulate new growth, particularly during a mild period during the winter. The succulent stems that are produced as a consequence are not cold hardy and can be easily damaged, even by a light frost. Even if growth is not stimulated by pruning, low winter temperatures can cause cambium damage beneath improperly executed pruning cuts. This is particularly true of plants which are marginally hardy. If in doubt about cold susceptibility, it is best to delay heavy pruning until just before growth begins in the spring.

## Pruning Techniques

Plants are pruned either by heading back or by thinning. **Heading back** is the selective cutting of the ends of twigs or young branches back to a bud or node. Heading back that involves using the thumb and forefinger to remove the tips of branches is referred to as **pinching**. Usually an increased number of shoots and leaves result, producing a denser plant. New growth is typically vigorous and upright, developing from two to several buds just behind the

pruning cut. On trees, this kind of pruning will result in undesirable multiple leaders (trunks) (Figure 34); however, if properly applied to shrubs, pleasing forms can be created and maintained. New foliage may be so thick that it shades the lower growth, forming a top heavy plant. To avoid this problem, head back the shrub's shoots to several different heights (Figure 35). When heading back, make the cut on a slight slant 1/4 inch above a healthy bud (Figure 36). The bud should be facing the direction preferred for new growth.

Heading back (or stubbing) trees is rarely warranted in landscape sites and often results in undesirable multiple leaders (trunks). If it is necessary, for instance, to prune beneath power lines or to clear a tree from interfering with a structure, always prune back to a fork where there is a live branch that is at least half the diameter of the limb being removed. This technique is called **drop-crotching** (Figure 37). Within several months, prune out all sprouts growing in response to the cut. Never "hat-rack" a landscape tree by cutting all of its branches back to an arbitrary length (Figure 38). This type of pruning has no place in horticulture.

**Thinning** (Figure 39) is the complete removal of branches back to a lateral branch or to the main trunk or, in shrubs, to the ground. Depending on how the plant is

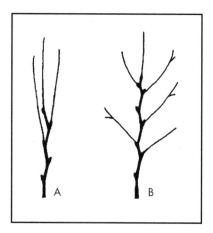

**Figure 34. (A) Young unbranched trunk that has been headed back. (B) Growth from an unpruned shoot. Note the horizontal branching habit and the desirable central leader.**

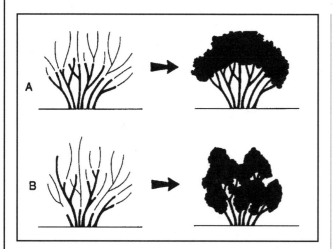

**Figure 35. (A) Shrub with all shoots headed back to same height. (B) Shrub when shoots have been headed back to different heights.**

thinned, thinning can give a plant an open appearance or can encourage new growth inside the crown. If thinning is heavy, interior sprouts will develop. If the plant is lightly thinned, interior shoots are not likely to develop. Shrubs are thinned primarily to control size while maintaining a natural appearance. This technique differs from hedging or heading to the same spot on all branches, which will give a shrub a formal, controlled appearance.

Trees can be thinned to increase light penetration and encourage turf growth beneath the tree. First remove branches that are rubbing, crossed over each other, dead, diseased or dying. Removing upright

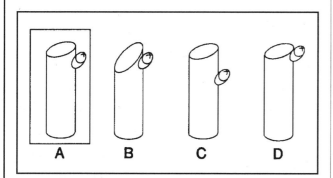

**Figure 36. (A) Proper location and angle of pruning cut. (B) Too slanted. (C) Too far from the bud. (D) Too close to the bud.**

branches creates a more spreading tree while removal of horizontal branches results in an upright form. If further thinning is desired, remove branches back to major limbs to create an open crown. (This is a specialized technique best performed by a professional arborist.) Space remaining branches along the major limbs so that each one has room to develop (see Figure 39B, right side). Trees with properly thinned crowns resist wind damage better than unpruned trees.

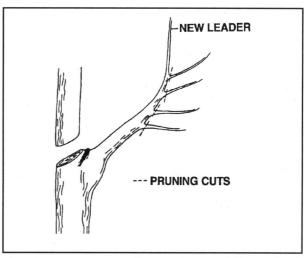

**Figure 37. Drop-crotching is the term for pruning back to a fork with a living branch that is at least half the diameter of the limb being removed. This branch will become the new leader.**

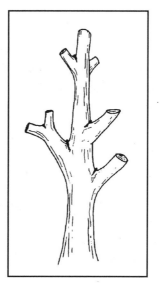

**Figure 38. Never "hat-rack" a tree.**

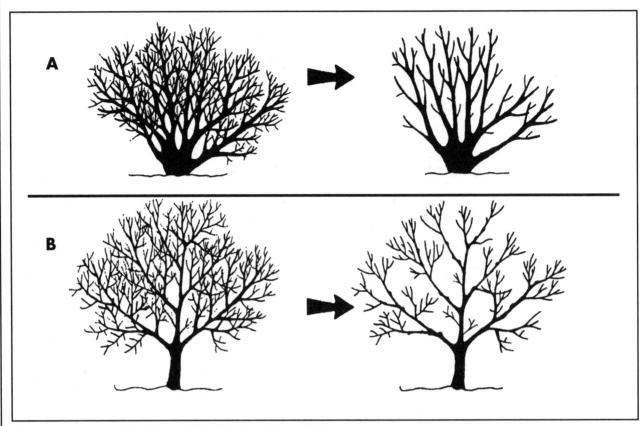

**Figure 39. Correctly thinned shrub (A) and tree (B).**

## Pruning Shrubs

A properly pruned shrub is a work of art and beauty and does not look as if it has been pruned. Pruning cuts should not be visible but located inside the plant where they will be covered by remaining foliage. The first step in pruning a shrub is to remove all dead, diseased or injured branches. Remove branches that cross or touch each other and those that look out of place. If the shrub is still too dense or large, remove some of the oldest branches. Head back excessively long branches to a bud or lateral branch that is 6 to 12 inches below the desirable plant height (Figure 35). Thinning (Figure 39) may also be desirable. Do not use hedge shears. Cut each branch separately to different lengths with hand pruners. This will maintain a neat informal shrub with a natural shape. (Plants sheared into hard geometric shapes look out of place in a landscape designed to look natural.) For a discussion of formal pruning, see "Hedge Pruning" later in this chapter.

## Rejuvenation of Shrubs

Rejuvenation is a drastic method of pruning old shrubs that have become much too large or have a large amount of nonflowering wood. The best time for rejuvenation is in late winter or early spring, just before growth begins. Large, old shrubs should not be rejuvenated during late summer. New growth will be stimulated and possibly killed by cold weather in the winter.

Multiple stem shrubs are rejuvenated by cutting back all stems at ground level over a period of 12 to 18 months. At the first pruning, remove 1/3 of the old, mature stems (Figure 40A). Six months later, take out 1/2 of the remaining old stems and head back long shoots growing from the previous pruning cuts (Figure 40B). At the third pruning in yet another 6 months, remove the remaining old wood and head back the long new shoots (Figure 40C).

On single stem shrubs that grow in tree form (e.g. ligustrum, gardenia), rejuvenation is carried out over a period of 12 to 18 months by severe thinning and heading back to the basic limb framework (Figure 41). One-third to one-half of the old growth is removed at 6 month intervals. Pruning cane-type shrubs such as nandina and mahonia is best done on a 2 or 3 year cycle. The tallest canes are pruned to stubs 3 to 6 inches above the soil line during the first spring, just as growth begins. By the second spring, last year's medium-sized canes have grown to become tall canes and should be cut back to 3 inch stubs. Canes from the first year's pruning have already begun to grow and are 1 to 3 feet tall by now. In the third spring, the canes which were the shortest in the first spring are now fairly tall and can be cut back. In this way, there is always foliage near the ground and the shrubs can be kept from becoming leggy. Cut nandina canes generally will not flower during the growing season that follows their pruning.

## Pruning Trees

Become familiar with the characteristic form of your tree before removing any live branches. In many landscapes, little or no attempt should be made to significantly change these characteristic growth habits. Instead, prune in such a way as to enhance and encourage the natural shape of the tree. First remove dead, diseased or broken twigs and branches. Now study the tree's form and select the best spaced and positioned permanent branches, removing or shortening the others (Figure 42). To shorten, use thinning cuts as previously described under "Pruning Techniques." Note that the tree represented in A and B of Figure 42 has a bad fork which should be eliminated. Pruning the upright portion of the left fork will slow growth on that branch and encourage growth in the central leader. (A central leader may be difficult to maintain higher than 15 feet in some large species such as live oak, royal poinciana and jacaranda. Such trees can be trained with several co-dominant leaders or trunks spaced 24 inches apart.) Permanent branches should be spaced 6 to 24 inches apart on the trunk, depending on the ultimate mature size of

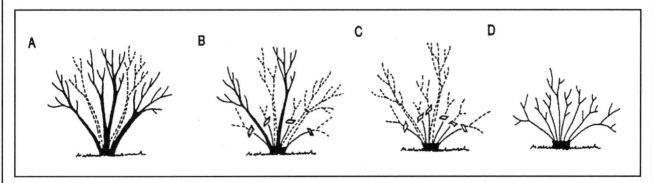

**Figure 40. Rejuvenation of multiple stem shrubs. (A) First pruning. (B) Second pruning. (C) Third pruning. (D) Rejuvenated shrub.**

**Figure 41. Rejuvenation on single stem and grafted shrubs is carried out by severe thinning then heading back to the basic framework.**

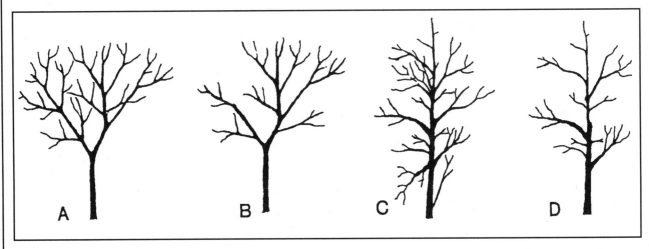

**Figure 42. A tree maturing at less than 30' tall before (A) and after (B) pruning. A large-maturing tree before (C) and after (D) pruning.**

the tree. On smaller trees like dogwoods, a 6 inch spacing is adequate whereas spaces of 18 to 24 inches are best for large maturing trees like oaks. Remove fast growing suckers that sprout at the base of and along tree trunks or on large, interior limbs.

To prune a young tree to a single leader (the stem that will become the trunk), locate the straightest and best leader to retain. In shaping the tree crown, remove lateral branches that are growing upright (Figure

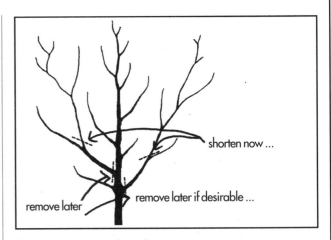

**Figure 43. Forming the tree crown.**

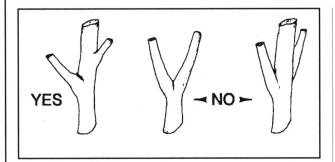

**Figure 44. Angles of branch attachment.**

**Figure 45. Temporary branches 8 to 12 inches long are left on a young tree to protect and strengthen the trunk.**

43). They will compete with the leader and form a weak, multiple leadered tree. (Most trees can be grown with a single leader when they are young, but the growth habit of some species will change to a multi-leader spreading form at maturity.) There should be no branches leaving the trunk at an acute angle or narrow forks either between branches or between a branch and the trunk (Figure 44). Branches that are less than 2/3 the diameter of the trunk are less likely than larger branches to split off the tree.

When training a young tree, prune back those branches below the lowest permanent branch to 8 to 12 inches from the trunk (Figure 45); these are temporary branches. Remove any lower branches that are larger than 1/4 inch in diameter. By keeping the smaller-diameter branches on the trunk, the tree will grow faster and develop a thicker trunk. The trunk will also be better protected from sunburn and vandalism or accidental damage. Removing the lower branches too soon will result in a poorer quality plant. When the tree trunk approaches 2 inches in diameter (measured 6 inches up from the ground), remove the temporary branches.

**Figure 46. Removing a branch over 1-1/2" diameter. First (A) and second (B) cuts prevent bark from tearing. Third cut (C) detailed in Figures 47 and 48.**

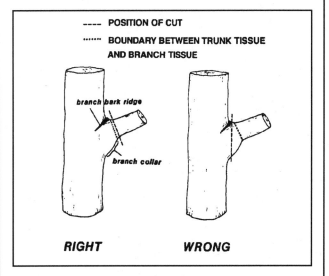

**Figure 47. Correct (left) and incorrect (right) final pruning cuts for branches of any size.**

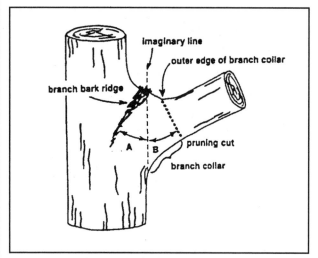

**Figure 48. The angle (A) created by the branch bark ridge and an imaginary line flush with the tree trunk is the approximate angle (B) at which to make the pruning cut. This calculation is useful when the bottom of the branch collar cannot be seen.**

## Removing Large Tree Branches

Large branches too heavy to be held by hand (i.e. 1 1/2 inches or more in diameter) require three separate cuts to prevent trunk bark stripping (Figure 46). The first cut is made on the underside of the branch about 15 inches away from the trunk and as far up through the branch as possible before the branch weight binds the saw. The second cut is made downward from the top of the branch about 18 inches from the main trunk to cause the limb to split cleanly between the two cuts without tearing the bark. The remaining stub can then be supported easily with one hand while it is cut from the tree. This final cut should begin on the outside of the branch bark ridge and end just outside of the branch collar swelling on the lower side of the branch (Figure 47). (The bark ridge is usually rough, always darker than the surrounding bark and fairly obvious on most species.) Note that the cut is usually made angling down and outward from the tree. If

the cut must be made straight down (parallel to the trunk), do not make it flush with the tree trunk. A flush cut will cause serious injury. Although this was once standard practice, research has conclusively shown that flush cuts cause extensive trunk decay because wood that is actually part of the trunk gets cut. When the bottom of the branch collar is hard to see, prune as shown in Figure 48. In this way, only branch tissue is cut, and there is no damage to the trunk.

Painting wounds with tree wound dressing has become a controversial practice. The standard recommendation was to paint wounds with a quality tree wound dressing to protect the cut surface from wood rotting organisms and from cracking upon drying. However, research has shown that wound dressings do not prevent decay. When exposed to the sun, the protective coating often cracks, allowing moisture to enter and accumulate in pockets between the wood and the wound covering. This situation may be more inviting to wood rotting organisms than one with no wound cover. In situations where aesthetics are important, the practice may be justified.

## Pruning Palms

Care must be taken when pruning palms not to cut or otherwise injure the terminal bud or the whole tree will die. See *Landscape Use and Pruning of Palms* in the PALMS section.

Old dead leaves on palms such as the Washington palm should be removed as they often harbor insects and rodents and may become a fire hazard. Remove palm leaves by cutting them from the underside to avoid tearing the fibers of the palm's stem. Palms such as the royal palm shed their leaves, which are heavy and could pose a hazard in some situations. In such cases, remove them

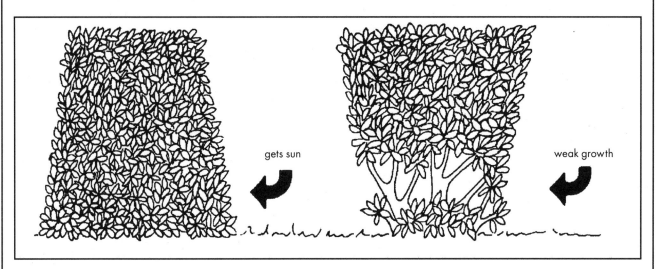

**Figure 49. Plants pruned as a solid hedge should be wider at the bottom than the top.**

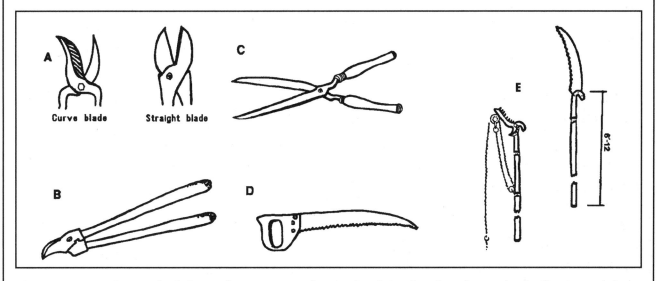

**Figure 50. Pruning tools. (A) Hand pruners are for cutting branches less than 1/4" in diameter. (B) Loppers cut branches up to 1/2" in diameter. (C) Hedge shears are used on formal hedges. (D) Saws are for removing large branches. (E) Some shears and saws can be attached to poles for pruning difficult-to-reach branches.**

before they drop. The large fruit of coconut palms can be dangerous in areas where pedestrians and automobiles pass beneath. Prevent formation of fruits by removing the flower stalks. On small-fruited palms such as Christmas and cabbage palms, such safety precautions are not necessary. However, the fruit from these and many other palms can become slippery. Consider removing the flower stalks if this is a concern.

## Hedge Pruning

The method you choose for hedge pruning will be determined by the type of hedge you want. An informal hedge is generally a row of closely planted shrubs which are allowed to develop into their natural shape. Annual pruning consists of thinning and heading back just enough to maintain desired height and width.

Formal or clipped hedges require a specialized pruning which may become a continuous job during the growing season. The desired appearance of a formal hedge is a sharply defined geometric shape. There are two important factors to remember when pruning formal hedges: 1) hedges should be clipped while new growth is green and succulent; 2) plants should be trimmed so the base of the hedge is wider than the top (Figure 49). Hedges pruned with a narrow base will lose lower leaves and branches because shading from the top growth will not permit sufficient light to penetrate (Plate 54). This condition will worsen with age resulting in sparse growth at ground level and an unattractive hedge which does not give desired privacy. Flowering hedges grown formally should be sheared after they have bloomed as more frequent shearing reduces number of blooms. If the blooms are of secondary importance, pruning may be conducted at any time.

## Pruning Tools

Various pruning tools are designed to handle different pruning tasks (Figure 50). Keep tools sharp for easier cutting and to prevent injuries to plant tissue. Injured tissues are susceptible to disease and decay which can in turn lead to long term health problems for the plant. Pruning shears and saws can be dipped in rubbing alcohol for 30 seconds before each re-use to prevent the spread of disease between plants.

— *Edward F. Gilman and Robert J. Black*

# IDENTIFYING and Managing Weeds

While it is frequently said that a weed is a plant growing where it's not wanted, the fact is that some plants are so generally unwelcome by so many landscapers and gardeners that they are safe to call weeds in any situation. Plants often earn their reputations as weeds if they grow without care or cultivation *and* despite efforts to get rid of them. Weeds compete with desired plants for space, water, light and nutrients and can harbor insect pests and diseases. The predominant weed species change from season to season in Florida. Because weed populations can explode if not kept in check, the amount of pressure from these pest plants remains consistently high.

This chapter will focus on types of common weeds, weed control principles and the non-chemical gardening practices that can be integrated with chemical management practices to form a weed control program.

## How Weeds are Classified

Weeds belong to one of three major categories and are further distinguished by the lengths of their life cycles. As to category, a weed will be considered a grass, a broadleaf weed or a sedge. Its life cycle will be annual, biennial or perennial. A weed's life cycle has great impact on the selection and success of a given control procedure so it is important to learn the life cycle characteristics of a weed when you first learn its identity. Visual inspection will not necessarily reveal information about a weed's life cycle.

## Weed Types
### Grass Weeds

Grass weeds are true grasses and, as such, have hollow and rounded stems and nodes (joints) that are closed and hard. The leaf blades alternate on each side of the stem, are much longer than they are wide and have parallel veins. Among the grass weeds are crabgrass, goosegrass (Plate 55), crowfootgrass, sandbur (sandspur), annual bluegrass, torpedograss and vaseygrass.

## Broadleaf Weeds

Broadleaf weeds abound in great variety. Most have net-like veins in their leaves, and many have showy flowers. Because of differences in their leaf structure and growth habits, they are easy to distinguish from grasses. Broadleaf weeds include common chickweed, Florida betony (Plate 56), cudweed, eclipta, Florida pusley (Plate 57), henbit (Plate 58), pennywort or dollarweed, wood sorrel (Plate 59) and spurge (Plate 60). Two broadleaf weeds which are becoming both troublesome and widespread are chamberbitter or leafflower (Plate 61) and long-stalked phyllanthus (Plate 62).

## Sedges

Sedges are a widespread group of grass-like weeds, however they are not true grasses. Sedges are characterized by stems that are solid and triangular in shape. Their grass-like leaves appear on the stem in clusters of three with each one extending in a different direction. Annual sedges are often called water grasses. Perennial sedges predominate and are difficult to control. Included in this latter group, yellow nutsedge (Plate 63, center) has a yellowish green seedhead and reproduces by seed, rhizomes and tubers. The rhizomes radiate from the plant and have at their ends a single bulb or tuber which may produce new plants. Usually smaller than yellow nutsedge, purple nutsedge (Plate 63, right) has reddish purple seed heads and also reproduces through series of bulbs on radiating rhizomes called tuber chains. Common in many areas but overall less widespread than the yellow and the purple, globe sedge (Plate 63, left) has spiked seed heads that look like but do not stick like sandburs.

# Weed Life Cycles

## Annual Weeds

Annual weeds germinate from seed, then grow, flower, produce seed and die in 12 months or less. Grasses, sedges and broadleaved weeds all include annuals among their varieties. Annual weeds are further categorized by the season in which they germinate and flourish. Summer or warm season annuals, such as chamberbitter, crabgrass and spotted spurge, sprout in the spring and thrive in summer and early fall. Henbit, common chickweed, and annual bluegrass are typical winter or cool season annuals. Such weeds sprout in the fall, thrive during the winter and early spring and die in late spring or early summer.

## Biennial Weeds

Biennials have a 2-year life cycle. They germinate from seed in the fall and develop large root systems and a compact cluster of leaves during the first year. In the second year, they flower, produce seed and die. Cudweed and Carolina falsedandelion are examples of biennial weeds. Compared to the annual weeds, species of biennial weeds are few in number.

## Perennial Weeds

Weeds that live more than 2 years are perennials. They reproduce using vegetative (non-seed) parts such as tubers, bulbs, rhizomes (underground stems) or stolons (above-ground stems), although some also produce seed. During the winter season, most perennial weeds are dormant, and many lose their above-ground foliage and stems. In the spring, they initiate growth from food reserves in their root systems. An exception is Florida betony, a perennial weed that, in this subtropical climate, initiates its growth in the fall, grows during the winter months and goes dormant during the heat of the summer. The shape of its edible tubers (Plate 56) gives Florida betony the common name rattlesnake weed.

Perennial weeds are the most difficult to control because of their great reproductive potential and persistence. Torpedograss, nutsedge and vines such as greenbrier (Plate 64) belong to this group of weeds.

Perennial weeds may also be categorized by type of root system and reproductive process:

- Simple perennials reproduce by seeds, but root pieces distributed by cultivation or other mechanical means will produce new plants. Florida betony is a typical simple perennial.

- Bulbous perennials reproduce by seed and above- or below-ground bulbs. Yellow nutsedge and wild onions have their bulbs below ground while wild garlic has an above-ground bulb.

- Creeping perennials produce seed but also produce rhizomes or stolons. Bermudagrass, torpedograss and purple nutsedge produce rhizomes and stolons which act as food storage organs and can initiate growth at each node along a stem.

Proper identification of weeds targeted for elimination is necessary in order to select effective control measures, be they cultural or chemical. Further assistance with weed identification is available from your county Extension office.

# Weed Control Principles

Weeds reproduce from seed, root pieces and special vegetative reproductive organs such as tubers, corms, rhizomes or bulbs. Seeds can be distributed by people, animals, birds, wind and water. Many of the weeds that show up in landscape beds come from seeds. Weeds also arrive in landscape beds when their reproductive tissues and organs (noted above) are in the soil of transplants. Additionally, weed rhizomes or stolons can creep into the bed from an infested area adjacent to the landscape bed. Plastic or metal edging that penetrates several inches into the ground around the perimeter of the landscape bed will reduce the likelihood of weed infestations arising from rhizomes or stolons.

Preventative weed control is the name of the game, especially for homeowners. Removing established weeds from a homeowner's landscape bed can be time consuming and/ or expensive. Weed infestations will probably have to be removed by hand as there are few herbicides available to homeowners that can be safely applied over the top and around most landscape plants. Application of most herbicides should be left to licensed pest control professionals. Although this is an expensive option, they have the proper equipment and take the appropriate measures to ensure that the job is done correctly and safely.

# Cultural Methods of Weed Control

Weed infestations in landscape beds can be effectively controlled using a program that integrates various approaches and in particular emphasizes cultural methods (i.e. gardening techniques). The following cultural methods of weed control will sharply reduce the need for herbicides and are usually all that is required in the home landscape.

## Mulching
Mulches provide an excellent means to keep the growth of weeds, especially annuals, in check. See *Mulches in the Landscape*.

## Reduced Irrigation
Some weeds will thrive if soil is wet or consistently moist. Dollarweed and some nutsedges are examples of weeds that thrive in a moist soil. By reducing the level of supplemental irrigation, it may be possible to eradicate them or prevent their occurrence. Consider using plants that have reduced water requirements or group plants in landscape beds with similar irrigation requirements.

## Dense Plantings
When planted densely, landscape plants themselves can keep weed growth in check. In essence, the landscape plants will out compete weeds for light, water and nutrients. Spreading shrubs such as low-growing junipers, annuals that fill in during the growing season and ground covers will all help reduce weed control costs.

## Well-Maintained Turf
Weeds growing in turf can easily spread into adjacent landscape beds, but turfgrasses are tough competitors for weeds if proper maintenance schedules are followed. Mowing at the recommended height and frequency, properly timing the correct rates of

fertilization and maintaining adequate soil moisture will help turf suppress weed growth and prevent the invasion of weeds into landscape beds.

## Weed-free Transplants

Weed seed, rhizomes and root pieces can be introduced into landscape beds by infested transplants. Remove any weeds growing in the root ball, being sure to remove the entire weed root system. Even when you remove weeds before transplanting, weed seed may remain on the surface of the root ball. You can reduce the likelihood that weeds will be introduced via transplants by purchasing only high-quality, weed-free plants. Healthy vigorous plants were probably produced under relatively weed-free conditions.

## Hand Weeding

No matter what preventative measures you use to control weeds, weeding by hand will probably be necessary sometimes. Be sure to remove the weeds before they flower and set seed. Discarded weeds can be composted. The heat generated by properly prepared compost will kill the weeds as well as seeds.

## Chemical Weed Control

Herbicides are a group of chemical compounds that control plant growth and development either by interrupting some metabolic pathway or by contact action. Plant response to such chemicals depends largely on the concentration at which the chemical is applied. For example, certain herbicides can effectively control broadleaf weeds but in some cases at lower concentrations will exhibit growth regulating properties and actually stimulate the rooting of cuttings.

Many herbicides registered for control of weeds in landscape beds are not available to home gardeners. Check with your county Extension agent before purchasing any herbicide to ensure that herbicide use is warranted. Also, realize that some of the herbicides sold are labelled for use in landscape beds but are not recommended for use in Florida because of our climate and soils. Be sure to read and follow all label directions.

## Herbicide Types

**Selective herbicides** control some plants without seriously affecting the growth of other plants. The majority of herbicides used are selective.

**Nonselective herbicides** are toxic to most plants. These are generally used to kill all plants, as when preparing for planting a new shrub bed, for spot treatment or as an edging material along sidewalks, etc.

**Contact herbicides** will kill only the plant tissue with which they come in contact. The foliage of perennial plants may be killed by contact herbicides but regrowth from the roots is likely. Repeat applications of contact herbicides are often needed in order to kill the regrowth from the underground plant parts such as roots or tubers.

**Systemic or translocated herbicides** are absorbed by and transported within the plant by the plant's vascular system, which also transports the nutrients and water necessary for growth and development. Systemic herbicides kill entire plants over a period of days or weeks.

## Herbicide Type by Timing of Application

Herbicides are also categorized by the timing of their application. **Preemergence herbicides** are applied prior to the germination of weed seeds. Consequently, the knowledge of weed life cycles is crucial when attempting preemergence control. Preemergence herbicides are generally not effective if applied after the weeds appear. The narrow "window" for timing application is a potential disadvantage for many homeowners and licensed pest control companies.

Because preemergence herbicides act by forming a uniform soil barrier, disturbing the treated soil layer by raking, for instance, may disrupt this barrier and deposit a fresh supply of weed seeds on the soil surface. The result is reduced herbicide effectiveness.

Adequate soil moisture before and after application is also necessary to activate most preemergence herbicides. Most preemergence herbicides are generally effective in controlling weeds from 6 to 12 weeks following application.

**Postemergence herbicides** are used on weeds that have already appeared. In general, the younger the weed seedling the easier it is to control. The effectiveness of postemergence herbicides is reduced when the weed is under drought stress, has begun to produce seeds or has been cut or trimmed before the chemical has had time to work (several days after application). Under any of these conditions, avoid application of postemergence herbicides.

## Herbicide Formulations

Herbicides are formulated in a variety of ways. Wettable powders (abbreviated *W* or *WP*) are, as the name suggests, powders that are mixed with water before applying. Dry flowables (*DF*) and water dispersible granules (*WDG*) come in a granular form that is mixed with water. Solutions (*L* or *S*) and emulsifiable concentrates (*E* or *EC*) are already in liquid form but must be diluted with water. Granular (*G*) herbicides are applied dry to landscape beds. Many preemergent herbicides (i.e. herbicides applied before weeds germinate) are granular formulations that ensure application to the soil surface with limited drift and contact with foliage. If given the choice, select a *G* formulation over one that must be sprayed. Granular formulations are more expensive, but are safer to apply. There is less potential for drift, no mixing is required, and cleanup is easier. For dry formulations of herbicides that must be sprayed, choose *DF* or *WDG* formulations over *WP* formulations. *DF*s and *WDG*s are safer for the person doing the application due to the reduced dust associated with these formulations.

All postemergent herbicides are mixed with water to facilitate thorough weed coverage. Good agitation in the spray tank is necessary to provide uniform application rates. The amount of active ingredient in a herbicide formulation is presented as a number in front of the formulation designation (*G, W, WP, DF, WDG, E, EC, L,* or *S*) on the label. For example, a 4% granular herbicide is identified as a 4G material and represents 4 pounds of active ingredient in 100 pounds of product. A 75% wettable powder (or dry flowable or water dispersible granule) is labeled as 75WP (or 75DF or 75WDG), which means that 75% of the product in the bag is active ingredient. Liquid formulations are labeled as pounds of active ingredient **per gallon** of product. For example, a 2EC (emulsifiable concentrate) or 2L (liquid) or 2S (soluble) contains 2 pounds of active ingredient per gallon of product.

Fumigants generally kill all living things in the soil including weeds, weed seeds, insects, nematodes and disease organisms. The nature of these chemicals makes them useful for treatment prior to planting. Because most fumigants are hazardous materials, they can only be applied by licensed pest control professionals.

Selection of a herbicide should be based on the weeds to be controlled, the existing weed population, length of control desired and specific landscape plants involved, rather than of a particular product.

Follow these **safety guidelines** when applying any herbicide and see *Safety with Pesticides*:

* Read and carefully follow all label directions, including those for protective clothing and precautionary statements. Remember, the label is the law.

* Prevent runoff of postemergent herbicides as this will minimize pollution and injury to your landscape plants.

* Do not use herbicides that are designed for use on lawns (especially 'weed-and-feed' type products) in landscape beds unless the herbicide is also labelled for use on ornamentals in landscape beds. Most landscape plants are very susceptible to damage from many of the herbicides commonly found in 'weed-and-feed' lawn products, so read labels with great care before applying.

* Avoid drift onto desirable plants by applying herbicides only on calm days (i.e. when the wind is less than 5 mph).

* Avoid herbicide use around lakes, ponds, sinkholes, rivers and streams.

—*Jeffrey G. Norcini*

# INSECTS
and Other Organisms

## Checking for Insects and Mites

Fewer than 1% of all insects are harmful to plants and many are actually beneficial, acting as predators or parasites of harmful insects and assisting in the cross pollination of certain plants. Remember that disease, nutritional deficiencies and environmental conditions can cause a plant to appear unhealthy or discolored, so it is important to be sure a problem is correctly diagnosed before remedial measures are taken. Most plants in the urban landscape are over-sprayed, resulting in unnecessary environmental contamination and often upsetting the natural predator/parasite - pest balance. Do not apply insecticides on a preventative basis. Spray only when plants have an active pest infestation and damage is occurring. Before using a control method for an active pest infestation, look around the landscape to see if predator or parasitic insects are present to control your pest problem. (See *Integrated Pest Management.*) If you must spray, use the least toxic remedy possible and exercise great care to avoid contaminating yourself and other living creatures. (See *Safety with Pesticides.*)

Sometimes the insect you spot on a plant is just resting while passing through the landscape, and often the insects you find will be a positive benefit to your plants. By identifying and learning about the insects in your landscape, you will avoid unnecessary pest management practices and help support a healthy, self-sustaining ecosystem in both your own and the larger landscape.

While many plants are relatively pest free, others are infested with particular pests virtually every year (e.g. mites on roses,

oleander caterpillars on oleanders, aphids on crape myrtles). Concentrate your scouting efforts on these "key" plants. Examine them weekly during spring, summer and fall. Look at several stems and the undersides of leaves. The use of a 10 to 15 power magnifying glass will aid in detecting and identifying insects and related organisms. To aid in locating mites or small insects such as aphids, lacebugs or thrips, hold a sheet of white paper or a white cloth beneath leaves and strike the foliage sharply. The insects or mites will fall onto the paper and are more easily observed and identified than when they are on the green foliage.

Watch for sooty mold on leaves (Plate 162). This fungus grows on the "honeydew" excreted by insects such as whiteflies, aphids and soft scales. Because ants also feed on this honeydew excrement, their presence on plants often indicates an insect infestation.

To combat insect pests successfully, you need to know something about the manner in which they develop and feed. Insects normally hatch from eggs deposited on or near the food supply. In some cases, as with aphids, they hatch within the female's body, and the active young emerge from the female. Adults usually have fully developed wings, although a few species of insects never develop wings.

Insects pass through several stages during their development. This process is known as metamorphosis. Some insects, such as plant bugs, leafhoppers, thrips and grasshoppers hatch from the egg in a form known as a nymph. The nymph resembles the full-grown insect except that it is smaller and lacks wings. It molts, or casts its skin, periodically as it increases in size. Insects such as moths, beetles and flies hatch from their eggs in a worm-like form called a larva. The larva is much different in appearance from the adult. Moth or butterfly larvae are called caterpillars, beetle larvae are known as grubs, and fly larvae are maggots. Larvae molt periodically and when mature, they transform to an inactive form known as a pupa. After a period of little activity and no feeding, the adult moth, beetle or fly emerges from the pupa. At this point, metamorphosis is complete.

The length of an insect's life cycle varies greatly among the species. Some develop from egg to adult in a few days or weeks, many require a year, and a few take 2 or more years to reach maturity.

The following list includes both beneficial and harmful insects as well as other organisms that may be found in the landscape. The most common insects and pests found in Florida have the notation "COMMON" following their descriptions. A description as well as information on common habitat or food source is also included. Refer to the color plates for further assistance with identification.

## Ambush bugs

Ambush bugs (beneficial) are small and stout-bodied, 1/4 to 1/2 inch in length and closely related to assassin bugs. There are 22 species in North America. Their front legs are thickened for grasping prey. Feeding primarily on wasps and flies, they wait on flowers where they are camouflaged by their greenish-yellow and brown body color (Plate 65).

## Amphipods

Amphipods are crustacea with a shrimp-like appearance. Often called "lawn shrimp," amphipods live on the top 1/2 inch of mulch and moist ground and are usually pale brown in color when alive. They are general scavengers but are not harmful. After rains, large numbers of amphipods can migrate into garages or under the doors of houses. They die quickly in the drier environment and turn a reddish color (Plate 66).

## Ants

Ants are often thought of as nuisance pests. However their roles range from benign to destructive in the landscape environment. For instance, acrobat ants may nest in rose canes causing little damage to the plant, yet they can inflict a painful sting when disturbed as the plants are pruned. Ghost ants may be beneficial because they prey upon spider mites. Many ants create a mere annoyance as they harvest honeydew left on plants by aphids, scales and related insects. Some of these ants will actually tend (assist) the aphids and protect them from predators and parasites. Probably the most notorious of all ant species in Florida is the imported fire ant. In addition to its painful sting, the red imported fire ant can cause direct damage to plants.

Because of the varied role each ant species plays in the landscape environment, it is important to correctly identify the ant. Ants can be distinguished from other insects by their narrow waists and elbowed (bent) antennae. Worker ants are used to further establish the identity of the ant. Ants may belong to species that are **monomorphic** (one size), **dimorphic** (two sizes) or **polymorhphic** (more than two sizes). Ants live in colonies or nests. Nest sites are as variable as the ants themselves and can be found in places ranging from soil to decaying organic matter to hollow plant stems. They are often difficult to find. The nest serves as the central site from which workers leave and find food, then return. These workers are called foragers. Once the food is brought back to the colony, special workers called brood tenders help distribute the food to the other members of the colony; these include the brood, the mated females (queens) and sometimes male and female reproductives. The brood consists of the immature stages: eggs, larvae and pupae. The larvae do not have legs and look like whitish sacs with a head. The male and female reproductives are unmated and usually still have their wings attached. Once a colony has been established, the main function of the queen is to lay the eggs. Colonies that contain one queen are called **monogyne** or, if there are many queens, **polygyne**. COMMON.

**Florida carpenter ants** are large, about 1/5 to 2/5 inch long (Plate 67). The thorax is evenly rounded when viewed from the side. The tip of the abdomen has a "circlet" of hairs. Workers are polymorphic, and colonies are monogyne.

The Florida carpenter ant nests in the ground beneath objects such as dead tree branches or wood piles, in the bases of palm fronds, in rotting logs and tree stumps, in dump sites along roadways and in abandoned fire ant nests. A colony can contain several thousand workers. Food sources include honeydew and insects, both live and dead. Carpenter ants forage throughout the day, with a greater percentage of the colony foraging at night. Though they don't sting, they have very sharp mandibles for chewing through wood and can subject a curious observer to a sharp, painful bite. A common name for this ant in Florida is "bull dog" or "bull" ant.

Quite often these ants nest outdoors and either forage indoors for water and food or form satellite nests indoors. Satellite nests may contain unmated sexual forms but usually do not contain a queen. Carpenter

ants do not consume wood, rather they excavate galleries in wood to form a nest. They will find untreated wood that has decayed and tear it into sawdust, but they are not responsible for the initial destruction of the wood.

**Ghost ants** (beneficial) are 1/25 inch long and have a sweet, musty odor when squashed. The head and thorax are black while the abdomen and legs are clear (Plate 68). Workers are monomorphic while colonies are polymorphic. Although found both indoors and out, ghost ant nests are often located in the decaying organic matter that collects at the base of palm tree fronds. Entryway to buildings is provided by contact between limb or frond and building. Ghost ants are opportunistic and will colonize almost any site in a greenhouse including potted plants, soil, gravel and aluminum doors. Because ghost ants can be shipped with potted plants, they are considered nuisance pests. Paradoxically, ghost ants are skillful predators that have effectively controlled spider mites in greenhouses. Ghost ants do not sting.

**Imported fire ants** are reddish brown and 1/9 to 1/4 inch long (Plate 69). There are two nodes on the waist. The antennae are 10-segmented with the last two segments enlarged to form a club. No spines are present on the thorax, and the mandibles (jaws) have four teeth. Imported fire ants are best known for their sting, which usually causes a white pustule to develop within a day and can create an even greater allergic reaction in some people.

Fire ant workers are polymorphic. Colonies are usually monogyne but are sometimes polygyne. Nests, which may contain 100,000 to 500,000 workers as well as other members of the colony, are usually found in soil but can also be found in decaying organic matter, rotten logs and moist mulch.

In soil, fire ants build dome-shaped mounds. Fire ants have the dubious distinction of being both beneficial and harmful. As beneficials, they can aerate the soil with their nest building and underground foraging, speed the decomposition of dead organisms and prey on insect pests of plants. However, their disadvantages greatly outweigh their advantages. In vegetable gardens, they can tunnel into potatoes, chew on okra fruit and buds and destroy young seedlings. They can also ruin irrigation systems as they chew into tubing in search of water. Young citrus are damaged when fire ants move a mound to the tree base and damage bark, allowing an entry point for pathogens. The ants also feed on young oranges. They are known to attack watermelon, cucumber, sunflower, peanuts and sorghum. Gardeners often come into contact with these ants when weeding and harvesting. Because they are attracted to heat and moisture, they are also a nuisance in compost piles and mulched areas.

**Little fire ants** are golden brown and very small, 1/25 to 1/12 inch long (Plate 70). The head is covered with grooves. Workers are monomorphic, and colonies are polygyne. Queens are slightly larger and a darker brown than the workers.

The little fire ant often nests under the bark of trees, in rotting wood, in pine cones, at the base of leaves, in structures and in exposed soil or in soil under objects. Nests are found in areas ranging from very dry to very moist; the nest's depth in the soil will vary according to moisture conditions. When conditions are dry, the ants nest deeper in the soil, and when conditions are very moist (flooding), the ants may move into trees. In the early 1900s these ants were a pest in the Miami area. Orange pickers refused to perform their job or demanded higher wages when the little fire ant was present in groves. This ant is sensitive to the cold and is typically found in Florida from Ocala south, but recently they have been found in Gainesville. Workers tend insects such as aphids, mealybugs, scales and whiteflies. They also feed on dead organisms such as insects, other arthropods and small animals. They may feed on live insects as well. The little fire ant is not aggressive like the imported fire ant, nor are the two related.

Little fire ants have a fire-like sting but will not usually sting unless caught or pressed by clothing. The sting is irritating and may last for several days. Individuals that are stung may become pale, nervous and/or shaky.

**Native fire ants** are generally reddish-brown and the same size as the imported fire ant, but their color may range from all orange to all black. They also build mounds in the soil but can be distinguished from the imported fire ant by the presence of major workers. Major workers have an enlarged head, wider than any other part of the body, that is rounded into the two lobes beyond the eyes (Plate 71). Only a small part of the colony contains majors. Native fire ants have incurved jaws with no teeth on them, two other characteristics that differentiate them from the imported fire ant.

Colonies are usually monogyne but may be polygyne. Workers can also sting but appear to be a less aggressive species. Native fire ant mounds are not as abundant as imported fire ant mounds which can range from 40 to 800 mounds per acre.

## Aphids

Aphids are soft bodied, pear-shaped insects generally less than 1/8 inch long. Though usually green in color, many are black, brown, pink, yellow, blue, or white.

The most distinguishing features in the identification of aphids are the two short tubes, or cornicles, which extend from the rear of the body (Plate 72). Also known as "plant lice," aphids may infest almost any plant and are commonly found on camellia, crape myrtle, gardenia, hibiscus, ixora, oleander, palm and rose as well as nearly all annual plants. Clusters or colonies of individual aphids feed on young, developing leaves and stems, distorting the new growth and causing the leaves to curl (Plate 73). Flower buds may become hardened, causing the flowers to be malformed.

Although the largest numbers of aphids are found in the early spring months feeding on new flushes of growth, they may be found throughout the year. Aphids seem to be especially troublesome on plants that are in shaded areas. With their piercing-sucking mouthparts, they cause damage by sucking plant juices. However, their ability to transmit viral plant diseases may be more harmful than any direct feeding damage.

Aphids are unlike most insects in that almost all aphids are female and can reproduce without mating. They seldom lay eggs and instead give birth to live young. Aphids have the ability to reproduce rapidly, and many generations are produced in a year. Each female aphid produces 50 to 100 daughters during her life, and each daughter begins reproducing in 6 to 8 days. Most aphids are wingless, but when colonies become overcrowded or the host plant becomes undesirable, winged aphids are produced which establish new colonies.

Aphids, as well as soft scales, mealybugs and whiteflies excrete large amounts of honeydew which provides an excellent medium for the growth of a black fungus called "sooty mold" (Plate 162). Besides being unattractive, sooty mold interferes with photosynthesis and retards the growth of the plant. Sooty mold usually weathers away once the insect infestation has been controlled. Ants feed on the honeydew so when ants are observed, look closely for sucking pests.

Aphids have natural enemies and can also be controlled through non-insecticidal methods, so do not use a pesticide as a first line of defense. Instead, follow the instructions for spotting insects and mites at the opening of this chapter. Check individual aphids to see if any have small holes in their bodies, as if stuck by a straight pin (Plate 188). This is evidence that they have been parasitized by tiny wasps. Delay applying a pesticide to provide such beneficials an opportunity to control the aphid population. Many homeowners are able to remove aphids and keep populations below damaging levels by spraying their landscape plants with a forceful stream of water. Use a garden hose with an adjustable nozzle and spray undersides of leaves and stems when the aphids appear. Soaps are available that are formulated for controlling insects and related pests. If one of the commercial soaps is unavailable, three to four tablespoons of liquid dishwashing detergent per gallon of water may be applied as a foliar spray to landscape plants. COMMON.

## Assassin bugs

Assassin bugs (beneficial) are usually 1/2 to 1 inch in length and generally black or brown (Plate 74), though many are brightly colored. The head is elongate with a short, curved beak. Assassin bug nymphs are very colorful (Plate 75), but they may not retain their bright coloration as adults. There are more than 160 North American species, one of which is the wheelbug (Plate 76). It gets its name from the wheel-like projection on its back.  Most assassin bugs are predaceous.  They are usually found on foliage and attack many harmful insects, however caterpillars are their favorite prey.  Most species will inflict a painful bite if handled.

## Beneficial pathogens

Beneficial pathogens are extremely important in naturally occurring biological control.  Beneficial pathogens are diverse and include fungi, viruses and bacteria.

The body of an insect infected with an entomophagous (insect eating) **fungus** becomes mummified and covered with white, grey, tan, pink or green powdery-looking mold (Plate 77).  As the disease progresses, the insect becomes covered as the growing fungus expands over the body.  One common fungus, *Metarhizium*, attacks mole crickets and other soil inhabiting insects (Plate 78).  When a fungus disease appears and weather conditions are favorable, an insect population can be drastically reduced in a short time.

**Viruses** are usually very host specific and can suppress pest populations without harming beneficial insects.  Insects infected with a viral disease rarely show symptoms of infection until just before death, when the body darkens and becomes shiny in color (Plate 79).

## Big-eyed bugs

Big-eyed bugs (beneficial) are 1/16 to 1/8 inch long and usually black with silver wings.  Stout bodied and somewhat flattened, they have the large, prominent eyes suggested by their name (Plate 80).  Big-eyed bugs are often found on the soil surface preying on many small pests, especially chinch bugs, small caterpillars and other soft-bodied insects.

## Booklice

Booklice are less than 1/4 inch long and range in color from pale brown to white (Plate 81).  The booklouse has a large swollen area above the mandibles (clypeus) and may or may not have wings.  Often found in books, on floor molding and in closets, booklice do not suck blood but feed on molds, mildews and certain stored materials.

## Boring insects

Boring insects are the many species of insects which injure trees and shrubs by burrowing into them.  Many burrow just under the bark, but some bore deeply into the wood.  Twig borers are found only in smaller twigs and in the tips of shoots while other types of borers injure the wood at about ground level and feed in the root crown of the plant and the large roots emerging from the crown.

In most cases, borers are not the primary cause of trouble to trees.  Plants are first weakened by something that makes them particularly susceptible to borer injury.  A plant does not have to be badly stressed to make it susceptible to attack by borers.  Insect problems may begin with such injuries or stresses to the plant as those caused by drought, salt water flooding, soil added or removed around the plants, soil compaction, root disturbances caused by the digging of house foundations, septic tanks or underground utilities, and injuries to the trunk or roots inflicted by the elements or by vehicles or machinery.  Also, the setbacks that trees receive in transplanting increase the possibility that borers may attack them.

Two major types of borers attack pine trees, "bark beetles" which burrow in the inner bark and feed on the cambium or living layer of the tree and "borers" which burrow deeply into the wood of the trunk. Several species of Ips beetles as well as the black turpentine beetle and southern pine beetle all feed under the bark. Signs that these insects are present are not exactly the same for all species, but generally a reddish dust left from the boring collects around the entrance holes and in bark crevices. Pitch or sap may flow from entrance holes and form small pitch tubes (Plate 82). In time the many exit holes of the beetles give the bark the appearance of being riddled with shotgun pellets. The turpentine borer and sometimes other large beetles may tunnel into the sapwood or heartwood of pines through open scars and wounds in the trees.

A very small Asian twig beetle, *Xylosandrus compactus*, bores in the twigs of many species of trees in Florida. Dogwood, redbud and magnolia seem especially susceptible. Dogwoods are also often attacked by the dogwood twig borer. Infested twigs become shrunken, often cracking and eventually dying (Plate 83). A series of holes with frass (insect debris) exuding can be seen along infested twigs. The trunks of weakened dogwoods may also be attacked by flatheaded borers. These beetles burrow deeply into the wood.

Oak trees, especially laurel and water oaks which have been damaged or stressed, are attacked by the red oak borer. The larva of this longhorned beetle bores into the trunk and the large lower limbs. Many species of hardwood, particularly damaged oaks, are sometimes infested by carpenterworms. These larvae also bore into the trunk and larger limbs. The most common signs that oak borers or carpenterworms are present is the boring dust and sap flow at the entry holes (Plate 84).

The seagrape borer is a caterpillar which causes concern to some growers of seagrape, a popular landscape plant in Florida. The caterpillars burrow down the shoots from the tips. The life of the plant is not endangered, but shoot tips may be killed back.

There are many other boring insects in Florida which may cause occasional or isolated instances of damage. The peach tree borer is a caterpillar which may damage or kill trees in the *Prunus* group such as wild plum, cherry laurel and ornamental peach.

Other beetles which are occasionally noticed include the red-headed ash borer, which may bore deeply into many kinds of trees, *Xylobiops basillare*, which has been found burrowing in the branches of the royal poinciana, and the Australian pine borer.

Preventing the borers from infesting the tree or shrub is the best control. The fact that weakened trees are especially susceptible to borer attack indicates, of course, that one of the best means of avoiding injury is to keep valued trees and shrubs in the healthiest possible condition. Provide ample watering during droughts. Be careful to avoid injury to the roots as well as above ground parts, and prune out dead or dying branches as outlined in *Pruning Trees and Shrubs*. COMMON.

## Broad and cyclamen mites

Broad and cyclamen mites are translucent and very small, about 1/100 inch long. Usually their presence is first detected by symptoms of plant injury rather than by observation of the mites themselves. New leaves that are curled or cupped and smaller than usual or newly-produced leaves that do not expand (Plate 85) are symptoms of broad and cyclamen mite damage. Heavy infestations often cause death of the shoot apex. See "Spider Mites" for more information.

## Bumblebees

Bumblebees (Plate 86) nest underground in colonies of several hundred individuals. The nests are usually in abandoned rodent burrows, in mulch or under logs or debris. The abdomen of the bumblebee is covered with hairs.

Wasps and bees can cause problems around people. Most are social insects that live in colonies and they will aggressively defend their nests by stinging. The sting usually involves the injection of a venom that is a nerve poison. A sting can cause death if a person is allergic or receives many stings at once. If stung, those allergic to bee stings should be transported to a hospital immediately.

## Caterpillars

Caterpillars are the larval stage of butterflies and moths. Some caterpillars can inflict painful stings with spines which are connected to poison glands. Entomologists prefer to refer to these species as "nettling caterpillars," because they do not actually "sting" in the truest sense of the word. The five major nettling caterpillars occurring in Florida are the buck moth caterpillar (Plate 89), hag caterpillar (Plate 97), Io moth caterpillar (Plate 98), puss caterpillar (Plates 101 and 102) and saddleback caterpillar (Plate 103). Less common nettling caterpillars are the flannel moth caterpillar (Plates 95 and 96) and the spiny oak-slug caterpillar (Plate 104). See individual listings for more information.

Some people experience severe reactions to the poison released by the spines and require medical attention. Others experience little more than an itching or burning sensation.

**First aid:** Place scotch tape over affected area and strip it off repeatedly to remove spines. Apply ice packs to reduce stinging sensation and follow with a paste of baking soda and water. If an individual has a history of hay fever, asthma or allergy, or if allergic reactions develop, contact a physician immediately.

**Azalea caterpillars** will defoliate azaleas. Young larvae skeletonize the leaves, and the larger ones eat the entire leaf. The 2-inch long mature larvae can be recognized by the red head, the red last segment and the broken yellow (occasionally white) lengthwise stripes. When disturbed, the caterpillar raises its front and rear ends into the air (Plate 87) but does not sting.

**Bagworm caterpillars** are general feeders that spin silk sacks or bags to which they attach small pieces of twigs and leaf material, usually cedar. The sacks are 1/4 to 1 1/2 inches in length and are usually found on foliage (Plate 88). The bag is carried by the insect wherever it goes, and the front end of the larva's body protrudes from the bag when it is feeding or moving.

**Buck moth caterpillars** are large, 1 3/4 to 2 1/4 inches long when mature, and are among the less common nettling caterpillars. Yellow-brown to purplish-black with numerous small white spots and a reddish head, the buck moth caterpillar (Plate 89) usually feeds on oaks but may also be found on willow, rose and other deciduous plants.

**Cabbage palm caterpillars** are larvae associated with the flower stalks of cabbage palm. Their development is synchronized with the flowering period of the palm. (The cabbage palm flower is a source of nectar for honey bees, and larvae may so damage the flower that the honey crop is reduced.) Mature larvae are purplish brown with numerous black spots from which hairs emerge (Plate 90). To pupate, cabbage palm caterpillars migrate from the plant and may enter houses. They are capable of cutting through fiberglass screens, and once inside the house they may chew up the fabric in draperies, upholstery and carpeting for use in forming their cocoons. The cocoon is formed from the caterpillar's own hairs plus the materials it chewed up and is variable in color and in texture.

**Eastern tent caterpillars** are covered with long, soft, light brown hairs. A white stripe bordered with reddish brown runs down the back, and along each side is a row of oval blue spots and brown and yellow lines (Plate 91). The caterpillars become fully grown and about 2 inches long in 4 to 6 weeks. Each caterpillar spins a white cocoon (usually on a tree trunk), pupates and then emerges as a light reddish brown moth. There is only one generation each year. About 9 months are spent in the egg stage.

Large, thick webs are constructed in the forks and crotches of many kinds of trees, especially cherry (Plate 92). Larvae will frequently infest and defoliate unsprayed oak, plum and poplar. These caterpillars do not feed within their webs but congregate there during the night and in rainy weather.

**Fall webworms** are pale yellow, black-spotted, hairy caterpillars about 1 inch long (Plate 93). Hatched from eggs deposited on leaves by satiny white moths, the caterpillars feed upon the surfaces of leaves for 4 to 6 weeks. As they feed, they construct loosely woven webs that enclose foliage at the ends of branches (Plate 94). Several branches are sometimes covered by a single web 3 to 4 feet long. The webs provide protection from natural enemies and the elements and also keep the developing caterpillars in touch with their food source. Webs contain many caterpillars which, when mature, spin cocoons in which they pass the winter. Co-

coons are found under trash on the ground or sometimes under bark.

**Flannel moth caterpillars** are about 1 inch long when mature. Their stinging hairs, or nettling organs, are intermixed with soft hairs in diffuse tufts. The larvae (Plate 95) are creamy white and turn dark as they mature (Plate 96). They feed on oak and various other shrubs and trees. See the introduction to "Caterpillars" for more information about nettling caterpillars.

**Hag caterpillars** are light to dark brown in color. Nine pairs of protruding body parts bear the nettling organs (Plate 97). The protrusions are curved and twisted, causing them to be likened to the disheveled hair of a hag. Found on various forest trees and ornamental shrubs, hag caterpillars do no significant damage. Though neither as common as the other nettling species nor found in great numbers, hag caterpillars can nonetheless appear in many different places. See the introduction to "Caterpillars" for more information about nettling caterpillars.

**Io moth caterpillars** are pale green caterpillars with yellow and red stripes (Plate 98). Often exceeding 2 inches in length, they are fairly stout bodied. The nettling organs are borne on fleshy tubercles (bumps), and the spines are usually yellow with black tips. Io moth caterpillars feed on a wide range of plants; however, ixora and roses are favorite hosts. See the introduction to "Caterpillars" for more information about nettling caterpillars.

**Oleander caterpillars** feed only on oleander, a plant poisonous to most animals. At maturity, the orange-red caterpillar with its black tufts of hair is 2 inches long (Plate 99). When environmental conditions are favorable, there can be as many as three generations a year. When larvae and adult moths (which are purplish black with white dots on the wings) are observed together, the generations are said to be overlapping.

**Palm leaf skeletonizers** incorporate tiny, brown fecal pellets in silk webs on palm fronds. The pellets look like fine sawdust and are usually found on the underside of leaves or where they have been woven together (Plate 100). Removing the web reveals creamy white caterpillars up to 5/8 inch long with eight faint reddish brown stripes running the length of the body. The caterpillars feed only on palms. The tiny moths have a 5/8 inch wingspan and are inconspicuous. They do not take part in the skeletonizing.

**Puss caterpillars** are convex, stout bodied larvae, almost 1 inch long when mature and completely covered with gray to brown hairs (Plate 101). When younger, the caterpillars are lighter in color (Plate 102). Under the soft hairs are stiff spines that are attached to poison glands. When touched, these poisonous spines break off in the skin and cause severe pain. Puss caterpillars feed on a variety of broadleaf trees and shrubs but prefer oaks and citrus. In Florida, there appear to be two generations per year, one in spring and the other in the fall. Natural enemies keep these caterpillars at low numbers during most years. Periodically, however, they become numerous. See the introduction to "Caterpillars" for more information about nettling caterpillars.

**Saddleback caterpillars** can exceed 1 inch in length and are stout bodied and striking in appearance (Plate 103). A green back and flanks set off a conspicuous brown oval-shaped central area that is usually bordered with white. This brown spot gives the appearance of a saddle and the green area appears to be a saddle blanket, hence the name. The main nettling organs are on the paired fleshy protuberances toward the front and hind ends of the body. There is also a row of smaller nettling organs on each side. This caterpillar feeds on many plants including hibiscus and palms but appears to show little host preference. See the introduction to "Caterpillars" for more information about nettling caterpillars.

**Spiny oak-slug caterpillars** are pale green and, at maturity, about 3/4 inch long (Plate 104). Favorite food plants include oak, willow and other deciduous plants. See the introduction to "Caterpillars" for more information about nettling caterpillars.

**Tussock moths** are members of a group of moths with basic similarities. They begin as caterpillars that hatch in late spring and feed on shade trees. They have three stiff tufts of long, black hairs — one on each side of the red head and a third posterior tuft that extends beyond the end of the insect. Several tufts of short, white, erect hairs sprout from the back, and there are two red spots on the back toward the rear end (Plate 105). They are not considered nettling caterpillars, although some people experience a stinging sensation from contact with the hairs. The fully grown 1 1/2-inch caterpillars spin their cocoons on trunks, branches or some nearby stationary object. Adult moths of this generation emerge about 2 weeks later. A second generation of caterpillars feeds during late August and early September. These emerge as moths in September and October. Flightless females deposit overwintering eggs on the cocoons, which usually are attached to the wall of a house. The tussock moth may produce two or three generations per year.

## Centipedes

Centipedes are wormlike and up to 6 inches long. Often called "hundred-leggers," they have one pair of legs per segment. The 40 to 50 body segments are flattened, and the head has one pair of antennae (Plate 106). Some species can bite and penetrate the skin with their mandibles (jaws). Centipedes are beneficial outdoors, feeding on insects, spiders and other small animals.

## Cicada killers

Cicada killers are 1 3/5 inches long and black with pale yellow markings on the last three abdominal segments (Plate 107). These wasps are solitary, but colonies will nest in the same location. Each female digs its own hole up to 10 inches deep then stings and paralyzes a cicada, placing it in the hole with an egg. Closely related species attack and kill flies. Although capable of stinging, cicada killers are usually not aggressive toward people. See "Bumblebee."

## Damsel bugs

Damsel bugs (beneficial) are small, slender insects 1/4 to 3/8 inch long. Yellowish to brownish in color with prominent eyes (Plate 108), they are important predators and feed on a wide variety of soft-bodied insects such as aphids and caterpillars.

## Damselflies

Damselflies (beneficial) are slender, delicate insects 1 to 2 inches in length (Plate 109). Like dragonflies, both adults and nymphs are predaceous. The nymphs live in the water, feeding primarily on the larvae of aquatic insects such as mosquitoes and midges.

## Dragonflies

Dragonflies (beneficial) are also known as "mosquito hawks" and have a wingspan of 1 to 4 1/2 inches depending on the species (Plate 110). Both adults and nymphs are predaceous. They are especially effective in reducing populations of mosquitoes and other aquatic flies. The nymphs live in ponds and streams and prey on mosquito larvae, while the adults catch mosquitoes in flight.

## Earwigs

Earwigs (beneficial) are 1/4 to 1 inch long as adults and have flattened bodies that are pale to dark brown (Plate 111). Their antennae are threadlike and about half the length of the body. They can use their forceps-like cerci (claspers) to capture prey or to defend themselves against predators. Active at night, they are attracted to light and often crawl into homes under doorsills.

Many earwigs prey on chinch bugs, small mole crickets, sod webworms and other insects that live on the soil surface. In laboratory experiments, earwigs commonly consume 50 chinch bugs in a day.

## Fungus gnats

Fungus gnats are small flies (Plate 112) that breed in damp soil or decaying vegetable matter. Often they are brought into houses in potted plants or are found in commercial buildings in planted areas. Adult fungus gnats are attracted to light and often are found around windows. In overly moist soil, fungus gnat larvae are pests that feed on leaves in contact with the soil and on the roots of house plants.

## Galls

Galls are growths that occur on a wide variety of plants (Plates 113 through 122). Although these growths may be the result of fungi, bacteria, nematodes or mites, insects are the prime cause. Gall-forming insects include aphids, phylloxerans, psyllids, midges (gall gnats) and cynipid wasps (gall wasps). Of the more than 2000 gall-producing insects in the United States, 1500 are either gall gnats or gall wasps. About 80% of the gall wasps produce galls specifically on oak trees. In fact, 60% of all known insect galls occur in the oak family and 30% occur in the daisy, rose and willow families. Galls contain large amounts of tannin, which has a very bitter taste, and were long ago known as "gallnuts" because they tasted as bitter as gall.

Galls are abnormal growths of plant cells that are stimulated by an insect's egg laying or by larval or nymphal feeding. In the spring, before leaves are fully developed, eggs are laid in the leaf or stem. The immature insects can often be found in a cell or cells within the developing gall. The insect becomes enclosed by the gall and feeds only on gall tissue during its development. Small holes on the outside of the gall indicate that the adult insects have emerged.

Galls are found most commonly on stems and leaves but also occur on trunks, flowers, fruit, leaf-shoot terminals, petioles and roots. Each gall-forming insect produces a gall that is characteristic of that particular insect. Some galls may be 2 inches in diameter while others are so small they are rarely noticed. Galls occur in almost every conceivable form and color, and their shapes range from spheres to tubes. The surface may be smooth, hairy or covered with spines. Susceptibility to galls varies greatly among species in the same location. This is probably due to the general condition of the particular plant and its natural resistance.

Although they seem to cause the general public a great deal of concern, galls do not generally do a plant serious harm. Even relatively large numbers of galls do not apparently injure most ornamental plants and trees. Some people actually look for plants which are susceptible to gall formation because of their unusual appearance.

Insecticidal control of galls is usually not practical for several reasons. First, application must be timed to control the adult pests before the gall is formed. Once formed, galls and their inhabitants are impossible to eliminate with insecticides because the organisms are enclosed and well protected by the gall. Secondly, environmental contamination and considerable expense are involved, especially when treating large trees. Finally, damage is not significant most of the time. Parasites normally build up and suppress populations of gall-makers before serious injury occurs. Galls that occur on leaves will drop off with the leaves; some of the galls on stems and limbs may be hand-picked and destroyed. However, those occurring on the trunk and roots may persist for several years. If a tree or ornamental plant is unhealthy or under stress, it will be damaged to a greater extent than a healthy one. Fertilize, irrigate, prune and carry out other approved practices to keep plants healthy.

## Ground beetles

Ground beetles (beneficial) are 1/4 to 1 inch in length when mature. They are generally black or brown, sometimes green, and often display a metallic luster (Plate 123). As their name suggests, they are usually found on the ground and are most active at night. Both the adults and larvae of ground beetles prey upon harmful insects including some of our most serious lawn, vegetable and field crop pests such as webworms, armyworms, cutworms, corn earworms and small mole crickets.

## Honey bees

Honey bees (beneficial for pollination of crops and ornamentals) live in colonies of 20,000 to 80,000 individuals. Raised for honey and beeswax, the honey bee (Plate 124) is essential for pollination of many crops. The bee's stinger has barbs, so that both the stinger and the poison sac are left in the skin after a sting. Unlike wasps, honey bees can only sting once.

Most honey bee colonies are in hives that are managed by beekeepers. However, some colonies swarm in large number and can be found outside (Plate 125). Colonies may become established in walls or eaves of houses. The nests in walls can contain a lot of honey. If the bees are controlled or removed, the nest and honey should also be removed to prevent problems to the house.

## Lacebugs

Lacebugs are broad, flat insects about 1/8 inch long and rectangular in shape. Their bodies are usually brown to black and their wings clear with a fine, lace-like appearance (Plate 126). Immature lacebugs are wingless, blackish in color and covered with many small spines (Plate 127).

Lacebugs deposit their eggs on the underside of the leaf along the midrib then secrete a brownish substance over the eggs to secure them to the leaf. These dark varnish- or molasses-like spots are very noticeable when leaves become heavily infested (Plates 126 and 127). The nymphs molt five times before reaching adulthood. The life cycle from egg to adult requires approximately 30 days. Three to five generations occur each year.

Lacebugs have piercing-sucking mouthparts; in feeding on the undersides of leaves, they create damage that appears as a whitish speckling on the top sides (Plate 128). This and the black spotting on the undersides of leaves are good indications of lacebug infestation. The most prevalent species are named after the host plants which they infest (azalea, hawthorn, pyracantha and sycamore). COMMON.

## Lacewings

Lacewings (beneficial) are common insects about 3/4 inch long and found on grass, weeds, cultivated row crops and shrubs. Most are greenish with copper colored eyes (Plate 129). The adults may be predaceous or feed on pollen. Lacewings attach their white eggs to foliage with thin stalks approximately 1/4 inch high to prevent the larvae from preying on any unhatched eggs. The predaceous larvae are elongate and have large sickle-shaped jaws (Plate 130). Because they feed primarily on aphids, lacewings are commonly called "aphid-lions."

Brown lacewings (beneficial) resemble green lacewings but are brownish in color (Plate 131), smaller and less common. Most larvae are elongate, soft bodied, active and have sickle-shaped jaws. However, some species cover themselves with the skins of their victims as well as other debris and so are also known as trash bugs (Plate 132).

## Lady beetles

Lady beetles (beneficial) range from 1/16 to 1/2 inch with most species about 1/4 inch long. Among the most beneficial insects in Florida, both adult and larval lady beetles are predaceous on aphids, scale insects, mealybugs, mites and other soft-bodied insect pests. Both adults and larvae are frequently found feeding among aphid populations. Adults are oval shaped, and most are orange or reddish with black markings (Plates 133 and 134) or black with yellow or red markings (Plate 135). Although not often seen, in their earlier stages larvae resemble mealybugs and are white, elongate, somewhat flattened and covered with small spines (Plate 136). When further developed, they are usually black or dark in color with bright spots or bands (Plate 137). About 475 species occur in North America.

## Leafminers

Leafminers are usually the larvae of flies or moths that mine between the upper and lower epidermal layers of leaf surfaces. The larvae tunnel through leaves creating narrow, whitish-colored serpentine (winding) mines or blotch (blister) type mines. Leafminers attack many ornamental plants, but azalea, bougainvillea, ixora, hollies, chrysanthemum, lantana and boxwood are some of their preferred hosts.

The **serpentine leafminer** (Plate 138) is the most common throughout Florida. The adult is a black and yellow fly about 1/20 inch long that inserts eggs in the underside of a leaf. In a few days, the eggs hatch into tiny yellowish maggots. As the maggots mine between the leaf surfaces and increase in size, the meandering mines gradually widen. When fully grown, the maggots pupate on the outside of the leaf. There are several generations per year.

Some of the most prevalent caterpillar leafminers are the azalea, palm and oak leafminers. The **azalea leafminer** is a yellow moth about 1/4 inch long. Its caterpillars mine between leaves until about half grown. They then emerge and fold the leaves over themselves by a series of silken threads. Known during this stage as leaf tiers, they continue to feed by chewing holes in the leaves. The **palm leafminer** (also known as the palm leaf skeletonizer, Plate 100) attacks

saw palmetto as well as Phoenix, sabal and coconut palms. The caterpillars feed on the fronds of palms and cover themselves with a silken web in which they incorporate pellets of frass (insect debris). **Oak leafminers** attack several different species of oaks and usually make a blotch type mine.

Leafminers usually cause no serious injury to their host, however when heavy infestations occur, plants appear bleached or faded and their aesthetic value is reduced. In some cases leaves turn yellow and drop. COMMON.

## Long-legged flies

Long-legged flies (beneficial) are about 1/4 inch in length and metallic green, blue or copper colored (Plate 139). There are about 1,250 North American species, and they are usually abundant near woodland swamps and streams. Both adults and larvae prey upon other insects.

## Mealybugs

Mealybugs are soft-bodied insects that vary from 1/8 to 1/5 inch in length when mature. They are covered with a white wax-like material that appears powdery or cottony (Plate 140). Short wax projections extend from the margin of the body, and some species have long filaments projecting from the rear of the body (Plate 141). Mealybugs are mobile and tend to congregate together, appearing like fluffs of cotton on the foliage (Plate 142). The mealybug life cycle requires approximately 30 days at 80°F. Common host plants are azalea, coleus, croton, cactus, rose, bedding plants and a large number of foliage plants. Mealybugs are one of the major pest problems affecting plants in greenhouses and interiorscapes. In feeding with their piercing-sucking mouthparts, they cause chlorotic (yellow) spots on leaves. COMMON.

## Millipedes

Millipedes vary in length from 1/2 to 4 inches long and are often called "thousand-leggers" because they have two pairs of legs on each of their many cylindrical body segments (Plate 143). A millipede has one pair of short antennae with seven segments. Millipedes feed on decaying organic matter and are found in decaying vegetation and mulched areas. They are nocturnal and are known to mass migrate from swampy areas of Florida.

## Minute pirate bugs

Minute pirate bugs (beneficial) are about 1/8 inch long and are black with white markings (Plate 144). The approximately 70 North American species are predaceous on many small insects and eggs. One species is an important predator on the eggs and larvae of the corn earworm.

## Mites

See "Spider mites" and "Predaceous mites."

## Nematodes

See the section *Nematodes.* Some nematodes are beneficial and attack harmful insects, especially soil inhabiting species. Among the beneficial nematodes is one introduced to Florida from South America that is a parasite of mole crickets (Plate 145).

## Palm leaf skeletonizer

See listing under "Caterpillars."

## Parasitic wasps

See listing under "Wasps."

## Pillbugs

Pillbugs (beneficial) are Crustacea in the order Isopoda and are about 5/8 inch long. They have seven pairs of legs and two pairs of antennae, one of which is very tiny (Plate 146). Because they roll into tight balls when disturbed, they are also known as "roly-polies." Pillbugs live in wet areas under logs, flower pots or mulch and feed on decaying organic matter.

## Plaster beetles

Plaster beetles are 1/25 to 1/9 inch long, reddish brown and elongate (Plate 147). Their wings have six to eight rows of punctures. They are in the family Lathridiidae and get their name from infesting newly plastered walls. They like to feed on molds growing on walls or on wet stored grain.

## Praying mantids

Praying mantids (beneficial) are large brown or green insects with adults usually over 2 inches in length. There are more than 1500 species worldwide, but only 20 are found in the United States and Canada. The front legs of praying mantids are modified for grasping and holding their prey. As they wait patiently in the foliage for unsuspecting insects, their forelegs are held in an upright position (Plate 148) that gives rise to the common name "praying mantid."

## Predaceous mites

Predaceous mites (beneficial) are large, active mites, orange to brown in color and about 1/25 inch in length (Plate 149). They prey upon spider mites, small insects and eggs. These mites are reared and released in greenhouses in Europe and to some extent in this country to reduce plant-feeding mite populations.

## Psocids

Psocids (Plate 150) are usually less than 1/8 inch in length. They construct webbing on tree trunks and limbs and feed underneath it on algae, lichens and fungi growing on the bark surface. Psocids are also known as "tree cattle" for their tendency to move about the bark in a herd. They cause no harm to trees.

## Robber flies

Robber flies (beneficial) are relatively large insects. Ranging from 1/4 to 1 1/4 inches in length, some are robust, and some are very long and slender. Legs are long and strong, the face is usually very hairy, and the top of the head is hollowed out between the eyes (Plate 151). There are nearly 1,000 species of robber flies occurring in North America. They attack a wide variety of insects, including wasps, grasshoppers and other flies, and usually capture their prey in flight.

## Scales

Scales are divided into two groups, armored scales and soft scales. The armored scales secrete a waxy covering over their bodies. This covering is not an integral part of the insect's body, but the scale lives and feeds under this covering, which resembles a plate of armor and supplies the name.

**Armored scales** vary in size from 1/16 to 1/8 inch in diameter and can be almost any color, depending on the species. In shape, they may be circular, oval, oblong, thread-like or pear-shaped. The female's armor is larger than that of the male though shape and color may be anywhere from similar to distinctly different, depending upon the particular species. Three hundred and fifty species of armored scales occur in the United States, and about 175 species are present in Florida. Examples of armored scales are the tea scale (Plates 152 and 153), Florida red scale (Plate 154), false oleander scale (Plate 155), oleander pit scale (Plate 156) and white peach scale (Plate 157).

**Soft scales** also secrete a waxy covering, but theirs is an integral part of the body. Soft scales vary widely in color, size and shape. They range from 1/8 to 1/2 inch in diameter and may be nearly flat to almost spherical in shape. Sixty of the eighty-five species of soft scales found in the United States occur in Florida. Examples of soft scales are hemispherical scale (Plate 158), green scale (Plate 159), pyriform scale (Plate 160) and Florida wax scale (Plate 161).

Life cycles of the various scales differ somewhat, but a generalized life cycle is as follows. Eggs are laid underneath the waxy covering and hatch in 1 to 3 weeks. The newly hatched scales (crawlers) move about over the plant until they locate succulent new growth. They insert their piercing-sucking mouthparts into the plant and begin feeding. Female scales molt two times before reaching maturity and do not pupate. Male scales go through two additional molts and pupate underneath the wax. The cast skins (exuviae) are incorporated in the waxy coating. Adult males are tiny two-winged, gnat-like insects without mouthparts. (The females never possess wings and are disseminated primarily by infested plant stock.

They are spread to a lesser extent in the crawler stage by humans, birds, other animals and wind currents.) In some armored scales the adult stage is reached in 6 weeks, and there are several generations per year. Some soft scales require 1 year to reach maturity.

Scale insects are the most serious pests of many ornamental plants. Most ornamentals are susceptible to one or more species of scales. Scales cause damage by sucking the juices from the plants. Scales feeding on the undersides of leaves may cause yellow spots to appear on the top sides (Plate 153), and these spots become progressively larger as the scales continue to feed. If the scales are not controlled, leaves will drop prematurely, sometimes killing portions of twigs and branches. Scales also feed on trunks and stems of plants. Heavy infestation results in plants that appear unhealthy and produce little new growth. Soft scales excrete large amounts of honeydew which provide an excellent medium for the growth of a black fungus called sooty mold (Plate 162, see listing below). Armored scales do not secrete honeydew.

Many species of scales are highly parasitized by tiny wasps. Pin-size holes in the scales' wax are evidence of this parasitism. Scales in the crawler stage are preyed upon by numerous beneficial insects. If signs of parasitism are present, make every effort to preserve the beneficial insects. Delay applying a pesticide and provide the beneficials an opportunity to control the pest population. Scale insects are more difficult to control as they become mature. Inspect plants weekly during the spring, summer and fall. If necessary, use a 10 power magnifying glass. Sometimes scales are overlooked as fungus growth or part of the plant. Scales may be somewhat hidden in the crevices of bark and the axils of leaves. COMMON.

## Sooty mold

Sooty mold is a black fungus that grows on the honeydew (excretion) of Homopteran insects such as aphids, mealybugs, soft scales and particularly immature whiteflies (Plate 162). This fungus detracts from the beauty of ornamental plants and reduces their photosynthetic activity. Sooty mold may be washed off the leaves with soapy water. Controlling the insects will keep sooty mold from recurring.

## Sowbugs

Sowbugs are slightly larger but otherwise similar in appearance to pillbugs. Unlike pillbugs, they cannot roll into a tight ball. They also have seven pairs of legs and two pairs of antennae. Sowbugs have prominent, tail-like appendages (uropoda) that project from the rear end of the body (Plate 163). They are active at night and often are found under debris, in mulch and under flower pots. They often enter homes by crawling under doors.

## Spider

Spiders (beneficial) are predaceous, feeding almost exclusively on a wide variety of insects. They paralyze their prey by injecting venom with their bites. They rarely bite people, and only a few (such as the widows and the brown recluse spiders) are dangerously venomous. The majority capture their prey in webs, but many of the more beneficial species such as the Carolina wolf (Plate 164), the jumping spider (Plate 165), the green lynx (Plate 166) and the crab spider (Plate 167) do not spin webs. Those that do not construct webs are especially effective in capturing insects that inhabit the soil surface or plant foliage.

## Spider mites

Spider mites are among the most common pests to attack ornamental plants in Florida. The two-spotted spider mite, *Tetranychus urticae* (Plate 168), is the most common. Mites are not insects and are more closely related to spiders and ticks. Adult spider mites, spiders and ticks have eight legs. Mature mites are usually less than 1/50 inch in length and are generally found on the undersides of leaves. Mite infestations are often not detected until the plants are already exhibiting damage.

Mites have needle-like, piercing mouthparts which puncture the leaf and suck the plant juices. Damage from light infestations appears as yellow or gray stippled patterns on the leaves (Plate 169). The undersides of infested leaves usually have fine silken webbing spun across them. Heavy infestations cause the leaves to turn yellow, gray or brownish and eventually drop off. Webbing may be spun over entire branches (Plate 170) or, in the case of small plants, over the entire plant. When the undersides of the leaves are examined closely with a 10 or 15 power magnifying glass, the small mites can be seen. They may be green, yellow, purple, black or virtually transparent. The body contents sometimes show through their transparent body walls giving them a spotted appearance. Cast skins may also be seen among the live mites, imparting a grayish residue to the undersides of the leaves.

Among the many species of mites, development differs somewhat, however the following is a description of the typical life cycle. The adult female is capable of laying several hundred eggs during her life. The eggs are attached to the fine silk webbing and hatch in approximately 3 days. Immature mites molt (cast their skins) three times before reaching the adult stage. The time required from egg to adult varies greatly depending on temperature. Under optimum conditions (80° F), mites complete their development from egg to adult in 7 to 10 days. There are many overlapping generations per year.

Plants on which spider mites are frequently found include azalea, camellia, chrysanthemum, citrus, ligustrum, orchid, pyracantha, rose, viburnum and bedding plants. Mites are also a persistent pest of interior foliage plants. Their damage is much more severe during dry weather. Large numbers of mites are commonly seen during the spring months, especially April and May, and again in September and October.

One of the most important aids in successful mite control is to begin treatment before damage becomes severe. (See introduction to this chapter for tips on scouting for pests.) Predaceous mites and beneficial insects such as lady beetles, praying mantids, assassin bugs and tiny, wasp-like insects may prey upon spider mites. However, these predators may not be able to keep the mite population below damaging levels. Nevertheless, do not apply an insecticide unless plant damage is becoming evident, and then spray only those plants affected. COMMON.

## Springtails

Springtails are tiny, wingless insects about 1/25 to 1/12 inch long (Plate 171). White to greyish in color, they have a forked structure (furcula) on the rear of the body that enables them to jump. Springtails live in mulch and wet soil, but can migrate into homes and swimming pools in large numbers. They feed on molds and decaying vegetation.

## Stinkbugs, Predaceous

Predaceous stinkbugs (beneficial) are usually oval or shield-shaped and brown (Plate 172), green or grey, though many are brightly colored. A common predaceous (beneficial) species in Florida is midnight blue and orange (Plate 173). As a general rule, beneficial species can be identified by spines projecting from the thorax, whereas harmful plant feeders have round "shoulders." The predaceous forms have short, stout beaks and prey on many insects, especially caterpillars. Plant feeding forms have long, thin mouthparts and generally damage vegetable and agronomic crops. There are over 200 species of stinkbugs found in North America.

## Syrphid flies

Syrphid flies (beneficial) vary greatly in color and size; most are yellow with brown or black stripes on the abdomen (Plate 174). Many resemble wasps, others closely resemble bees, but none sting. Adult flies feed primarily on pollen and are so commonly found on flowers that they are also known as flower flies. Many syrphid larvae are predaceous, especially on aphids. The larvae (Plate 175) are slug- or maggot-like, have no legs or visible head and are usually a greenish, translucent color. There are about 900 North American species of syrphid flies.

## Tachinid flies

Tachinid flies (beneficial) are parasitic in the larval stage and a valuable asset in keeping many of our serious pests in check. Many tachinids resemble the common house fly but are a little larger (Plate 176). Others are bee-like or wasp-like in appearance (Plate 177). Most tachinids deposit eggs directly on the hosts' bodies, and it is not uncommon to find caterpillars and other insects with several eggs on them (Plate 178).

Upon hatching, the larvae burrow into the host and feed internally. Other tachinids lay their eggs on foliage, and the eggs hatch inside the host insect that has consumed the foliage. The tachinid that parasitizes mole crickets locates the mole crickets by their song and deposits live larvae on or near them. (This particular fly was imported from South America and has been released at numerous locations in Florida as a biological control agent.) There are about 1300 North American species of tachinid flies.

## Thrips

Thrips are small, slender, yellow-brown or black insects that range in length from 1/8 to 1/25 inch (Plates 179 and 180). With their rasping-sucking mouthparts, thrips withdraw a plant's juices by rasping or shredding its tissues. Thrips injure both foliage and flowers, feeding primarily on young tissues in the bud or shoot apexes where new leaves are expanding. Infested leaves dry out and have a silver flecked or stippled appearance (Plate 181). Small, brownish specks of excrement can usually be seen on the undersides of the leaves. Infested flower buds fail to open, or the flowers are deformed, becoming streaked and discolored. Flowers or leaves suspected of being infested with thrips can be shaken over a white sheet on which the thrips may then be detected.

The life cycle from egg to adult requires from 2 to 4 weeks and produces three to five generations per year. Thrips populations are at their peak during the spring months. The most significant thrips species attacking flowers and buds are the Florida flower thrips and gladiolus thrips. Red-banded thrips, Cuban laurel thrips and greenhouse thrips are the most common species on foliage. COMMON.

## Tiger beetles

Tiger beetles (beneficial) are active, usually metallic or iridescent and 1/2 to 3/4 inch long (Plate 182). Their well developed jaws (mandibles) can be easily seen, and they can run and fly rapidly, making them difficult to approach. The adult beetles feed on a variety of insects. The larvae live in vertical burrows in the soil and pull captured insects into their tunnels.

## Tussock moths

See listing under "Caterpillars."

## Wasps

Wasps are characterized by a constriction between the thorax and abdomen called a "wasp waist." They include some of our most familiar and beneficial insects. The vast majority of beneficial wasps are small parasitic insects that often escape our notice; the larger beneficial species are generally more familiar to us because they are capable of stinging.

**Mud dauber wasps** are about 1 inch long and black with long, thin waists (Plate 183). The mud dauber is not a social wasp, nor is it very aggressive. Though its mud nest is often built close to human activity, it rarely stings people. The mud dauber uses the sides of buildings and the areas under eaves to construct brood chambers from mud. The wasp stings and paralyzes a spider, lays an egg on it and seals it inside a chamber. When the wasp larva hatches, it feeds on the body of the spider. An emergence hole in the mud means that the young wasp has exited the chamber (Plate 184).

**Paper wasps** (beneficial) are very common in Florida and are usually yellow with brown markings or black with red or yellow markings (Plate 185). These 3/4 to 1 1/2 inches wasps are aggressive and readily sting. People are generally stung while trimming shrubbery or otherwise accidentally or intentionally disturbing a nest.

A nest consists of a single circular tier that is shaped like an inverted umbrella and attached by a short stalk to an "underside" area like a building eave or the ceiling of a porch. Made of a papery material, the nest usually has a single comb that houses up to 250 wasps (Plate 186). Paper wasps are primarily predators of caterpillars which they sting and paralyze, then place in the individual cells or chambers of the nest as food for the developing larvae.

**Parasitic wasps** (beneficial) are usually less than 1/8 inch long and so small they are rarely noticed. Nonetheless, they are an extremely important and large group of beneficial insects with about 16,000 species occurring in North America. An adult wasp lays eggs on or injects them into the body of a host insect. The larvae feed on the host and may consume it entirely. Some wasp larvae construct numerous small, white cocoons (Plate 187) on or in the body of the host. Pupation may occur in or on the host. Species that pupate inside the host leave small circular holes in the host's body upon emerging (Plate 188). Many harmful insects such as scales, whiteflies, aphids, leafminers and caterpillars are parasitized by these wasps.

**Yellowjackets** are about 1/2 inch long and have alternating yellow and black markings on the abdomen (Plate 189). The stinger is not barbed so the wasp can sting repeatedly. Closely related to the paper wasp, this wasp is very aggressive in defending itself or the nest. The nest is made of a papery material and can be quite large. Inside the nest are layers of combs to raise the brood. Some nests are aerial (Plate 190), but most often the nests are subterranean. People are usually stung when they step into or otherwise disturb a nest.

## Whiteflies

Whiteflies in the adult stage resemble tiny, white moths (Plate 191) but are more closely related to scale insects. Only 1/16 inch long, their four wings and bodies are covered with a fine white powder of wax. Two of the most prevalent whiteflies on ornamental plants are the sweetpotato whitefly (silverleaf whitefly) and the citrus whitefly. It is difficult to distinguish between the two species, and positive identification can only be determined by close examination of the pupal stage under relatively high magnification. One field identification characteristic is that sweetpotato whitefly tends to fold its wings over its body while the citrus whitefly does not.

During recent years, the sweetpotato (silverleaf) whitefly has become the major species attacking ornamental plants, especially in central and south Florida. This whitefly is not yet parasitized to any extent and possesses the genetic ability to rapidly become resistant to chemical pesticides.

Whiteflies are common pests on many ornamental plants. Among the plants most frequently attacked are allamanda, chinaberry, citrus, crape myrtle, ferns, fringe tree, gardenia, hibiscus, ligustrum, viburnum and many annuals, bedding and foliage plants. The sweetpotato whitefly has a much wider host range and is currently known to attack over 500 species of plants from 74 plant families. They have been a particular problem on tomatoes, members of the squash and cucumber family, eggplants, okra, beans, peanuts, Gerbera daisies, hibiscus and many other ornamental plants. The poinsettia is a favored host with leaf damage expressed as loss of bract color on affected plants.

Whiteflies have piercing-sucking mouthparts which puncture the leaf and suck the plant juices. Top sides of leaves on infested plants become pale or spotted when these insects feed on the undersides of the leaves (Plate 192). Whiteflies (as well as soft scales, mealybugs and aphids) excrete large amounts of honeydew which provides an excellent medium for the growth of a black fungus called sooty mold (see "Sooty mold"). Ants feed on the honeydew, so when ants are noticed, plants should be examined closely for sucking pests.

Whiteflies deposit 50 to 400 eggs on the undersides of the leaves (Plate 193). In 1 to 2 weeks, the eggs hatch into active, six-legged nymphs that are also called crawlers. Flat, round and slightly smaller than a pinhead, nymphs are light green to whitish and somewhat transparent. After moving around for several hours, the newly hatched nymphs insert their mouthparts into the undersides of leaves and then remain stationary throughout the remainder of their immature stages. After molting three times, they pupate (which is a resting stage) and transform into adults. The length of the life cycle from egg to adult varies considerably, requiring from 4 weeks to 6 months (for winter generations).

*Authors (in alphabetical order):*
*James L. Castner, Dale H. Habeck, Freddie A.*
*Johnson, Philip G. Koehler, Paul F. Ruppert,*
*Donald E. Short and Karen M. Vail*

# PLANT NEMATODES:
## What They Are and What They Do

## What Are Plant Parasitic Nematodes?

Nematodes are small, unsegmented round-worms, generally transparent and colorless; most are slender, with bodies from 1/100 to 1/8 inch long (Plate 194). Nematodes reproduce by eggs. Some kinds deposit eggs in the soil or in plant tissue as they are passing through. Other kinds of nematodes keep their eggs in a jelly-like mass that is attached to or inside the female's body which (when she completes her life cycle and dies) becomes a tough protective cap-sule called a cyst. Each female produces a few dozen to over 500 eggs in her lifetime. Eggs of some species survive for years without hatching, then they hatch quickly when a host plant grows near them. Rates of growth and reproduction increase as soil temperature rises, from about 50°F to about 95°F. Under ideal conditions (i.e. when the temperature is between 80° and 86°F), as little as 4 weeks is all that is required for many kinds of nematodes to complete the life cycle from a newly deposited egg to egg-depositing adult (Plate 195).

Only about 10% of all of the kinds of nema-todes on earth are estimated to be parasites of plants. About 15% may be parasites of higher animals (including domestic animals and people), and about 75% have no direct effect on humans or the plants and animals upon which we depend for life. (This 75% includes free-living nematodes that live in soil, fresh water, decaying organic material and the bottoms of oceans. In fact, there are different kinds of nematodes nearly any place on earth you can think of: in the Arctic tundra; around the roots of cactus in desert soils; in hot springs and salt lakes; in decay-ing fruit on the ground; in the galleries of insects under the bark high up in a tree; and, of course, in your garden soil.) Many of the nematodes that do not directly parasitize people, higher animals or plants perform important environmental tasks. Some feed on bacteria and microbes and may play key roles in the natural cycle of decay and the return of nutrients from organic materials to the soil. Your compost heap is teeming with these kinds of nematodes. Predatory nema-todes are important in keeping down the numbers of nematodes that are parasitic on plants. Many of the nematodes that are parasitic on insects are being studied and developed as environmentally acceptable pest control agents.

The nematodes that attack plants are aquatic animals that live in moisture on soil particles or in plant tissue. They are obligate para-sites, meaning they must feed on **living** tissues. Plant parasitic nematodes feed with a hollow stylet or oral spear with which they puncture cell walls, inject digestive juices into cells and draw liquid contents from cells.

Plant parasitic nematodes may be classified as **ectoparasites** (which always live outside of roots and feed only on tissues they can reach from outside the root) or **endopara-sites** (which spend at least part of their life cycle inside the roots on which they feed). Endoparasites may be either **migratory** or **sedentary**. With the exception of the egg, all stages of an ectoparasite or a migratory endoparasite can move freely in, through and out of root tissues. Most of the life cycle of a sedentary endoparasite is spent in a permanent feeding position with only one or two life stages free to move. If a nema-tode problem has occurred on a site in the recent past, it is likely to recur when a plant or crop susceptible to that kind of nematode is planted again on that site.

## How Do Nematodes Damage Plants?

Most if not all plant nematodes inject saliva into plant cells as they feed on them. The saliva apparently contains digestive enzymes to increase the amount of food that the nematode can take in. In some cases, the saliva may also contain:

- toxins that kill the cell and even other cells nearby, sometimes causing root elongation to stop, root tips to swell and/or proliferation of lateral roots.

- growth-regulating chemicals that change the way the root tissues develop and grow, which can lead to knotting or galling of roots or other changes in patterns of root growth.

Some nematodes can store and transmit some plant viruses.

As nematodes move through root tissues, direct injury to the cells causes open wounds and allows invasion by rot and wilt disease organisms. Nematode infection sometimes reduces plant resistance to disease.

## When to Suspect Nematodes as Plant Pests

Above-ground symptoms of nematode infestations (Plate 196) are:

- premature wilting or other evidence of unusual sensitivity to heat or moisture stress

- stunting or abnormally slow growth

- chlorosis (yellowing) of leaves

- premature loss of leaves (older first) and fruit, especially during stress periods

- thinning out of turf and its failure to compete with weeds

- irregular shape and distribution of the affected areas (i.e. not all plants are equally affected).

Below-ground symptoms of nematode infestations (Plate 197) are:

- galls or "knots" anywhere along a root (typical of root-knot nematode infection of many plant species)

- abbreviated roots, often with swollen tips or lateral root proliferation near tip

- discolored (dark color) roots

- root decay caused by fungi or bacteria that often follows nematode attack

- very small roundish bodies (cyst nematodes) attached to the roots; ranging in color from white to yellowish or golden to brown, they are about the size of a period on this page and may be visible to a careful observer, especially with the help of a hand lens or low power microscope

- general stunting of the roots; roots otherwise appear normal.

## Nematode Samples

Laboratory analysis of soil and/or plant tissues is the only way to learn all of the kinds of plant parasitic nematodes present, their approximate population levels and, if there is enough research information available to support and estimate, the relative risk that nematodes pose to the plant that is presently on the site or is to be planted. Information about the University of Florida's

Nematode Assay Laboratory is provided in the section GETTING HELP.

— *Robert A. Dunn*

# NEMATODE Management

As you will recall from the preceding chapter, *Plant Nematodes: What They Are and What They Do*, only a small percentage of the various kinds of nematodes that inhabit the earth are parasites on plants, and some are actually beneficial. But nearly everyone who grows plants in a garden or landscape in Florida eventually does have problems with nematodes. Parasitic plant nematodes damage so many different kinds of plants that many people just throw their hands in the air and give up. Is there any way to prevent nematode damage in the permanent landscape?

Perennial landscape ornamentals accumulate pest problems as do other perennial crops. If there are serious nematode infestations in the roots or soil ball or in the planting site, the chances of satisfactory growth are slim, and the longevity of the planting may be substantially reduced. The kind of start given perennial ornamentals and the care that follows can substantially affect their performance in the landscape.

# Nematode Symptoms and Diagnosis
## Above Ground Symptoms

Above ground symptoms of nematode damage are similar to those produced by many kinds of root injury. Foliage loses its luster and wilts more readily than it should. Prolonged stress because of nematode injury to the root system may result in yellowing and eventual loss of foliage (Plate 198). New flushes of growth are weak and display fewer and smaller leaves than healthy plants. Woody plants may suffer twig dieback if the stress continues. This weak condition may persist despite use of extra fertilizer and water. The distribution pattern of damage is usually irregular like the distribution in the soil of the nematodes themselves.

## Root Symptoms

Root symptoms vary widely. Some kinds of nematodes such as root-knot and some foliar nematodes cause host tissues to grow strangely while others stop the growth of the roots. Still others kill cells on which they feed, leaving patches of dead tissue as they move on. Fungi and bacteria which cause root rots, wilt and other plant diseases often infect nematode-damaged roots earlier and more severely than they do uninjured roots. Depending on the kinds of nematodes involved, nematode damage to landscape ornamentals may include galls, stunting and decay of roots. Nematode damaged roots are often darker in color than healthy roots.

Among the dozens of nematode species associated with landscape ornamentals, relatively few cause most of the serious problems. The root-knot nematodes (*Meloidogyne* spp.) are by far the most important in Florida. Their easily recognized galls on roots make their presence obvious (Plate 199, right side). Galls result from growth of plant tissues around juvenile nematodes which feed near the center of the root. The tissue of a root-knot gall is firm and does not have the hollow center of other types of galls. Removing a root-knot gall from a root will tear the root's cortical tissue. Other structures are commonly seen on roots and often mistaken for root-knot. Nodules form on the roots of many legumes (plants in the bean family) because of the beneficial nitrogen-fixing bacteria, *Rhizobium* spp. Most other natural nodules or bumps are loosely attached to the roots and have hollow centers. Active *Rhizobium* nodules have a milky fluid in their centers.

The root-knot nematodes cause more damage to more kinds of ornamentals than do any other kinds of nematodes; fortunately, their symptoms are also the most easily recognized. Popular woody ornamentals known to be susceptible to root-knot nematodes include many hollies (*Ilex* spp.), ixora (*Ixora coccinea*), hibiscus (*Hibiscus* spp.), Barbados cherry (*Malpighea glabra*), ti plant (*Cordyline terminalis*), most *Gardenia* spp., *Pittosporum* spp., boxwoods (*Buxus* spp.), rose (*Rosa* spp.) and figs (*Ficus* spp.).

Many other plants, such as *Citrus* spp. and wax myrtle (*Myrica cerifera*), may occasionally be damaged by root-knot nematodes even though they are not normally affected by them (Plates 200 and 201). We do not know why these unusual infections occasionally happen, but it is likely that plant stress from environmental factors or other pests may promote them.

The less obvious discoloration, stunting and decay of roots caused by nematodes other than root-knot are easily masked by or confused with the effects of numerous pathogens and other root problems. Nematodes such as lesion (*Pratylenchus* spp.), burrowing (*Radopholus similis*) and reniform (*Rotylenchulus* spp.) probably cause far more damage to landscape plantings than is recognized because their effects are not as readily identified as those of root-knot nematodes. Susceptibility to one kind of nematode is not necessarily related to the reaction of the same plant to other nematodes.

## Laboratory Soil Sample Analysis

Laboratory soil sample analysis is the only way to determine all of the kinds of nematodes associated with a problem and may be necessary to identify the most effective control measures. Information on proper sampling techniques is provided at your county Extension office. See GETTING HELP.

# Managing Nematode Pests

First, it is important to realize that there are a few plant parasitic nematodes in nearly every square foot of soil in Florida. However, it is obvious that most plantings of landscape ornamentals in Florida are healthy assets to their surroundings. In most cases, any number of attractive plant varieties can be planted in a given site without serious damage or immediate losses. With proper site selection and preparation, appropriate plant selection and continued care during the life of the planting, anyone can establish and maintain an attractive landscape in Florida despite the nematodes that infest the soil nearly everywhere. The keys to minimizing the effects of nematodes on Florida landscape ornamentals are good horticultural care and preventative maintenance as outlined below.

## Prepare new planting sites properly

Give plants the best chance to become rapidly established. Horticulturists may disagree on how desirable it is to incorporate soil amendments into the soil which is used to fill in around perennial woody ornamentals (trees and shrubs), but they do generally agree that it is important to dig a much wider (but not deeper) hole than is needed to encompass the root spread or root ball of the plant. A wider hole provides plenty of loose soil into which new roots can grow.

Native soil into which annual beds are to be planted should be prepared well. Old roots and any debris should be removed from the site. The water and nutrient-holding capacity of the soil and the activity of natural enemies of nematodes will be enhanced by organic amendments incorporated into soil before planting.

## Treat soil

If nematodes built up to high levels on the preceding plant(s) in the site, or if vegetables or other plants that are especially favorable for nematodes were recently removed from the site, some soil treatments may give the new plant(s) a better chance. Chemical treatments sometimes can be used to reduce nematode populations before planting in perennial sites or annual beds. However, no pesticide treatment can eliminate all pests from a treated area nor can a chemical's effects last forever. Nematodes not reached by a fumigant treatment usually reinfest the bed during the growing season, so the soil may have as many nematodes by the end of the season as it did before fumigation. Currently, all chemical treatments require that a professional pesticide applicator treat soils.

**Soil solarization** is a method of soil treatment using energy from the sun to heat the soil enough to reduce populations of nematodes and some other soil-borne problems. It seems likely that much and perhaps all of the effect is obtained by increasing soil temperatures in the normal root depths. Many gardeners and other growers desire a soil treatment that can substantially reduce nematodes without pesticides. Soil solarization may provide that alternative.

Soil solarization consists of covering the soil with a clear polyethylene tarp for 4 to 6 weeks during a hot period of the year when the soil will receive maximum direct sunlight (Plate 202). This method has been used to reduce damage caused by a wide range of soil-borne fungi, weed seeds and nematodes in fields in Israel, Jordan and California. In Florida, solarization has worked well in some trials but has failed in others. In several California tests, temperatures of tarped soil 6 inches deep were 111°F to 122°F, 14° to 23°F higher than those of uncovered soil. Many nematodes and other soil pests will be controlled by prolonged exposure to these temperatures. The procedure described here provides guidelines for those who wish to try it.

**Soil should be covered** at least 4 weeks, preferably longer, during the hottest and sunniest time of the year. June and July appear to be most suitable in Florida, since air and soil temperatures are highest then, and day length and the angle of the sun provide for maximum solar energy hitting the soil at that time.

**Soil must be well tilled** before tarping. This destroys clods and plant debris which might interfere with uniform conduction of heat through the soil and thus protect some organisms from the full effects of the treatment. When soil is well tilled and its surface very smooth before the tarp is applied, there can be maximum contact between the tarp and the soil surface, with few air pockets to interfere with direct heating of the soil by incident sunlight. All other soil preparations such as fertilizing and placing drip irrigation tubes should be completed before placing the tarp over the bed. This will minimize the need to disturb the treated soil before planting.

**Soil moisture must be high** when the tarp is applied. Wet soil conducts heat better than dry soil, so moistening the soil before tarping will provide for a deeper treatment. Also, most pest organisms are more susceptible to lethal effects of heat in moist soil; they may be dormant if dry.

**Use clear polyethylene, not black polyethylene.** Clear plastic produces higher soil temperatures faster than black plastic. Sunlight passes through clear plastic to heat the soil directly. Black plastic intercepts the light, and soil is heated primarily by conduction only where the plastic actually touches the soil. Some of the heat generated when sunlight hits black plastic is lost directly to the outside air.

**Thin plastic** (1 to 2 mil) may permit more sunlight to penetrate to the soil and has been reported to favor more rapid and deeper control of soil-borne fungi than thicker plastic (6 mil). However, both eventually provided equal control, and thicker plastic is less likely to tear.

**Leave the tarp in place** until planting time. It has no detrimental effect on the soil, so it will only maximize the period of treatment and reduce the chance of recontamination before planting. When ready to plant, it may be possible to remove the plastic carefully enough to save it for re-use, especially if 4 to 6 mil thick plastic was used. It probably should be removed before planting any crops that require relatively cool soil for best growth.

**Avoid bringing contaminated plants** or untreated soil into the treated bed when planting, and do not till or otherwise disturb treated soil if possible. Deep tillage can bring soil up from depths that were not adequately heated, thus contaminating the crop root zone.

## Replace infested (contaminated) soil

When fumigation is objectionable, illegal or has failed, landscapers sometimes simply remove all soil or planting mix from an annual bed and replace it with new sterile planting medium. Although this may seem to be an extreme measure, it is sometimes much more convenient. New plantings can be put in the site immediately, unlike those sites that have been treated chemically. Nematodes will eventually invade the new medium, and bedding plant roots can grow out of the new medium into the infested native soil. Using barrier fabric between the shrub bed and the annual bed apparently can delay infection of the plants.

## Use nematode-free plants

No matter how perfect and pest-free the planting site, a nematode infection already started in roots of transplants (Plate 203) is right where it must be to do the most damage. Buy only top quality plants. Reject any that have clear evidence of nematodes or other hard-to-control pests.

## Select plants that are well adapted

Plants should be suited to the climate, soil type, hours of sun and shade, drainage characteristics and other features of the location. (See chapters on selection in the sections TREES; PALMS; and SHRUBS, VINES AND GROUND COVERS.) Plants that are out of place are more likely than well-adapted ones to suffer environmental stress at any given time and to be under stress more of the time. Just as you may be more apt to catch pneumonia when a cold places unusual stress on you, stress makes plants more susceptible to potential pests which are common in their environment. Moreover, a plant species that is well adapted to an area probably has some degree of tolerance or resistance to locally common pests such as nematodes.

## Avoid nematode-susceptible plants

Do not use plants that are highly susceptible to nematodes in a planting site where those nematodes are known to occur. Just as they vary in form, flower color and season of bloom, plants also vary widely in their susceptibility to different nematodes. Most references to nematode susceptibility in magazine articles and Extension Service literature refer to one or more root-knot nematode species unless otherwise noted. Although lists from these sources are often incomplete, it is still probably correct to assume that any plant identified as nematode susceptible is not to be planted where root-knot nematodes are known to be serious.

Susceptibilities of 22 common woody ornamentals to four widely distributed nematodes are compared in Table 17. Many plants that are rated susceptible (S) or highly susceptible (HS) to root-knot nematodes are tolerant (T) to one or more

**Table 17. Susceptibility of some popular woody ornamentals to four common nematodes at the NCSU Central Crops Research Station, Clayton, NC.***

**HS** - Plants highly susceptible (severe stunting, branch die-back and death), **S** - Plants susceptible (some stunting but plants will grow satisfactorily), **T** - Plants will grow satisfactorily, **O** - Have not been tested

| | Nematode Reaction | | | |
|---|---|---|---|---|
| Host Plant | Root-knot | Stunt | Lesion | Ring |
| Azalea | T | S | O | T |
| *Aucuba japonica* | HS | S | O | S |
| *Buxus microphylla* (Japanese Boxwood) | HS | O | O | O |
| *Buxus sempervirens* (American Boxwood) | O | T | HS | O |
| *Camellia japonica* | T | T | O | O |
| *Camellia sasanqua* | T | T | O | O |
| *Gardenia jasminoides* | S | T | T | T |
| *Gardenia radicans* | HS | T | O | T |
| *Ilex cornuta* (Chinese Holly) | | | | |
|     cv. *Burfordi* | T | T | O | T |
|     cv. *Rotunda* | S | S | O | S |
| *Ilex crenata* (Japanese Holly) | | | | |
|     cv. *Compacta* | HS | T | O | S |
|     cv. *Convexa* | HS | T | O | S |
|     cv. *Helleri* | HS | S | O | S |
|     cv. *Rotundifolia* | HS | S | O | S |
| *Ilex vomitoria nana* | T | T | O | T |
| *Juniper spp.* | | | | |
|     Blue rug | T | T | HS | T |
|     Shore juniper | T | T | O | T |
|     Spiney Greek | T | T | S | T |
| *Ligustrum* (Privet) | T | T | O | T |
| *Nandina domestica* | T | T | T | T |
| *Photinia fraseri* (red tip) | T | T | O | T |
| Rose | S | S | S | T |

*Data in part courtesy of R.H. Jones, D.M. Benson, and K.R. Barker, Department of Plant Pathology, North Carolina State University at Raleigh. Many are likely to be more susceptible to root-knot nematode populations in Florida than resulted in these tests.

of the others, and vice versa. This table is based on many years of research at the North Carolina State University Research Station at Clayton, N.C. Because of the extreme sensitivity of plants to drought stress in our sandy soils, the same plants may suffer greater damage from the same nematodes in Florida than they would in North Carolina. That is, some plants rated T in the chart for North Carolina probably deserve an S in Florida.

## Keep other pests under practical control

Stress from pests can set plants up for nematode infection just as readily as over- or under-supply of nutrients or water. Overuse of pesticides can also injure plants; use them carefully and only when needed.

## Maintenance

Give your plants optimum care from the start and for as long as you want them to perform well. "Optimum" does not mean "maximum." Fertilize as needed to maintain healthy growth, not to produce excessive, succulent growth that invites attack by nematodes and other pests. Water deeply, to encourage development of a deep root system which can exploit a large volume of soil for water and nutrients. (Frequent shallow watering causes plants to develop a shallow root system.) A large root system can better withstand a small amount of nematode damage without major compromise to the overall health of the plant than can a shallow, already minimal root system.

## Do not allow maintenance to lapse

Sudden dry periods or pest outbreaks can weaken plants in an incredibly short time.

Even under normal conditions, erratic or inadequate watering can weaken a plant so that it can no longer tolerate a modest nematode population that had existed on/ with it for years.

## Mulches

Keep the plant root zone mulched to keep roots cool in hot weather and minimize evaporation of water from the soil surface. Organic mulches also contribute organic matter to the soil, thus enhancing the capacity of the soil to retain water and nutrients. Mulches reduce stress on the plant as a whole and the root system specifically, improving the plant's chances to do well in spite of some nematode damage to roots. (See *Mulches for the Landscape*.) Greater organic matter content in soil also stimulates the activity of natural enemies such as certain fungi, predatory nematodes, etc. which apparently help suppress harmful nematode populations.

Avoid using chipped wood mulches that may contain stump or root tissues from woody plants that were infected with the mushroom root-rot fungus, *Armillaria* spp. or the *Ganoderma* fungus that causes butt-rot of palm trees. These fungi may kill woody plants which are mulched with chips that carry them.

— *Robert A. Dunn*

# PLANT DISEASES

## What are Plant Diseases?

Whenever a plant stops growing as it should and loses its normal vigor, appearance or productivity, disease is a prime suspect. Some disease symptoms, like leaf spots and wilting, are easily seen or measured. Others, such as a root decay, are difficult to observe or are very subtle (e.g. shorter growth flushes). Detecting the less obvious symptoms is more difficult when the diseased plant is the only specimen of its kind in the landscape and cannot be compared to a healthy one.

## Cases of Mistaken Identity

When it comes to plant disease, appearances can be deceiving. People who have come to Florida from other parts of the country may mistakenly view some of the plants they see here as diseased when, in fact, their apparently abnormal appearances are normal. Similarly, because of how they look or where they grow, certain of Florida's native plants and fungi are treated as harmful when they are not. Take time to learn the natural components of Florida's landscapes and accept them. This will save much time, energy, and expense in unnecessary management activities directed toward the control of a problem that isn't one!

The variation among ornamental species that we so highly prize can also be a source of confusion. For example, one common expression of mutation (to which all plants are subject) is the loss of green pigment in foliage that causes variegation (Plate 204). Variegation that occurs on a part of a plant can resemble the symptoms produced by a viral pathogen. Similarly, the loss of variegation in a normally variegated shrub may be thought to be a result of disease when in fact it is just a mutation back to the original appearance of the plant. Different bark characteristics among plants may also prove confusing. Certain woody species of elm, sweet gum and euonymus may exhibit wings of cork from around the stem (Plate 205) which could be mistaken for a canker-type disease. This bark characteristic is highly prized in the nursery trade and is a trait in these species for which breeding programs select. Some plants like crape myrtle and sycamore shed their outer bark, a characteristic that might be alarming if you didn't know it was natural for those plants.

Similar confusion is created by other unique and native life forms found in Florida. Perhaps the two most distinctive plants in Florida's landscapes are the epiphytic plants Spanish moss (Plate 206 and back cover) and ball moss (Plate 207 and back cover). Although these plants appear to parasitize landscape plants, they simply use them as support structures for growth. Sunlight along with water and nutrients from the air permit these plants to grow as easily from telephone wires as in oak trees. Occasionally, Spanish moss will become dense enough to cause twig breakage when wet or to reduce sunlight to tree foliage. Neither condition is irreversible or lethal.

Like the epiphytes, lichens are frequently misidentified as disease-causing agents. In fact, a lichen is composed of a fungus and an alga that have co-evolved into a complex and symbiotic life form. The fungus contributes support, nutrients and water, while the algal component photosynthesizes complex foods to support the life form. Lichens (Plate 208 and back cover) are commonplace on tree trunks, but when they develop on branches and twigs, they are blamed for decline. Lichens can only colonize interior twigs and branches **after** the leaf canopy has thinned. They follow the sunlight into the

163

plant interior, and though they take advantage of declining plants, they do not cause decline. Increased lichen density should be taken as an indication that a particular plant is under stress and has lost leaf cover. Real causes of this decline could include nematodes, root diseases, environmental or cultural stress.

Many of the diverse, native saprophytic fungi also get blamed for causing plant diseases. Perhaps the most obvious are the stinkhorn fungi, *Clathrus* (Plate 209 and back cover), *Mutinus* and *Phallus* spp. These large and offensive smelling fungi are often found near thickly mulched areas, old stumps or declining trees. They do not cause plant disease but rather colonize deposits of organic matter. Their colonies are often extensive in an area and may arise from deep within the soil. Their odor attracts carrion flies which spread the fungus spores throughout the environment. If you cannot tolerate stinkhorns, remove them before they mature. No controls on these fungi are needed.

# Causes of Plant Disease

Symptoms of plant disease can be seen or measured and are limited in their variety. Furthermore, although a symptom may indicate disease, it may also be evidence of a problem other than disease. For example, a poorly growing or stunted plant may be the work of a plant pathogen (a microbe that causes plant disease), a nematode population in the root zone or, possibly, an unsuitable growing site. Remember to consider all the possible causes of a given symptom.

Plant diseases are divided into two major categories which are based upon whether the symptoms are caused by a plant pathogen or by some non-living factor associated with the culture of or the environment surrounding the plant in the landscape. Plant pathogens include such diverse organisms as viruses, phytoplasmas, bacteria, fungi, nematodes (see *Plant Nematodes: What They Are and What They Do*) and certain plant species. Worldwide, plant diseases are caused by over 8,600 distinct plant pathogens. Most of these plant pathogens can only cause disease in a narrow range of plant species; however, some pathogens possess the ability to infect hundreds of plant species across different genera and families.

## Virus Pathogens

There are about 500 viruses that cause plant disease throughout the world, but their impact is greater on food and feed crops than on landscape ornamentals. Too small to see, even with a light microscope, a virus is simply a chemical molecule consisting of a strand of nucleic acid (the genetic blueprint of all life) surrounded by a protective protein coat. (Some viruses, known as viroids, lack the protein coat.) It can be argued that viruses are not living since they lack cells and the ability to reproduce. However, their genetic blueprint does replicate by commandeering the plant cell metabolic machinery. It is during this activity that plant disease develops. Few viruses persist outside the host plant. In fact, many viruses depend on a second organism to move about the environment and invade a plant. These other organisms are known as **vectors** for the virus and can be fungi, nematodes, mites, insects or even parasitic plants. Viruses can be seedborne and are commonly spread through the vegetative propagation of plant material.

## Phytoplasmas and Similar Pathogens

The phytoplasmas are pathogens that are also submicroscopic in size. By colonizing the food conducting cells of a plant, they produce "yellowing" type diseases that are characterized by loss of vigor, plant decline and death. In Florida, the most significant disease of this type affects certain palm trees and is known as Lethal Yellowing (Plate 25). Mycoplasmas do not persist outside their host plants or their vector insects (plant hoppers or treehoppers).

## Bacterial Pathogens

Bacterial pathogens are extremely simple microbes. Most bacteria are single cells with no organized nucleus and a cell membrane but not a cell wall. There are about 100 species or biotypes of bacteria that infect plants. Although you can often smell the presence of certain bacterial pathogens or see the ooze of hundreds of thousands of cells, observing single cells requires the use of a light microscope. Bacteria survive in soil, organic debris, insects and on or in various plant parts. The spread of these pathogens is most often tied to the movement of water in the soil or, from overhead, as rain or irrigation splash. However, certain insects are also responsible for bacterial movement within the environment and can vector bacteria into plants. Some bacteria are seedborne or carried internally during vegetative propagation of plant species.

Bacterial pathogens can produce a wide variety of plant symptoms that include leaf spots and blights, cankers, galls, leaf scald, soft decays of fruit and roots, scabs, wilts and other problems. Many of these plant symptoms overlap with those caused by fungal pathogens, making diagnosis difficult without a laboratory. In the landscape, foliar diseases caused by bacteria can often be distinguished from those caused by fungi by certain differences in appearance. Spots caused by bacteria are often located along the edges of the leaf and are angular in shape. The lesions are often bounded by leaf veins, which creates the angular shape. Early in the morning or after heavy irrigation or rainfall, the margins of bacterial lesions (Plate 210) have a characteristic watersoaked look that fades away as the tissue dries.

## Fungal Pathogens

The largest group of microbes that cause plant disease are fungi. Over 8000 species of fungi are known to damage plants. When one considers the numbers of fungi and the range of hosts each can infect (i.e. between 1 and over 400), the number of possible plant diseases is staggering. Thankfully, they do not all occur in Florida!

Once considered primitive plants, fungi are vegetative forms comprised of branched filaments with definite cell walls. Each filament is called a hypha: the aggregation of many hyphae into a layer or mat of fungus is called mycelium. Fungi are diverse in size, shape and complexity of reproductive structures. Many fungal pathogens have an asexual life cycle, multiplying by non-sexual or vegetative means; this is most important in the initiation of repeated disease cycles in Florida. Fungi and their various reproductive stages are visible to the naked eye or certainly with the aid of microscope magnification.

Many fungi can exist as saprophytes, degrading organic matter, and can also cause plant disease. Others cannot actively live and grow in the absence of the host plant and are considered obligate parasites. For part or all of their life cycles, fungal pathogens can persist in living hosts, in dead host plant debris, in the soil or in water. Air, water, insects, birds, animals and humans are responsible for long distance movement of fungi. People often spread fungal pathogens along with the soil, plants or plant products they are moving.

## Non-living Causes of Plant Disease

The environment or the cultural management of a plant is often responsible for producing the disease symptoms observed in the home landscape. Environmental and cultural factors such as nutrient and moisture levels, temperature extremes, sunlight, toxic chemicals and mechanical damage can often explain abnormal plant growth. The greatest challenge is to account for the damage days, weeks or months after it has occurred. Statewide, the most common among the non-living agents of disease are nutrient-related problems. The low organic, highly porous soils of Florida do not sustain a high level of soil fertility; with the added complication of alkaline soil pH, minor elements are often unavailable to plant roots. (See *Nutritional Deficiencies in the Basic Plant Groups*.)

Plant diseases may also be brought on by changes in available water or light, temperature extremes, toxic chemicals and mechanical damage. When, for instance, a storm front deposits excessive rainfall, plant roots may experience oxygen depletion and literally suffocate in water-saturated soil. The resultant feeder root death can be directly damaging and may also allow soil fungi that cause root disease easy entrance into a plant's roots. On the other hand, plants that receive too little water may exhibit marginal and interveinal leaf scorch on the newest leaves (Plate 211), especially under conditions of bright light and drying winds. Often high temperature periods will combine with low soil moisture conditions to produce plant wilt and leaf scorch. Low tempera-

tures, although rare in Florida, also cause considerable damage when they occur. A drastic drop in temperature close to or below freezing will kill soft herbaceous tissue. Woody plants sustain equal damage on soft new growth and may sustain frost damage on branches, stems or trunks. Frost cracks (Plate 212) often are not visible for months after the damage has occurred, commonly causing diebacks in early summer (see *Protecting Plants from the Cold*). Rapid changes in light intensity, as when the tree canopy is suddenly thinned, can result in sunburn on the plants below (Plate 213).

Readily preventable damage is caused by toxic chemicals and mechanical wounding of plants in the landscape. Such common practices as cleaning brick and concrete with muriatic acid solutions can produce virus-like symptoms on the leaves of plants that come in direct contact with the solution (Plate 214). Use of weed and feed type lawn products (containing active ingredients that regulate growth) can leach through soil into the root zones of less tolerant plants and cause growth distortions (Plate 215). Enthusiastic use of lawn mowers, line trimmers and other edging equipment can result in repeated trunk wounds to woody plants in the landscape, especially when these plants do not have mulched buffer zones. Similarly, woody plants that are used to line driveways and parking areas often sustain repeated stem or trunk wounds from vehicle doors or bumpers (Plate 216).

## Conditions that Favor Disease

Florida's climate provides a rich, nurturing environment for plant species as well as for the organisms that cause plant diseases. Despite the diversity of plants and microbes throughout the state, disease is still the exception rather than the rule. Plant disease

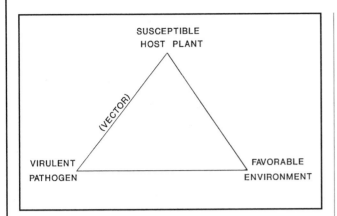

**Figure 51. Plant disease triangle.**

occurs only through the concurrence of a number of factors that can be thought of as a set of traffic signals that will either allow disease development or prevent it. For a plant disease to occur, these factors must be in a "green light" situation. This relationship is most easily expressed through the disease triangle (Figure 51).

The infection process can proceed only when a susceptible host plant, the appropriate aggressive plant pathogen and a set of exacting environmental conditions all exist in the same time and place. Among the favorable environmental factors may be particular temperatures, certain relative humidities, a wet plant surface, saturated soil or specific periods of exposure to such factors. For certain pathogens like the viruses or phytoplasmas, the disease triangle becomes more complex because a vectoring organism must be present to move the pathogen into the host plant.

A plant disease is a slow but dynamic biological phenomenon. Once the requirements of the disease triangle are met, the pathogen infects the susceptible host, and the disease begins and continues until the environment changes to disfavor the pathogen.

*Cercospora* leaf spot disease of ligustrum (Plate 217) provides a good example of the time involved in the development of a disease (Figure 52). This disease begins when the reproductive spores of one of three species of the fungus *Cercospora* is carried by wind or water to a ligustrum leaf surface. If the surface remains wet for six to eight hours, conditions are ripe for disease to set in. The *Cercospora* spore absorbs water like a seed and proceeds to germinate into a leaf stomate (air pore). This process occurs overnight. If the leaf dries off prior to fungus penetration of the leaf, disease is stopped. If the fungus is below the leaf surface by sun-up, it has successfully infected the plant and disease has begun. Examining an infected leaf the next day would yield no evidence of this disease. *Cercospora* requires a colonization period within the leaf of 14 days before enough leaf cells are killed to produce a visible leaf spot. Seven more days are required for fungus reproduction to begin from the first leaf spot. Every wet night from that of day 21 after infection, can mean a new disease cycle is starting.

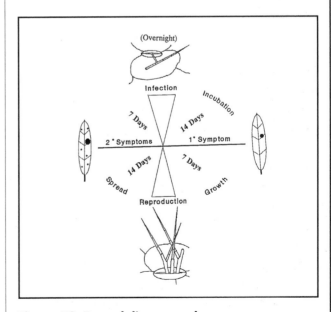

**Figure 52. Fungal disease cycle.**

Other kinds of fungal diseases may be faster or slower. Bacterial diseases are often faster in development. Few true diseases caused by plant pathogens invade and cause visible damage overnight.

# Disease Diagnosis

With the thousands of plant diseases found in Florida, diagnosis is difficult at best. Plant symptoms themselves are finite in variety, and one symptom may reflect a variety of different causes. Remember that many of the pathogens that cause disease, particularly the bacteria, phytoplasmas, viruses and many fungi are not visible to the eye. Often a plant may have a complex of pathogens contributing to disease development. Get assistance in identifying plant disease problems. (The GETTING HELP section at the end of this book lists IFAS resources for plant disease diagnostic assistance.) You will find that you need to be an astute observer of all the elements of your landscape. Plant disease diagnosis requires a good sample of the diseased plant as well as complete information regarding cultural and environmental conditions and a thorough description of symptoms and their onset.

All plant diseases provide two types of evidence that can be used in diagnosing a problem. One type of evidence is that created by the pathogen itself. Either the vegetative or the reproductive state of one or more pathogens may be seen in, on or near the affected plant, although many of the signs dealing with viruses, phytoplasmas, bacteria and fungi are too small to be seen without magnification. Some, however, are identifiable through their obvious and distinctive appearance. The powdery mildews, for example, are fungal pathogens whose vegetation and reproduction are manifested in a powdery, white growth (Plate 218). Other pathogens may produce large reproductive structures such as the woody shelf created by *Ganoderma* fungus on palms (Plate 24).

The plant itself provides the second type of diagnostic evidence. Learning to recognize the various symptoms plants express will help you narrow down the probable causes and will also enable you to select appropriate samples when seeking assistance with diagnosis.

# Managing Plant Disease

The more that science discovers about the cause and nature of plant diseases, the more insights we have into their management. Depending on the characteristics of your landscape as well as factors like cost, your disease management strategy will incorporate one or more of the following techniques: 1) cultural management; 2) chemical actions; 3) regulation; 4) biologicals; and 5) physical activities. (See also *Integrated Pest Management*.)

## Cultural Management

For the average homeowner, the greatest flexibility in managing plant diseases comes through managing the culture surrounding plant growth. That is, by taking time to plan and by seeking sound horticultural advice, you can design a landscape that favors the growth of specific ornamentals in each of your planting sites. Furthermore, you can manage plant nutrition, irrigation and spacing of plants in a way that discourages the incidence and spread of plant pathogens in the landscape. The following are practical methods of disease control:

- Match the plant to the landscape site to avoid sub-optimal levels of plant vigor.

- Do not overplant new landscapes. Overplanting creates pockets of poor air circulation and slow drying.

- Install gutters and downspouts on roofs or install the plants below well away from areas where rainwater cascades down.

- Use mulching materials to manage soil moisture more effectively.

- Irrigate the roots, **not the foliage**. Water for longer periods less often, to encourage deep rooting.

- Avoid late season fertilization. Let plants go dormant to avoid cold weather injury which predisposes plants to canker diseases.

- Identify disease problems so you can decide whether to control the disease or remove the plant.

- Remove diseased plant parts or entire plants early in the disease cycle to slow disease development.

## Chemical Actions

Fungicides are one type of pesticide used specifically to manage plant diseases. Some fungicides control bacterial pathogens as well and could be termed bactericides. Although these products are readily available for landscape use, they are generally not used effectively in Florida's landscapes. To use a fungicide effectively, one must be able to distinguish serious diseases from those that are merely cosmetic. One must also be willing to take on the task of disease identification so that the right fungicide ingredient can be applied. Fungicide products have different strengths and weaknesses, and no one product works for all disease situations. Effective fungicide use also requires appropriate application equipment to deliver the product to the soil or leaf canopy according to label instructions. Single applications of fungicides are seldom of value because these chemicals are designed to be suppressants more often than fungus killers. The product often needs to be reapplied at intervals specified on the label.

## Regulation

Florida's intensive agricultural production has resulted in strong federal and state regulations. Personnel from the Florida Department of Agriculture and Consumer Services safeguard Florida's environment from the unwanted introduction of new diseases, pests and weeds. Plants bound for import or export are inspected and, if necessary, quarantined at inspection stations along Florida's borders. In this way, officials hope to protect the quality of production of both food and ornamental plants grown in the state.

## Biologicals

The development and use of plants that resist certain pathogens is a fast-developing disease management strategy. Throughout the United States and abroad, breeding programs for popular ornamental species produce cultivars resistant to certain diseases that typically plague them; examples include rose cultivars with tolerance or resistance to black spot disease and crape myrtle cultivars resistant to powdery mildew. These and other such cultivars may be available at your local nursery.

## Physical Activities

The least applicable option for managing disease in the Florida home landscape involves physical actions such as the use or control of temperature, light or radiation to protect plants from pathogens. These measures take place largely on the industrial and commercial level. The use of soil solarization to control soilborne pathogens is the only physical method of practical use in Florida's landscapes. This is an excellent method for both nematode and soil pathogen control in flower and vegetable garden areas and is described in detail in the chapter entitled *Nematode Management.*

Whether one or more of the above options will prove appropriate and effective will be determined by the growing site of the plant, the magnitude of the problem and the specific biology of the pathogen involved. Remember that the first step in constructing a disease management strategy, **if one is needed**, is to correctly identify the disease involved.

## Common Diseases of Florida Ornamentals

Florida encompasses four plant hardiness zones within the geographical boundaries of the state (see *The Planting Site*, Figure 1). Yet, when you look at the plants that actually grow throughout Florida, you'll find many that were brought here from other zones. Within bounds, many plants can adapt to various weather conditions, but remember: where the plant material goes, so go many of the plant diseases. In fact, many new diseases result from the introduction of plants foreign to Florida's environment.

There are thousands of important plant diseases, and a complete listing is not within the scope of this book. Among the following examples are common diseases that affect some of the more popular Florida landscape ornamentals.

### Mushroom Root Rot Disease

Mushroom root rot disease occurs statewide and is caused by the pathogen *Armillaria*

*tabescens.* The fungus naturally colonizes old roots and stumps as well as living woody and herbaceous plant species in a host range that exceeds 200 plants including common ones such as azalea, juniper, loquat, pittosporum and viburnum. Symptoms include a slow decline that takes a year or more and yields a thinning canopy. Usually during the high temperatures of summer, the affected plant will dessicate quickly, holding onto its greyish-green leaves for a period of time (Plate 219). Single stemmed plants are killed outright, while multistemmed plants may partially survive. Sampling below the bark at the soil line will reveal the creamy white mycelium of the fungus (Plate 220). Often after the plant has died, the mushroom reproductive stage will appear in the immediate area of the dead trunk (Plate 221). The fungus is a fleshy mushroom that persists for only a week or so, but may reappear 2 to 3 times each year. The fungus spreads by airborne spores, by direct vegetative growth through soil or by hyphal growth through root grafts of adjacent plants.

Management of this disease is very site specific. Removal of the diseased plant is mandatory as this fungus is a wood rot organism. Root system excavation is recommended followed either by a fallow period of several years or by use of fumigation (where possible) prior to replanting. Deep spading to sever root grafts may slow the fungus' movement along hedges or in beds of woody plants.

### Wet Root Rot Diseases

This group of plant diseases is caused by a pair of soil fungi (*Phytophthora* and *Pythium* spp.) that are common throughout Florida's landscapes and nurseries. These fungi function as saprophytes in the soil but have the ability to invade a diverse group of plants, causing feeder root death and plant decline. Many species of these fungi exist within Florida with different host ranges from narrow to broad. The initial stage of the disease is triggered by periods of excessive soil moisture which allows the fungus to invade roots and reproduce. Disease development depends on plant size, vigor, environment and other factors. Above-ground symptoms of this disease (Plate 222) include loss of leaves from the plant's oldest to its newest, leaf yellowing or browning, reduction in growth flushes, plant wilt, loss in dark coloration of leaves and plant death. Below ground, the fine feeder roots are decayed throughout the outer cylinder (cortex) of the roots. This layer slips off between two fingers leaving the thread-like center of conductive tissue (Plate 223).

Wet root rot diseases can occur as a direct result of the planting of infected nursery stock. Landscape situations that favor disease development include: 1) poor water management; 2) poorly drained or saturation-prone areas; 3) planting too deep; 4) shallow root establishment. Such disease should be managed by more critical water management and/or use of fungicides specified upon laboratory diagnosis.

## Ganoderma Trunk Rots

As landscapes within Florida age and maintenance activities become more reliant on motorized tools, the incidence of wood rots increases. As trees grow older, they may become more susceptible to wood decay fungi. Additionally, increased use of motorized maintenance results in more instances of mechanical wounding which in turn provides airborne fungal spores easy entrance to the tree.

Perhaps the most serious of the wood decay fungi is the genus *Ganoderma*. At least five species of this fungus exist in Florida. *Ganoderma zonatum* (Plate 24) is a major pathogen of palms statewide and has caused widespread and expensive tree loss (see *Pest and Other Problems of Palms*). Two other species of *Ganoderma*, *G. applanatum* and *G. lucidum*, are commonplace on such trees as oak, maple, sweet gum, citrus and bald cypress. These fungi have large, woody shelf-like reproductive structures that emerge either from the tree trunk or in close proximity to it. These pathogens can cause limb or tree death or can enter after the tree has died from another cause. Because they are wood decay organisms, the trees they infect should be removed before they snap in a storm and damage vehicles or structures. These fungi can move through root grafts or can be airborne. Remove the reproductive shelves as they appear and before they mature to release spores. Discrete infections in a limb can sometimes be eradicated by tree surgery.

## Lethal Yellowing of Palms

Through its destruction of the Jamaican Tall coconut palm as well as other palm species, this disease has changed the face of Florida's coastline in the southern third of the state. Lethal yellowing is caused by a phytoplasma; description of its symptoms (Plate 25), biology and management are included in the chapter entitled *Pest and Other Problems of Palms*.

## Sphaeropsis Gall

Gall diseases can be caused by both fungal and bacterial pathogens. Diagnosis can be confusing. *Sphaeropsis* gall is a serious landscape disease statewide affecting such common species as bottlebrush, holly, oleander and wax myrtle. This fungus produces a range of symptoms from swollen, woody galls in limbs and twigs of holly and bottlebrush (Plate 224) to a witches' broom growth in wax myrtle, oleander and holly (Plate 225). Severity of this disease is on the rise due primarily to improper pruning practices. When the disease is first detected, remove infected tissue at a point 4 to 6 inches below obvious symptoms. Pruning should be scheduled for dry periods. Do not prune while shrubs are wet. More superficial pruning will leave the fungus in the plant's wood to continue producing symptoms. All prunings should be destroyed. Fungicides are not recommended for this problem.

## *Hypoxylon* Canker of Oak

Very little of habitable Florida is without at least one native oak (*Quercus* spp.). Many of these oaks are large and desirable for landscaping purposes. However, even with good intentions during construction, oak habitat is seriously altered or the oaks themselves wounded. Operations such as land clearing or digging house footings or septic tanks can result in root and/or trunk damage. Movement of heavy construction equipment or the occasional lightning strike can seriously wound some trees. The wounding or stress imposed upon these oaks results in oak susceptibility to a canker fungus named *Hypoxylon*. A number of species of this fungus exist in Florida, and the collective host range includes the oaks, magnolia, mahogany and fig.

Symptoms of *Hypoxylon* infection may be localized on one branch or may occur on the main trunk. On oak, green-to-brown reproductive tissue develops on the bark near the wound sites in spring to early summer. In late summer through fall, a compact layer of

mycelium develops on the bark (Plate 226). The mycelium may be silver-grey, brown or black depending on the fungus involved. These patches may range in size from several inches to several yards upward on the trunk. Often black, dot-like structures emerge in this mycelial layer and produce the rain-splashed, wind-borne sexual stage of the pathogen. A tree surgeon can remove a small, contained infection, but in most cases this disease has no control, and the tree must be removed.

## Fusiform Rust on Pine

Fusiform rust has a complicated fungal life cycle that spans at least 2 years and requires two types of host plants to complete itself. *Cronartium quercuum* f. sp. *fusiforme* uses loblolly, slash and other pine species for one host and various oak species for the second.

Symptoms of fusiform rust disease are most severe on the pine hosts. Galls of various sizes are produced on twigs, branches or trunks. In moist spring weather, the gall's surface erupts into a creamy yellow spore mass (Plate 227) that is carried by the wind to new oak leaves. The newly infected oak leaves produce a late spring stage that then reinfects the oak leaves. In early summer, a sexual stage is produced which is again windborne, this time back to tender pine shoots. A pine infected in mid-summer begins a 1 to 2 year gall development period that completes the disease cycle.

Management of fusiform rust in the landscape requires detection of the problem. While damage to oaks is cosmetic, damage to pines can be serious. Trunk galls can cause trunks to snap in a strong wind, and tree removal is advised if the falling tree could cause damage. Young branch galls should be pruned out several inches below the gall if within 1 foot of the main branch or trunk. No other management is required.

## Powdery Mildews

Perhaps the easiest disease group to diagnose in the landscape is that of the powdery mildews. Caused by a group of closely related *Oidium* fungi, the disease produces a characteristic powdery white mycelial growth over leaves as well as soft shoots and buds. Powdery mildews prefer the cool, drier weather of fall through spring. Common hosts of powdery mildews (Plates 228 and 229) include azalea, *Cassia* spp., crape myrtle, dogwood, elm, hibiscus, honeysuckle, hydrangea, ixora, Jerusalem thorn (*Parkinsonia aculeata*), magnolia, oak and rose. Severe infections can curl and brown leaves as well as distort shoot growth and blooms. Powdery mildews are more severe in shady locations and may require fungicide applications.

## Fire Blight

Caused by the bacterium *Erwinia amylovora*, this disease is labelled a blight due to the rapid death of leaf and twig tissue that occurs during the cool wet spring weather that favors its growth. Fire blight is a more widespread and serious problem in the more northern temperate region of the country and in Florida affects only certain plants in the rose family, most often apple, pear, photinia, firethorn (*Pyracantha* spp.) and loquat (Plate 230). The bacteria can be spread by water splashing from the previous year's small twig infections or, during flowering, by pollinating insects. The bacteria rapidly invade leaves, flowers or soft shoots and cause a dieback with a characteristic terminal crook of dead tissue (Plate 231). The outer shoot will appear dark-brown to

black in color while the internal tissues will be a chocolate brown. Fire blight is often confused with certain fungal diebacks that occur in the spring.

Always get lab verification of fire blight before you initiate control. Avoid applications of fertilizer with readily soluble nitrogen sources. Prune 4 to 6 inches below obvious external disease symptoms. Between cuts, dip cutting tools into rubbing alcohol for 30 seconds prior to reuse.

## *Rhizoctonia* Aerial (Web) Blight

*Rhizoctonia solani* has one of the broadest host ranges of any plant pathogen. This fungus is versatile and causes seed decay, seedling damping-off, root rot, stem rot, fruit rot and, of course, a foliar blight. Conditions favoring the aerial blight phase include warm to hot summer temperatures with ample rainfall like that of the June to August rainy period in Florida. Although soilborne, the fungus is splashed up onto lower leaves by rain and irrigation water, thus initiating the disease. The fungus colonizes the lower, innermost leaves first and then moves upward and outward on the plant. Symptoms include irregular brown leaf lesions, frequent matting together of several leaves and retention of dead leaves on the plant due to attached fungal strands (Plate 232). Web blight on junipers appears as random areas of dead, scale-like leaves (Plate 233). Both old and new growth are involved.

The hyphae of *Rhizoctonia solani* (Plate 234) can be seen with the naked eye or with a magnifier of at least 10x. Common landscape plants affected by this fungus include azalea, *Carissa* spp., ferns, holly, ixora, juniper, nandina, pittosporum and Texas sage (*Leucophyllum frutescens*). At the first sign of disease, minimize the frequency of overhead irrigation. Collect and destroy diseased leaves on and below infected plants, and prune them to improve air circulation and enhance drying. Fungicides may be needed to avoid severe defoliation.

## Algal Leaf Spots

The alga *Cephaleurus virescens* is one of the more unusual plant pathogens in Florida. This algal species has the unique ability to parasitize plants causing a leaf spot on hosts as diverse as banana shrub (*Michelia figo*), camellia and magnolia in north Florida and black olive, citrus and palms in south Florida. Symptoms of this disease appear as grayish-green patches or lesions on plant leaves (Plate 235). The spots are slightly raised and can be quite numerous on foliage. Damage is primarily cosmetic unless the plant is growing in an unfavorable planting site. Infected plants growing in humid, shady areas may experience leaf loss and a reduction in vigor. Because damage is mostly cosmetic, control activities are generally not needed. The pathogen reproduces and spreads through a swimming spore stage in the wet summer months, so long range solutions include avoidance of overhead irrigation that wets the canopy and select removal of severely infected leaves before the rainy interval of summer. Pruning selectively will improve air circulation. Fungicides are not legally available nor are they particularly useful.

## *Cercospora* Leaf Spots

One of the largest genera of pathogenic fungi is the genus *Cercospora*. Many ornamental plants have at least one leaf disease caused by a *Cercospora* sp. Common landscape ornamentals affected by these fungi include azalea, dogwood, eucalyptus, ficus, ligustrum, nandina, palms, pittosporum, sweet gum and viburnum. Generally, these diseases

predominate in late summer through fall and consist of leafspots that are often maroon to purple and round (Plate 236) or angular (Plate 237). Some *Cercospora* diseases coincide with leaf senescence (Plate 238).

The spores of this pathogen are needle-like and easily windborne for long distances. The fungi persist where shrubs are planted too densely in rows or beds, are placed below drip lines from unguttered roofs or are planted in excessive shade. Such situations foster poor air circulation and slow drying of the canopy. Avoid frequent, overhead watering, especially during the early evening or at night. Fungicides can be useful only if both the surfaces and the undersides of the leaves can be treated. Appropriate spray equipment is required.

## *Entomosporium* Leaf Spots

The fungal pathogen *Entomosporium mespili* affects only certain plant genera in the rose family, specifically the genera that include loquat, photinia (Plate 239) and Indian hawthorn (Plate 240) as well apple and pear in north Florida. Although the host range is small, the damage created by this fungus in both the nursery and the landscape is severe, causing maroon-to-purple leaf spotting followed by leaf drop. The disease can be active almost year-round, with the fungus surviving on infected leaves and possibly on small bark infections on some plants. Susceptible plants should be planted in optimal growing sites only. Avoid overhead irrigation and watering cycles that occur toward evening or night. Avoid tight plant spacing and landscape areas with poor air circulation. Excessive usage of photinia or Indian hawthorn will tend to magnify the problem. Fungicides and daytime watering cycles are mandatory for satisfactory control of this plant disease.

— *Gary W. Simone*

# PROTECTING
# Plants from the Cold

Florida homeowners enjoy a vast array of plant materials. Because we often desire a tropical or semitropical appearance to our landscapes, we sometimes install plants past their northernmost limits. Tropical and subtropical plants can be used effectively in the landscape, but they must be protected or replaced when necessary. A combination of tender and hardy plants should be planted in order to prevent total devastation of the landscape by extremely cold weather.

Winter temperatures in Florida are frequently low enough to cause cold injury to tropical, subtropical and, occasionally, temperate plants not adapted to Florida climatic conditions. Tropical plants do not adapt or harden to withstand temperatures below freezing, and many are injured by temperatures below 50°F. Subtropical plants can harden or acclimate (become accustomed to a new climate) to withstand freezing temperatures. Properly conditioned temperate plants can withstand temperatures substantially below freezing. Freezing conditions occur annually in north and central Florida, while below freezing temperatures are rare for south Florida.

Freezes can be characterized as radiational or advective. **Radiational freezes or frosts** occur on calm, clear nights when heat radiates from the surfaces of objects into the environment. These surfaces can become colder than the air above them due to this rapid loss of heat or long wave radiation. When the air is moist, a radiant freeze results in deposits of ice or frost on surfaces. Dry radiational freezes leave no ice deposits but can cause freeze damage. Plant damage from a radiational freeze can be minimized by reducing radiant heat loss from plant and soil surfaces.

Although radiant heat loss occurs during an advective freeze, the conditions are quite different from a radiational freeze. **Advective freezes** occur when cold air masses moving from northern regions cause a sudden drop in temperature. Windy conditions are normal during advective freezes making plant protection difficult.

The ability of plants to withstand freezing temperatures is affected by temperature fluctuations and the lengths of the days prior to a freeze. A gradual decrease in temperature over a period of time increases the ability of plants or plant parts to withstand cold temperatures. A sudden decrease in temperature in late fall or early winter usually results in more damage than the same low temperature in January or February. Short durations of warmer temperatures in midwinter can deacclimate some plants resulting in bud break or flowering. Deacclimated plants are more prone to freeze injury.

Cold injury can occur to the entire plant or to plant parts such as fruits, flowers, buds, leaves, trunks, stems or roots. Many plant parts can adapt to tolerate cold, but fruits and roots have little ability to acclimate or develop cold tolerance. Cold injury to roots of plants in exposed containers is a common occurrence and usually is not evident until the plant is stressed by higher temperatures. Leaf and stem tissue will not survive ice formation inside the cells (the result of a rapid freeze), but many plants can adapt to tolerate ice formation between cells.

One type of winter injury is plant desiccation or drying out. This is characterized by marginal or leaf tip burn in mild cases and totally brown leaves in severe cases. Desiccation occurs when dry winds and solar radiation result in the loss of more water from the leaves than can be absorbed and/or transported by a cold or frozen root system. Root systems in the landscape are seldom frozen in Florida, but the roots of plants in small containers in north Florida can be frozen for several consecutive hours.

# What to do Before the Freeze

Homeowners can take steps to help acclimate plants to cold temperatures and to protect plants from temperature extremes. These steps range from selection of a proper planting site to alteration of cultural practices.

## Planting Site Selection

The microclimate of a location is determined by factors such as elevation, land form, surface reflectivity, soil properties, degree of canopy cover, proximity of structures or plants and the solar heat exchange. Both temperature and fluctuations in temperature can vary from one location to another, even within a residential landscape. Existing microclimates and/or possible modifications of microclimates should be considered when choosing the planting site for cold sensitive plants.

Tender plants should be planted in a site with good air drainage rather than in a low area where cold air settles. Arrange plantings, fences or other barriers to protect tender plants from cold winds and especially from advective freezes. Soils with poor water drainage can result in weak, shallow roots which are susceptible to cold injury.

## Proper Plant Nutrition

Plants grown with optimal levels and balances of nutrients will tolerate cold temperatures better and recover from injury faster than plants grown with suboptimal or imbalanced nutrition. Most established landscape plants grow well with two or three fertilizer applications per year. Applications are normally scheduled around February and October for south Florida, March and September for north Florida. A third application can be made during the summer.

A complete fertilizer with a ratio of approximately 3:1:2, 3:1:3 or 4:1:2 (e.g. 12-4-8, 15-5-15 or16-4-8, respectively) of nitrogen (N), phosphorus as $P_2O_5$ and potassium as $K_2O$ is generally recommended unless the soil test reveals that phosphorus and potassium are adequate. For each application, apply a maximum of 1 pound of nitrogen per 1000 square feet. Fall applications help with the plant's use of nutrients during the cool months. However, late fall fertilization of nutrient deficient plants or fertilization before an uncharacteristic warm period in winter can cause a late flush of new growth. New growth is more susceptible to cold injury. Therefore, fertilizer amounts are decreased in the fall because plant nutrient consumption declines during the colder season. Plants grown in colder portions of the state require one-third to one-half the standard fertilization rate in the fall, and two-thirds the standard rate should be applied in the warmer sections of Florida.

## Shading

The cover provided by tree canopies can reduce cold injury caused by radiational freezes. Plants in shaded locations usually go dormant earlier in the fall and remain dormant later in the spring. Tree canopies elevate the minimum night temperatures beneath them by reducing radiant heat loss from the ground to the atmosphere. Shading from early morning sun may decrease bark splitting on some woody plants.

Plants that thrive in light shade usually display less winter desiccation than plants in full sun. However, plants requiring sunlight that are grown in shade will be unhealthy, sparsely foliated and less tolerant of cold temperatures.

## Windbreaks

Windbreaks created by fences, buildings, temporary coverings and adjacent plantings can protect plants from cold winds and are especially helpful in reducing the effects of short-lived advective freezes and their accompanying winds. The height, density and location of a windbreak will affect the degree of wind speed reduction. Injury due to radiational freezes is influenced little by windbreaks.

## Irrigation

Watering landscape plants several hours before a freeze can help protect plants. A well-watered soil will absorb more solar radiation than dry soil and will re-radiate heat during the night. Under test conditions, this practice elevated minimum night temperatures in a canopy of citrus trees by as much as 2°F. Prolonged saturated soil conditions will, however, damage the root systems of most plants.

## Other Cultural Practices

Avoid late summer or early fall pruning which can alter the plant hormonal balance and result in growth of lateral buds. Such new growth is more susceptible to cold injury.

Healthy plants are more resistant to cold than plants weakened by disease, insect damage or nematode damage. Routine inspection for pests and implementation of necessary control measures are essential. Contact your county Extension office for information on pest identification and recommended controls. See also *Integrated Pest Management* and the sections on INSECTS AND PESTS; NEMATODES and DISEASES.

## Methods of Protection

Plants in containers can be moved into protective structures where heat can be supplied and/or trapped. Containers that must be left outdoors should be pushed together and protected by mulches to reduce heat loss from container sidewalls. Leaves of large canopy plants may be damaged if crowded together for extended periods.

Heat radiating from soil surfaces warms the air above the soil or is carried away by air currents. Radiant heat from the soil protects low-growing plants on calm cold nights but tall, open plants will receive little benefit. Radiant heat loss is reduced by mulches placed around plants to protect the roots.

Coverings placed over plants offer more protection from frost than from extreme cold. Covers that extend to the ground and are not in contact with plant foliage can lessen cold injury by reducing radiant heat loss from the plant and the ground. If foliage is in contact with the cover, it may sustain injury from the heat transfer between the foliage and the colder cover. Cloth sheets, quilts and black plastic are examples of materials that can be used for coverings. Remove plastic covers during a sunny day or otherwise provide for the escape of trapped solar radiation. When it is necessary to provide heat to ornamental plants in the landscape, a light bulb can be placed under a cover.

# What to do After the Freeze

## Water needs

A plant's water needs should be checked after a freeze. The foliage might be transpiring (losing water vapor) on a sunny day after a freeze while its water supply in the soil or container medium remains frozen. Irrigate to thaw the soil and provide available water for the plant. Soils or media with high soluble salts should not be allowed to dry because the salts would then be concentrated into a small volume of water, leaving plant roots susceptible to burn.

## Pruning

To ensure that live wood is not removed, severe pruning should be delayed until new growth appears. If a high level of maintenance is required, unsightly dead leaves may be removed as soon as they have turned brown. Cold injury may result in the absence of spring buds on part or all of the plant or as an overall weak appearance. Branch tips may be damaged while older wood is free of injury. Cold injured wood can be identified by examining the cambium layer, which is the food conducting tissue under the bark. If scratching into the bark reveals black or brown coloration, prune back to live wood which shows green when scratched. See the chapter on *Treating Cold Damaged Palms* for information on palms.

— *Thomas H. Yeager and Dewayne Ingram*

# SAFETY with Pesticides

The safe use of pesticides should be a concern of every home gardener. Pesticides include insecticides, fungicides, herbicides and nematicides. Safe handling of these toxic materials involves a combination of knowledge, common sense and the ability to follow directions. Misuse of pesticides can result in poisoning of the gardener, family members, neighbors, pets or the environment.

## Is a Pesticide Really Needed?

Home gardeners can follow many practices that will reduce the need for pesticides. Here are some of them:

- Avoid over-application of fertilizer and water, which aggravate many insect and disease problems.

- Keep the landscape free of weeds that might harbor insects and disease.

- When available, purchase plants which are resistant to disease, nematodes and insect pests.

- Use mechanical means of pest control: cultivate to control weeds, pick off insects, and destroy diseased plants.

Use biological controls when available. For example, *Bacillus thuringiensis* can control moth, butterfly and mosquito larvae. *Bacillus thuringiensis*, a naturally occurring bacterium found in soil, has been manipulated to act as a microbial insecticide on specific families of insects. This bacterium produces spores that enable it to survive in adverse environments. During the process of spore formation, *B. thuringiensis* manufactures unique crystalline bodies as a companion product. When a susceptible insect pest ingests the *B. thuringiensis*, the crystals soon

dissolve and act as a paralyzing agent in the wall of the insect's gut, disintegrating the digestive tract of the larvae. The resulting "stomach ache" prevents the larvae from further feeding on foliage. The spores then invade the insect's tissues and multiply in its blood until it dies. Death usually occurs within 1 to 5 days without further feeding. *Bacillus thuringiensis* is biodegradable and safe for humans, wildlife, the environment and many beneficial insects. See the individual product label for the name of the specific pest and rate of application.

## What Pesticide to Use

Before applying any pesticide, several questions should be answered:

- What pests or pest problems exist?

- Is the problem a disease, insect, nematode or weed?

- Is the problem serious enough to warrant pesticide treatment?

- Can the problem be corrected with a pesticide, and does it need to be?

- What is the safest pesticide to use? Remember to consider runoff potential, ground water leaching potential, chemical half-life and toxicity to non-target organisms.

- When and how should the pesticide be applied?

Many home gardeners do not know the answers to these questions. As a consequence, they may make too many pesticide applications or apply the wrong pesticides at the wrong time, in the wrong way and in the wrong amounts. This hit-or-miss method of using pesticides can do more harm than good. Improper pesticide use can endanger the environment by killing beneficial insects, poisoning wildlife and contaminating soil,

179

water and air. The hit-or-miss method can also result in the poisoning of people.

Home gardeners can obtain answers to the important pesticide questions from their county Cooperative Extension Service office or from a reputable garden center. A sample of the suspected pest and a sample or thorough description of the damage done by the pest will need to be supplied. Only when the problem is correctly identified can the appropriate treatment be recommended.

## Purchasing a Pesticide

When a decision is made that pesticides should be used, price should not be a major consideration in the selection. More important considerations are safety, ease of application and the effectiveness of the product.

Pesticide labels have signal words to inform the user of their "toxicity" or "poisonousness." Beginning with those that signify the most toxic, they are:

**DANGER—POISON.** (The words are in red and usually accompanied by a skull and crossbones symbol.) Pesticides with these signal words are not usually available to the home garden market. They are the most toxic pesticides and are intended for commercial agriculture or industrial use. Handle with extreme care.

**WARNING.** These are moderately toxic materials, but they should still be handled with care and respect.

**CAUTION.** These are slightly toxic materials that are still poisonous and should be handled accordingly.

When two or more recommended pesticides are available to control a pest problem, use the least toxic material. Pesticides labeled CAUTION are much safer to use than those labeled WARNING or DANGER—POISON.

A second consideration should be the ease with which the pesticide can be applied safely. Pesticides can be purchased in the following forms:

**Gas, vapor or mist.** Pesticides in these forms come in aerosol cans. This makes them easy to use but expensive.

**Granules.** Pesticides in this form are normally processed into particles that run from the size of fine sand to the size of rice kernels. The granules are usually incorporated into the soil to control soil insects, nematodes, diseases and germinating weeds.

**Wettable powders.** Wettable powders are dry, finely ground formulations that are mixed with water for application as a spray. Wettable powders do not dissolve in water and settle out unless constantly agitated.

**Soluble powders.** In appearance, soluble powders resemble wettable powders. However, when mixed with water, soluble powders dissolve readily and form a true solution that requires no additional agitation. Few pesticides are available in this formulation because so few active ingredients are soluble in water.

**Emulsifiable concentrates** (liquids). These pesticides are dissolved or suspended in oil bases and an emulsifier, which allows the formulation to be mixed with water.

**Dust.** This powdery form of pesticide is not usually mixed with water, but is applied only with application equipment designed to apply dusts. Sometimes the pesticide container itself is designed to apply dust.

**Baits.** A bait formulation is an active ingredient mixed with an attractive substance. The bait attracts the pest, which dies from eating the pesticide it contains.

Most pesticides can be purchased in more than one form. Normally, wettable powders or liquids are recommended for home gardeners. Most pesticides are available in these forms, and a small sprayer can then be used for application. Wettable powders or liquids are as safe as pesticides in other forms and are normally the most economical.

Pesticides frequently are available in different concentrations. A formulation with 10% active ingredient has twice the concentration as one containing 5% active ingredient. To determine value, a gardener must look at both concentration and quantity of active ingredient to get the best buy.

A frequent error that home gardeners make is to purchase too much product. Do not purchase more than you will use in one season. Some pesticide products deteriorate with time. Moreover, excess products create safety problems in storage and disposal.

Before purchasing any pesticide, know what is needed. Read the labels. Will the product do the job? Is it the safest product to apply? Do you have the proper application equipment? Can it be used on the ornamental plants, garden crops or other sites you need to use it on? These should be major considerations.

When a pesticide has been purchased, handle it with care to prevent accidental spills. Never transport a pesticide with food products or in the passenger area of a car.

## Storage of Pesticides

Pesticides should be stored in a dry, well-ventilated location and securely locked away to prevent children, unauthorized adults, pets and livestock from accidentally coming in contact with the materials. Only adults experienced in using pesticides should have access to this area. A secure wood or metal cabinet or closet will serve the purpose. Other toxic household chemicals, sprayers, dusters, fertilizers and other garden equipment could also be stored in this area, but do not store personal protective equipment or food products in this area. They could become contaminated.

Always store pesticides in their original containers, never in unmarked containers or containers which have held food or drink. When storing pesticides, always place dry products above liquid products. Clean up any spills immediately. Vermiculite, oil absorbents and even "kitty litter" can be used to soak up liquid spills. Finally, follow all directions on the pesticide label for storage and handling of spills.

## Personal Protective Equipment

Always read the label to determine the personal protective equipment required when working with a particular pesticide. Then wear it! Keep pesticide residues off skin and out of eyes, nose and mouth.

Always wear, as a minimum, a long-sleeved shirt and long pants. Cover feet completely (i.e. never wear sandals). The pesticide label may also specify additional items like waterproof gloves, hats and extra footwear. Sleeves should be worn **over** gloves, when sprays are directed downwards, and trousers **over** footwear. Do not use leather products, since they tend to absorb and retain pesticides. Even hatbands should be made of cloth or plastic. Disposable clothing for application of pesticides is also available. Check with a garden center or safety supply store for these products.

Other protective equipment might include goggles or a face shield and a respirator (along with the proper clean filter pads or cartridges) approved by the National Institute for Occupational Health and Safety (NIOSH). NIOSH is a governmental agency which tests and approves protective equipment. Look for safety equipment approved by NIOSH and read the labels to make sure the equipment is specifically approved for the intended use.

After each pesticide application, use warm, soapy water and wash the goggles, face shield, respirator (but not the filter pads or cartridges) and other waterproof equipment. Then rinse in clear water. Air-dry these items and store them away from pesticides.

All washable clothing should be washed immediately in hot water, using a strong detergent. Thoroughly rinse the clean clothing and air-dry. Do not wash other clothing with the clothing worn while applying pesticides.

One more important practice: Immediately after removing and cleaning personal protective equipment and placing clothing in a washer, take a hot shower. Use plenty of soap and wash your hair. Don't wait until after you have finished other landscape work! Make pesticide application the last garden task of the day.

## Mixing and Applying Pesticides

Remember, always read the pesticide label and understand it. The pesticide used should be the safest product for the pest problem, and proper personal protective equipment should be worn. Now inspect the sprayer, duster or spreader. See that it is functioning properly. There should be no loose or leaking hoses and connections. The cover gasket on a sprayer must fit securely.

For home garden spraying, a 1 to 3 gallon hand-carried sprayer is recommended. Partially fill the sprayer with water, and test it to make sure that the nozzle is not clogged. Make sure that there are no leaks and that the tank holds pressure.

Backpack sprayers are not recommended. They have been known to leak without the operator's knowledge, resulting in the poisoning of the operator. Hose-end sprayers, while economical and easy to use, are difficult to calibrate, and excessive application of pesticides is common with them.

Mixing is the most dangerous pesticide activity. This is the time you are working with the concentrated material. Know the symptoms of poisoning, first aid recommendations and how to get appropriate medical assistance.

Have soap, towels, water hose and other necessary supplies available in case of a spill or other accident. Never eat, drink or smoke while handling pesticides. Always mix the pesticide exactly as recommended on the label. Mix the pesticide and fill sprayer in a well-ventilated, adequately lighted area. Do this on a concrete floor to facilitate easy cleanup of any spills. Never mix more pesticide than needed. There is no good way to dispose of excess pesticide materials.

When applying a pesticide, never apply more than the recommended amount. Any application of a pesticide in a manner not consistent with its labeling is a violation of the law. In addition, improper application can result in damage to plants.

If a respirator is needed, be sure that it is working properly. If you can smell or taste any pesticide, check the respirator and correct the problem. The fit may be wrong, the filter may be saturated, or it may be the wrong type. Few home garden products require use of a respirator. If one is needed, a dust/mist respirator is usually the type required.

Keep humans and pets away. Do not apply pesticides when air currents will carry the pesticide into other areas. Pesticides should be applied when the air is still.

Maintain accurate records of all pesticides used: name, registration number, amount, date applied, and the plant and pest treated. Read the label. It is recommended that children and pets be kept away from treated areas. Only a fenced yard can keep un-wanted children and pets from entering. Follow the restrictions on the use of food products which have been treated. Heed all instructions.

Read the label to see how long people and animals should be kept off or out of treated areas. If no time is specified, keep them out or off at least until the sprays have thoroughly dried. If the pesticide was ap-plied to a food crop, check the label to see how long to wait before harvesting. Read the label for this information before applying the pesticide.

## Cleanup/Disposal of Pesticides and Pesticide Containers

If pesticide remains in the tank after a spray job is complete, you should use it up. Spray it out on **other** crops or sites listed on the pesticide label. (Putting more pesticide than recommended on the target plant can cause plant damage.) However, a better approach is never to mix more material than needed. There is no good way to dispose of excess spray materials. Dusts and granules can be saved for the next application, but not a liquid material.

Never pour pesticides down a drain. The pesticide could stop the bacterial action in a septic tank and create additional problems, or it could contaminate a municipal sewage system, surface water or ground water. Pouring pesticides in a storm sewer also leads to environmental contamination.

Thoroughly clean the pesticide applicator. A dust applicator or granular spreader can corrode rapidly if pesticide residue remains in it. Sprayers should be rinsed three times, and a portion of the rinse material should be sprayed through the nozzle. A small amount of detergent in the first rinse will help remove any residue. This is particularly important if you have been applying an oil-based pesticide or herbicide. You would not want any herbicide residue to remain in the sprayer, since the next use of the sprayer may be an application of an insecticide on a plant which is susceptible to minute am-ounts of the herbicide. For this reason, many home gardeners have two sprayers, one for herbicides and the second for insecticides.

Once the sprayer is clean, disassemble the nozzle, remove the tank cover, make certain the hose and spray mechanism is drained, and allow the sprayer to air-dry. When it is dry, reassemble the sprayer, and store it in a clean, dry location.

Proper disposal of empty pesticide contain-ers is equally important. Paper or cardboard containers should be shaken and inspected to remove all pesticide materials. If the container has a plastic liner, rinse the con-tainer three times.

Empty liquid containers should also be triple-rinsed. Allow the container to drain into a spray tank for 30 seconds. Fill the container one-fourth to one-third full of rinse, secure the cover, then shake and pour out the rinse material, again allowing the container to drain for 30 seconds. Repeat two more times. All rinse material should be poured into the spray tank and then used up, as if it were pesticide. Once rinsed, plastic and cardboard containers should be punctured several times in order to prevent them from being used again.

Some Florida counties offer a special service for the collection and safe disposal of unused or unwanted pesticides. Once empty and properly rinsed, garden pesticide containers can be disposed of at appropriate sanitary landfills. Place punctured plastic containers in the garbage can just prior to collection to prevent them from being taken and used for other purposes.

## Pesticide Accidents and First Aid

Know the symptoms of pesticide poisoning. The first symptoms to appear include:

> Fatigue
>
> Excessive sweating or salivating
>
> Headache
>
> Nausea, vomiting
>
> Dizziness
>
> Stomach cramps
>
> Blurred vision
>
> Diarrhea

Don't wait for the more severe symptoms of pesticide poisoning to occur. These symptoms include:

> Difficulty in walking
>
> Muscle twitching
>
> Weakness
>
> Secretions from mouth
>
> Chest pains
>
> Difficulty in breathing
>
> Dilated pupils
>
> Unconsciousness, coma, death

Some pesticides may irritate the nasal passages. Exposure to others may cause inflammation of the skin. Labels for such products contain instructions for wearing protective clothing or following certain practices to help prevent this from occurring.

If you do have a pesticide accident, basic first-aid practices should be followed:

**Pesticide on the clothes and skin**. Remove clothes at once. Rinse the skin immediately with clean, cool water, then wash with large amounts of soap and water.

**Pesticide in the eyes**. Flush the eyes immediately with clean cool water, and continue for at least 15 minutes. A garden hose with low water pressure works fine.

**Pesticide has been swallowed**. Read the label to determine if vomiting should be induced. Never attempt to induce vomiting in an unconscious or convulsing victim.

**Pesticide inhalation**. Get victim into fresh air immediately. Open doors and windows. Loosen victim's clothing. If the victim is not breathing, take steps to resuscitate at once.

In all cases of pesticide poisoning obtain medical advice and treatment as rapidly as possible. The pesticide label should be given to the medical team or physician. Do not transport the pesticide container inside the passenger compartment of a vehicle. Never permit a victim of pesticide poisoning to drive, since dizziness or drowsiness can occur with little or no warning.

## The Keys to Pesticide Safety

- **Stop and read the label** before using a pesticide.

- Use pesticides only as a last resort.

- Purchase the safest pesticide for the problem.

- Purchase or mix only needed amount of pesticide.

- Store pesticides securely.

- Wear proper personal protective equipment.

- Prevent drift/contamination during application.

- Clean up and wash up immediately.

- Dispose of pesticide containers properly.

- Get medical help immediately for all exposures.

— *O. Norman Nesheim and Michael Aerts*

# KEEPING Cool

Working on a Florida landscape means working in the heat. The same sunshine which makes living in the south so special can become dangerous to people working outdoors. With heat and humidity comes heat stress, one of the serious health problems of those who spend hours outdoors. Heat cramps, heat exhaustion and heat stroke, as well as sunburn and safety problems, may be caused by exposure to Florida's sun. All of these problems may be avoided, however, by using common sense and recognizing early warning signals.

## When It's Hot, Play It Cool

When we get too hot or too thirsty, we become irritable, frustrated, impatient and careless. We begin to hurry, our ability to think clearly evaporates, and serious accidents can happen. These problems are more common when individuals are not conditioned to working under the hot, humid conditions of a Florida summer. Fortunately, the human body has the ability to adjust to hot weather within a week or two.

The National Institute for Occupational Safety and Health (NIOSH) recommends that those not conditioned to strenuous activity in hot, humid weather limit their exposure to no more than 2 hours per day for the first week. This time can gradually increase to half- and then full-time activity over the next couple of weeks. This allows the body's temperature control mechanism to adjust gradually. Without a gradual acclimation to the heat, we are vulnerable to heat-induced medical problems.

The major health problem caused by working under hot conditions is dehydration, the loss of body fluids through perspiration. Energetic activity on hot days can cause the body to lose 1 to 1 1/2 quarts of fluid per hour. If this continues for a few hours, as much as 2 to 6% of body weight may be lost.

**Heat cramps** are the first and least severe sign of heat stress. Caused by loss of fluids, these painful muscle spasms in the legs and abdomen should be regarded as a warning of possible heat related injury.

Continued strenuous activity may lead to **heat exhaustion**, a condition which occurs when the body's cooling system fails. Loss of fluids decreases blood circulation. This leads to extreme discomfort and thirst, along with an increase in body temperature and a rapid pulse. Pale, clammy skin, dizziness, headaches, excessive sweating and a feeling of weakness are symptoms of heat exhaustion; heat cramps may accompany this condition.

Left untreated, heat exhaustion can lead to **heat stroke**, a potentially fatal condition.

Heat stroke is a true emergency which occurs when the body stops perspiring and the body temperature increases rapidly. Common symptoms include red, hot, dry skin, rapid pulse and rapid, shallow breathing. Convulsions, loss of consciousness and death become very real possibilities without proper and immediate treatment.

## First Aid and the Prevention of Heat Related Illness

The primary goal in aiding a victim of a heat-related illness is to cool the victim as quickly as possible and restore fluid balance. **Heat cramps** may be treated by having the victim lie in a cool place. Provide cool water or a sports drink, and lightly massage and stretch the affected muscles. The victim may resume activity when cramps stop and other symptoms disappear, but be sure to maintain adequate fluid intake.

The treatment of **heat exhaustion** and **heat stroke** are similar. Get the victim out of the heat. Loosen any tight clothing, and remove clothing which is soaked with perspiration. Apply cool, wet cloths to the skin; DO NOT apply rubbing alcohol. Allow conscious victims to drink slowly. Watch the victim closely, and do not allow normal activity to resume the same day.

If the victim refuses water, vomits or begins to lose consciousness, call an ambulance. While waiting for help to arrive, continue to cool the body any way you can. Use cold packs if they are available, sponge bare skin with cold water, or place the victim in a tub of cool water.

The best way to treat heat-related illnesses is to prevent them. Recognize the early symptoms, and follow simple precautions. Avoid working during the hottest part of the day from 10 a.m. to 3 p.m. Fight dehydra-tion; take a short break every half hour and drink 10 to 12 ounces of water, even if you do not feel thirsty. Include sodium-rich beverages such as sports drinks and tomato juice. Refrain from drinking alcoholic beverages.

When working outside, wear lightweight, light-colored, loose-fitting cotton clothes as well as long-sleeved shirts and pants. Initially, you may feel cooler in sleeveless tops and shorts, but under a hot sun your body temperature will increase more rapidly. Protect yourself from sunburn and the possibility of skin cancer as well. Wear a sunblock, a wide-brimmed hat, and keep your neck covered. Remember that the sun's rays can still burn on cloudy days and during the cool days of winter.

The foods we eat also influence body temperature. Hot foods add directly to body heat. Heavy meals also reduce the body's ability to get rid of heat. Keep the noon meal light and cool.

In summary, when it is hot:

Take frequent breaks, and allow your pulse to return to normal.

Drink lots of cool water, 10 to 12 ounces each half hour. Keep meals light and cool.

Wear cool, light-colored, loose-fitting clothing. Protect yourself from the sun's harmful rays with a wide-brimmed hat and sunblock.

Save the most strenuous work for the cooler hours of the day.

Know the symptoms of heat stress. At the first sign of heat stress, move to a cooler location, drink plenty of water and rest. Know and respect your limitations and capabilities. When it's hot, play it cool!

*— Carol J. Lehtola, William J. Becker and William G. Griswold*

## The University of Florida's IFAS and Cooperative Extension Service/ Resources and Services

Though this handbook covers basic landscaping principles and provides general guidelines for planning and caring for a Florida home landscape, you are almost certain eventually to encounter a problem or difficulty not discussed in these pages. Florida's plant life is remarkably diverse and so are the pests and diseases that can affect plants. Climates vary from one part of the state to the next, and within a given zone, micro-climates exist. A landscape's soil frequently has an inherent problem or deficiency or one that is due to the effects and methods of development in the area. In many parts of the state, the cost or availability of water for irrigation purposes may heavily affect landscaping decisions. No single reference book can hope to address all the variables that, separately or together, influence the design, maintenance and health of your home landscape. For certain problems, you will need the assistance of an expert.

If you are fortunate enough to have a local nursery staffed by personnel who know and take good care of their plants, you will probably find them to be not only an excellent source for plants adapted to the area but also a storehouse of information on growing conditions in your locale. Whether or not this is the case, you can still get expert assistance from your county Extension office and, in many instances, from one of the other services, clinics or laboratories of the Institute of Food and Agricultural Services (IFAS) of the University of Florida. Descriptions and listings of the various services follow.

## The Cooperative Extension Service

Before contacting the services, clinics or laboratories shown in the listings for IFAS at the University of Florida, please call your county Extension office. Your Extension agent may have information or publications that will resolve your problem and, if not, he or she will know about the forms, fees and samples that you will need to submit. Extension agents can also verify that you are making the correct contact at IFAS.

Your county Extension office is a great source for information about the plants and growing conditions in your vicinity. Additionally, many of the Extension offices select, train and certify volunteers as Master Gardeners. As "payment" for the horticultural training they receive, Master Gardeners perform various services for the Extension Service. Primarily, they handle general information and answer questions the Extension office receives from home gardeners.

Established in Florida in 1915 and directed by IFAS at the University of Florida, the Cooperative Extension Service has offices in every Florida county. The Extension Service is supported cooperatively by the U.S. Department of Agriculture as well as state and county governments.

## County Cooperative Extension Service Offices

**Alachua**
2800 N.E. 39th Ave.
Gainesville, FL 32609-2658

**Baker**
Rt. 3, Box 1074-B
Macclenny, FL 32063-9640

**Bay**
2234 E. 15th St.
Panama City, FL 32405-6096

**Bradford**
2266 N. Temple Ave.
Starke, FL 32091-1028

**Brevard**
3695 Lake Drive
Cocoa, FL 32926-8699

**Broward**
3245 College Ave.
Davie, FL 33314-7798

**Calhoun**
340 E. Central Ave.
Blountstown, FL 32424-2206

**Charlotte**
6900 Florida St.
Punta Gorda, FL 33950-5799

**Citrus**
3600 S. Florida Ave.
Inverness, FL 34450-7369

**Clay**
2463 State Road 16 W.
P.O. Box 278
Green Cove Springs, FL 32043-0278

**Collier**
14700 Immokalee Rd.
Naples, FL 34120-1468

**Columbia**
P.O. Box 1587
Lake City, FL 32056-1587

**Dade**
18710 S.W. 288th St.
Homestead, FL 33030-2309

**DeSoto**
P.O. Box 310
Arcadia, FL 34265-0310

**Dixie**
P.O. Box 640
Cross City, FL 32628-1534

**Duval**
1010 N. McDuff Ave.
Jacksonville, FL 32254-2083

**Escambia**
3740 Stefani Rd.
Cantonment, FL 32533-7792

**Flagler**
150 Sawgrass Rd.
Bunnell, FL 32110-9503

**Franklin**
33 Market St., Suite 305
Apalachicola, FL 32320-2310

**Gadsden**
2140 W. Jefferson St.
Quincy, FL 32351-1905

**Gilchrist**
P.O. Box 157
Trenton, FL 32693-0157

**Glades**
P.O. Box 549
Moore Haven, FL 33471-0549

**Gulf**
200 E. 2nd St.
P.O. Box 250
Wewahitchka, FL 32465-0250

**Hamilton**
P.O. Drawer K
Jasper, FL 32052-0691

**Hardee**
507 Civic Center Dr.
Wauchula, FL 33873-9460

**Hendry**
P.O. Box 68
Labelle, FL 33975-0068

**Hernando**
19490 Oliver St.
Brooksville, FL 34601-6538

**Highlands**
4509 W. George Blvd.
Sebring, FL 33872-5803

**Hillsborough**
5339 County Road 579 South
Seffner, FL 33584-3334

**Holmes**
201 N. Oklahoma St.
Bonifay, FL 32425-2295

**Indian River**
1028 20th Place, Suite D
Vero Beach, FL 32960-5360

**Jackson**
2741 Pennsylvania Ave., Suite 3
Marianna, FL 32448-4014

**Jefferson**
275 N. Mulberry St.
Monticello, FL 32344-2249

**Lafayette**
Rt. 3, Box 15
Mayo, FL 32066-1901

**Lake**
30205 State Road 19
Tavares, FL 32778-4052

**Lee**
3406 Palm Beach Blvd.
Ft. Myers, FL 33916-3719

**Leon**
615 Paul Russell Road
Tallahassee, FL 32301-7099

**Levy**
P.O. Box 219
Bronson, FL 32621-0219

**Liberty**
P.O. Box 369
Bristol, FL 32321-0368

**Madison**
900 College Ave.
Madison, FL 32340-1426

**Manatee**
1303 17th St. W.
Palmetto, FL 34221-2998

**Marion**
2232 N.E. Jacksonville Rd.
Ocala, FL 34470-3685

**Martin**
2614 S.E. Dixie Hwy.
Stuart, FL 34996-4007

**Monroe**
5100 College Rd.
Key West, FL 33040-4364

**Nassau**
P.O. Box 1550
Callahan, FL 32011-1550

**Okaloosa**
5479 Old Bethel Rd.
Crestview, FL 32536-5513

**Okeechobee**
458 Hwy. 98 North
Okeechobee, FL 34972-2303

**Orange**
2350 E. Michigan St.
Orlando, FL 32806-4996

**Osceola**
1901 E. Irlo Bronson Hwy.
Kissimmee, FL 34744-8947

**Palm Beach**
559 N. Military Trail
West Palm Beach, FL 33415-1311

**Pasco**
36702 State Road 52
Dade City, FL 33525-5198

**Pinellas**
12175 125th St. N.
Largo, FL 33774-3695

**Polk**
Drawer HS03
Bartow, FL 33831-9005

**Putnam**
111 Yelvington Rd., Suite 1
East Palatka, FL 32131-8892

**St. Johns**
3125 Agriculture Center Dr.
St. Augustine, FL 32092-0572

**St. Lucie**
8400 Picos Rd., Suite 101
Ft. Pierce, FL 34945-3045

**Santa Rosa**
6051 Old Bagdad Hwy., Rm. 116
Milton, FL 32583-8944

**Sarasota**
2900 Ringling Blvd.
Sarasota, FL 34237-5397

**Seminole**
250 W. County Home Rd.
Sanford, FL 32773-6197

**Sumter**
P.O. Box 218
Bushnell, FL 33513-0218

**Suwannee**
1302 11th St., S.W.
Live Oak, FL 32060-3696

**Taylor**
203 Forest Park Dr.
Perry, FL 32347-6396

**Union**
35 N.E. 1st St.
Lake Butler, FL 32054-0701

**Volusia**
3100 E. New York Ave.
DeLand, FL 32724-6497

**Wakulla**
84 Cedar Ave.
Crawfordville, FL 32327-2063

**Walton**
732 North 9th St., Suite B
DeFuniak Springs, FL 32433-3804

**Washington**
1424 W. Jackson Ave., Suite A
Chipley, FL 32428

## The University of Florida's IFAS

In 1862, the United States Congress passed the Morrill Act, which established colleges in each state to be financed through grants of land from the federal government. These land grant colleges were to emphasize teaching practical subjects such as agriculture and home economics. Then in 1887, the Hatch Act provided for experimental stations at land grant colleges to conduct research for those colleges' agricultural problems. A second Morrill Act, in 1890, established land grant universities for minorities. To facilitate cooperative work between the U.S. Department of Agriculture and the land grant colleges, the Smith-Lever Act of 1914 established the Cooperative Extension Service, which began to serve in Florida in 1915.

The University of Florida in Gainesville and Florida A & M University in Tallahassee are Florida's land grant colleges and together coordinate work on several programs. The University of Florida's Institute of Food and Agricultural Sciences, known as IFAS, directs Extension Service efforts in all 67 Florida counties; Florida A & M University also conducts a number of Extension programs. In addition to Extension activities, IFAS is both a teaching and research institute offering a broad range of services in the fields of food, agriculture, natural resources, environmental science and aspects of veterinary medicine. Funding comes from various government agencies, grant support and private sources.

## IFAS Resources and Services

Because many of the following services require you to submit certain forms, specimens and/or nominal fees, contact your county Extension agent first. The agent will have forms and other information, including current telephone numbers. For reference purposes, a mailing address and brief description of the various services available through IFAS is provided below.

## Florida Extension Plant Disease Clinic Network (FEPDC)

Sometimes plant ailments cannot be attributed to incorrect management or insect pests. Bacteria, fungi and viruses are infectious agents that can also cause disease; the FEPDC can determine if one of these agents is involved in the plant's disorder.

The FEPDC network consists of a core laboratory located on the University of Florida campus in Gainesville and three regional diagnostic laboratories located in Quincy (North Florida Research & Education Center), Immokalee (Southwest Research & Education Center) and Homestead (Tropical Research & Education Center).

The mailing address for the FEPDC core laboratory is:

**Florida Extension Plant Disease Clinic**
Building 78, Mowry Road
P.O. Box 110830
University of Florida
Gainesville, FL 32611-0830

The addresses for the three regional diagnostic laboratories are:

**North Florida Research & Education Center**
Route 3, Box 4370
Quincy, FL 32351-9500

**Southwest Florida Research & Education Center**
2686 State Road 29 North
Immokalee, FL 34142-9515

**Tropical Research & Education Center**
18905 S.W. 280th St.
Homestead, FL 33031-3314

## Insect Identification Service

Of the thousands of species of insects in Florida, some are harmful, and many are beneficial. A large number of insects are difficult to identify even under optimal conditions. An effective recommendation for control, if needed, can be made only if the insect is correctly identified.

The Department of Entomology and Nematology of IFAS provides an Insect Identification Service which will promptly identify insects as far as genus or to the degree that permits management recommendations to be made with little delay. (The degree to which identity is determined depends both on the quality of the sample and on how common the insect is.)

For more details or for questions about the Insect Identification Service, contact:

**Insect Identification Service**
Building 970
P.O. Box 110620
University of Florida
Gainesville, FL 32611-0620

## Nematode Assay Laboratory

The Florida Nematode Assay Laboratory, provided by the Department of Entomology and Nematology of IFAS, determines the identity (to genus) and number of each kind of plant parasitic nematode recovered from the sample you submit. These results and the appropriate management recommendations will be written on a *Nematode Assay Record Form*. You, your county Extension agent and any outside consultants or experts that are involved will each be sent a copy of this form no later than 10 working days after the laboratory receives the sample.

In some instances, selecting the best management program requires identifying the species (rather than just the genus) of nematode. Two to three months additional time may be needed to culture the organism in question. When such a delay is required, the normal report will still be returned within 10 days of receiving the sample, and a supplementary report will be provided when final results are available.

The contents and quality of the sample you submit are crucial. Your Extension agent should be able to supply you with a kit and instructions for collecting your sample, however if you find you need further information about collecting and submitting samples or the functions of the Laboratory, please contact:

**Biological Scientist**
**Nematode Assay Laboratory**
Building 78, PO Box 110820
University of Florida
Gainesville, FL 32611-0820

The Biological Scientist can also refer you to the Extension Nematologist if you need assistance interpreting assay results.

## Extension Soil Testing Laboratory (ESTL)

The Soil and Water Science Department of IFAS provides soil and water testing through the Extension Soil Testing Laboratory. To obtain information on types of tests, sample collection and the nominal fees involved, contact your county Extension agent. The agent will provide you with sample information sheets, soil sample bags, mailing kits, supporting literature and assistance in interpreting the results, when you receive them.

The ESTL mailing address is:

**Extension Soil Testing Laboratory**
631 Wallace Building, Box 110740
University of Florida
Gainesville, FL 32611-0740

## IFAS Publications

IFAS uses a variety of media to publish information on a wide range of topics of both specialized and general interest. Your county Extension agent should be able to provide you with the *Catalog of Publications, Software, Videos, and Other Media* published by IFAS Publications. The catalogue includes printed materials, computer software, CDs and videos that are for sale. In many cases, your local Extension office will either order or have on hand free publications that pertain to landscaping issues in your area.

IFAS Publications handles orders for and questions about catalogs and publications but does not provide landscaping information or advice. Instructions for ordering and paying for publications are included in the catalog. If not available from your Extension agent, the *Catalog of Publications, Software, Videos, and Other Media* can be ordered free of charge from the following address:

**IFAS Publications**
PO Box 110011
University of Florida
Gainesville, FL 32611-0011

**Plate 1.** Freshly dug root ball of a single stemmed palm.

**Plate 3.** Nitrogen deficiency (right) on bamboo palm.

**Plate 2.** Proper support for a newly installed palm.

**Plate 5.** Later stages of potassium deficiency showing marginal necrosis on coconut palm.

**Plate 4.** Early flecking stage of potassium deficiency on princess palm.

**Plate 6.** Potassium deficiency of spindle palm showing frizzling of older leaves.

**Plate 7.** Potassium deficiency on pygmy date palm.

**Plate 9.** Early stages of manganese deficiency on Paurotis palm.

**Plate 8.** Magnesium deficiency on Canary Island date palm.

**Plate 11.** Manganese deficiency on coconut palm showing scorched new leaves.

**Plate 10.** Frizzletop caused by manganese deficiency on queen palm.

**Plate 12.** Severe iron deficiency (left) on young queen palm.

**Plate 13.** Early stages of iron deficiency on queen palm.

**Plate 14.** Palm aphid.

**Plate 15.** Coconut mite damage.

**Plate 16.** Royal palm bug.

**Plate 18.** Palmetto weevils.

**Plate 17.** Royal palm bug damage.

**Plate 19.** Palmetto weevil larvae.

**Plate 20.** Palmetto weevil damage.

**Plate 21.** *Helminthosporium*-complex leaf spot.

**Plate 23.** *Phytophthora* bud rot.

**Plate 22.** *Graphiola* leaf spot or false smut.

**Plate 24.** *Ganoderma* bracket or "conch."

**Plate 25.** Symptoms of lethal yellowing.

**Plate 26.** Trunk splitting or cracking.

**Plate 27.** Lightning damage on palm.

**Plate 28.** Scale insects on a stem.

**Plate 29.** Leaves infected with scale insects.

**Plate 30.** Branch covered with scale insects.

**Plate 31.** Open wound on plant stem.

**Plate 32.** Sliding container off root ball.

**Plate 33.** Pot-bound plant.

**Plate 34.** Recently repotted plant.

**Plate 35.** Plant with black roots on root ball.

**Plate 36.** Plant with escaping roots.

**Plate 37.** Plant with obvious weed problems.

**Plate 38.** Magnesium deficiency on *Podocarpus nagi*.

**Plate 39.** Manganese deficiency on sago palm.

**Plate 40.** Sulfur deficiency on queen palm.

**Plate 41.** Boron deficiency on *Philodendron* spp.

**Plate 42.** Calcium deficiency on sandankwa viburnum.

**Plate 43.** Copper deficiency on ligustrum.

**Plate 44.** Iron deficiency on Formosa sweet gum.

**Plate 46.** Magnesium deficiency on althaea.

**Plate 45.** Iron deficiency on St. Thomas orchid tree.

**Plate 48.** Manganese deficiency on ixora.

**Plate 47.** Manganese deficiency on gardenia.

**Plate 49.** Normal hibiscus shoot (left). Symptoms of severe molybdenum deficiency (right).

**Plate 50.** Nitrogen deficiency on *Rhododendron* spp.

**Plate 51.** Potassium deficiency on black olive.

**Plate 52.** Potassium deficiency on orchid tree.

**Plate 54.** Results of improper pruning.

**Plate 53.** Zinc deficiency on dogwood.

**Plate 55.** Goosegrass.

**Plate 56.** Florida betony with tubers. Tubers grow underground and are edible.

**Plate 57.** Florida pusley.

**Plate 58.** Henbit.

**Plate 60.**
Spotted spurge
or milk purslane.

**Plate 59.**
Woodsorrel.

**Plate 61.** Chamberbitter or leafflower.

**Plate 62.** Long-stalked phyllanthus.

**Plate 63.** Globe sedge (left), yellow nutsedge (center) & purple nutsedge (right).

**Plate 64.** Smilax or greenbriar.

**Plate 65.** Ambush bug.

**Plate 66.** Amphipods.

**Plate 67.** Florida carpenter ant.

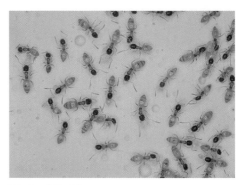

**Plate 68.** Ghost ants.

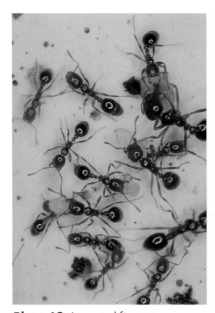

**Plate 69.** Imported fire ant.

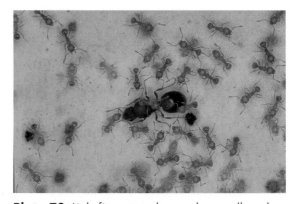

**Plate 70.** Little fire ant workers and queen (large).

**Plate 72.** Aphids.

**Plate 71.** Native fire ants: major worker (large) surrounded by workers.

**Plate 73.** Aphid damage.

**Plate 74.** Assassin bug.

**Plate 75.** Assassin bug nymph.

**Plate 76.** Assassin bug (wheel bug).

**Plate 77.** Caterpillar with pathogenic fungus.

**Plate 78.** Mole cricket with fungus (*Metarhizium*).

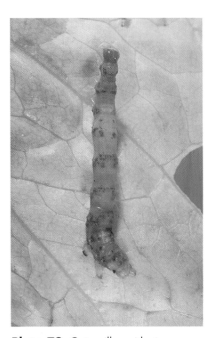

**Plate 79.** Caterpillar with virus.

**Plate 80.** Big-eyed bug.

**Plate 82.** Ips bark beetle pitch tubes.

**Plate 81.** Booklouse.

**Plate 84.** Sap flow at entry hole of red oak borer.

**Plate 83.** Dogwood twig borer damage.

**Plate 85.** Broad or cyclamen mite damage.

**Plate 86.** Bumble bee.

**Plate 87.** Azalea caterpillar.

**Plate 88.** Bagworm caterpillar sack.

**Plate 89.** Buckmoth caterpillar.

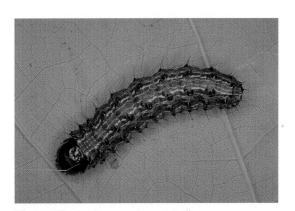

**Plate 90.** Cabbage palm caterpillar.

**Plate 91.** Eastern tent caterpillar.

**Plate 92.** Eastern tent caterpillar tent.

**Plate 93.** Fall webworm.

**Plate 94.** Fall webworm web.

**Plate 95.** Young flannel moth caterpillar.

**Plate 96.** Mature flannel moth caterpillar.

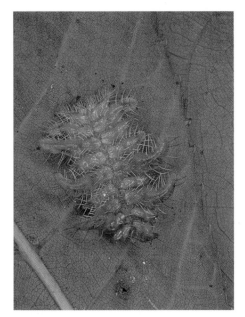

**Plate 97.** Hag caterpillar.

**Plate 98.** Io moth caterpillar.

**Plate 100.** Palm leaf skeletonizer damage.

**Plate 99.** Oleander caterpillar.

**Plate 101.** Mature puss caterpillar.

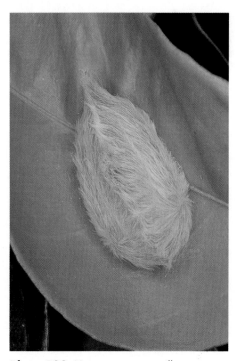

**Plate 102.** Young puss caterpillar.

**Plate 103.** Saddleback caterpillar.

**Plate 104.** Spiny oak-slug caterpillar.

**Plate 105.** Tussock moth caterpillar.

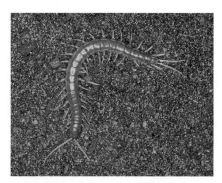

**Plate 106.** Centipede.

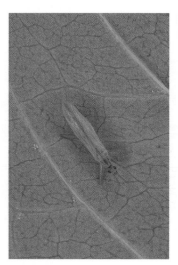

**Plate 108.** Damsel bug.

**Plate 107.** Cicada killer.

**Plate 109.** Damselfly.

**Plate 110.** Dragonfly.

**Plate 111.** Earwig.

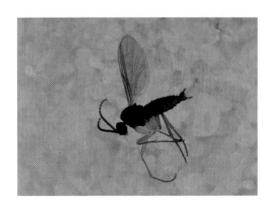

**Plate 112.** Fungus gnat.

**Plate 114.** Goudy oak gall.

**Plate 113.** Horned oak gall.

**Plate 115.** Oak apple gall.

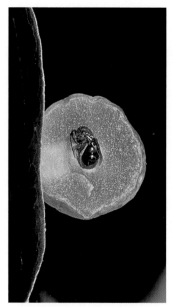

**Plate 116.** Gall wasp inside oak apple gall.

**Plate 117.** Gall formed by *Phytophagia wellsi*.

**Plate 118.** Hickory midge fly gall.

**Plate 119.** Roly-poly oak gall.

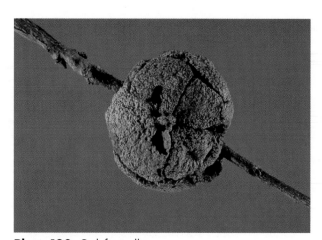

**Plate 120.** Oak fig gall.

**Plate 121.** *Phylloxera* gall on wild grape.

**Plate 122.** *Psyllid* gall on red bay.

**Plate 123.** Ground beetle.

**Plate 124.** Honey bee.

**Plate 126.** Lacebug.

**Plate 125.** Honey bee swarm.

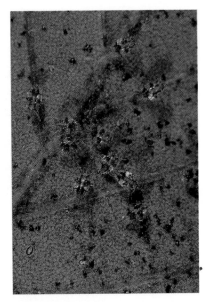

**Plate 127.** Lacebug nymphs.

**Plate 128.** Lacebug damage.

**Plate 129.** Lacewing.

**Plate 130.** Lacewing larva.

**Plate 131.** Brown lacewing.

**Plate 132.**
Lacewing (trash bug).

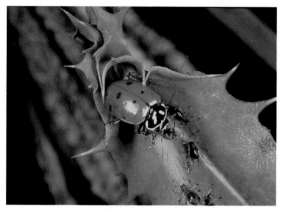

**Plate 133.** Lady beetle.

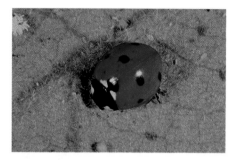

**Plate 134.** Lady beetle.

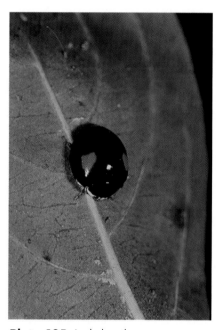

**Plate 135.** Lady beetle.

**Plate 136.** Lady beetle larva (early stage).

**Plate 137.** Lady beetle larva.

**Plate 138.** Serpentine leafminer damage.

**Plate 139.** Long-legged fly.

**Plate 140.** Mealybug.

**Plate 141.** Mealybug with filaments.

**Plate 142.** Mealybugs congregating.

**Plate 144.**
Minute pirate bug.

**Plate 143.** Millipede.

**Plate 146.** Pillbug.

**Plate 145.** Parasitic nematodes on mole cricket.

**Plate 147.** Plaster beetle.

**Plate 148.** Praying mantid.

**Plate 149.** Predaceous mite.

**Plate 150.** Psocid.

**Plate 151.** Robber fly (many robber flies mimic bees and wasps).

**Plate 152.** Tea scale.

**Plate 153.** Tea scale damage.

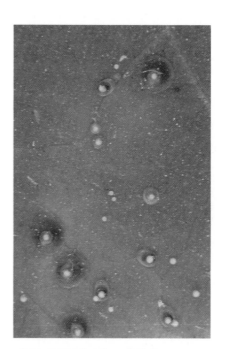

**Plate 154.** Florida red scale.

**Plate 155.** False oleander scale.

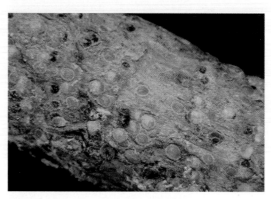

**Plate 156.** Oleander pit scale.

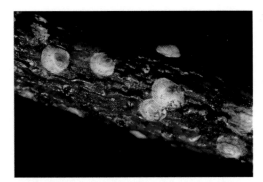

**Plate 157.** White peach scale.

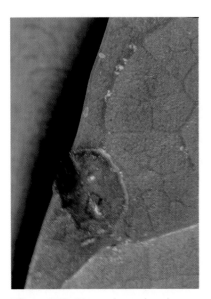

**Plate 158.** Hemispherical scale.

**Plate 159.** Green scale.

**Plate 160.** Pyriform scale.

**Plate 161.** Florida wax scale.

**Plate 162.** Sooty mold.

**Plate 163.** Sowbug.

**Plate 164.** Carolina wolf spider.

**Plate 165.** Jumping spider.

**Plate 166.** Green lynx spider.

**Plate 168.** Two-spotted spider mite.

**Plate 167.** Crab spider.

**Plate 169.** Spider mite damage.

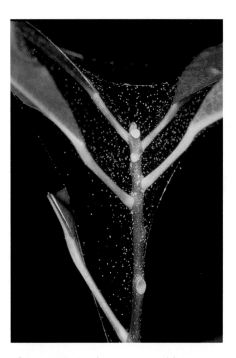

**Plate 170.** Spider mites in webbing.

**Plate 171.** Springtail.

**Plate 172.** Predaceous stink bug.

**Plate 173.** Predaceous stink bug.

**Plate 174.** Syrphid fly adult.

**Plate 175.** Syrphid fly larva.

**Plate 176.** Tachinid fly.

**Plate 177.** Tachinid fly.

**Plate 178.** Tachinid fly eggs on caterpillar.

**Plate 179.** Thrips (mature).

**Plate 180.** Thrips (immature).

**Plate 181.** Thrip damage.

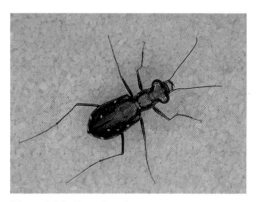

**Plate 182.** Tiger beetle.

**Plate 183.** Mud dauber wasp.

**Plate 184.** Mud dauber chambers.

**Plate 186.** Paper wasps on nest.

**Plate 185.** Paper wasp.

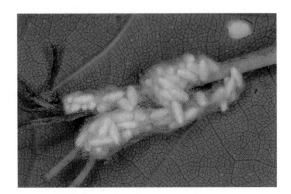

**Plate 187.** Parasitic wasp cocoons.

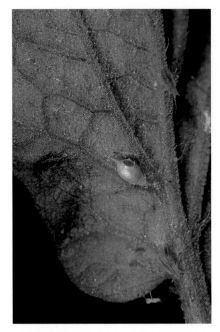

**Plate 188.** Wasp emergence hole in aphid.

**Plate 189.** Yellowjacket.

**Plate 190.** Yellowjacket nest.

**Plate 191.** Adult sweetpotato whitefly.

**Plate 192.** Poinsettia infested with sweetpotato whiteflies; note pale leaves due to feeding of the flies.

**Plate 193.** Sweetpotato whitefly adults and eggs.

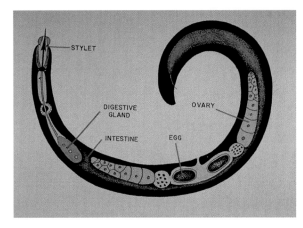

**Plate 194.** The body of a nematode.

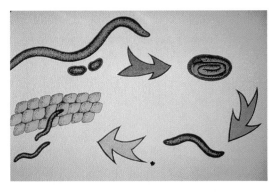

**Plate 195.** The typical life cycle of many nematodes.

**Plate 196.** Nematode stress on bottlebrush tree. Note poor vigor and thin canopy.

**Plate 197.** Severe galling caused by root-knot nematodes on ligustrum roots.

**Plate 198.** The yellowed foliage on boxwood is a typical reaction to root stress caused by root-knot nematodes.

**Plate 199.** Extensive galling by root-knot nematodes on boxwood roots (pair on right) compared to healthy roots (pair on left).

**Plate 200.** Root-knot nematode stress on wax myrtle tree. Note extremely thin canopy and poor vigor caused by root stress.

**Plate 201.** Wax myrtle roots heavily galled and decaying as a result of nematode infection followed by many other decay organisms.

**Plate 202.** Garden plots undergoing soil solarization.

**Plate 203.** Root-knot nematodes on roots of container-grown gardenia.

**Plate 204.** Leaf variegation on viburnum.

**Plate 205.** Winged bark on sweetgum.

**Plate 206.** Spanish moss.

**Plate 207.** Ball moss.

**Plate 208.** Crustose lichen on a limb.

**Plate 209.** Stinkhorn (*Clathrus columnatus*).

**Plate 210.** Angular bacterial spot on *Hibiscus* spp.

**Plate 211.** Leaf scorch on viburnum.

**Plate 212.** Frost crack on loquat.

**Plate 213.** Sunburn on magnolia leaves.

**Plate 214.** Muriatic acid burn on maranta.

**Plate 215.** Redbud leaf distortion due to "weed and feed" herbicides.

**Plate 216.** Bumper blight—mechanical injury on pittosporum.

**Plate 217.** *Cercospora* leaf spot on ligustrum.

**Plate 218.** Sign of powdery mildew fungi on oak.

**Plate 219.** Mushroom root rot disease on loquat.

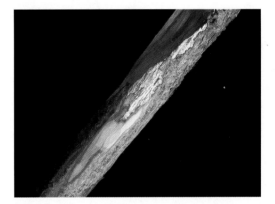

**Plate 220.** Mycelium of *Armillaria tabescens* under root surface.

**Plate 222.** Wet root rot disease on azalea.

**Plate 221.** *Armillaria tabescens* mushroom stage.

**Plate 223.** Root decay on juniper.

**Plate 224.** *Sphaeropsis* gall on bottlebrush.

**Plate 225.** *Sphaeropsis* witches' broom on holly.

**Plate 227.**
Fusiform rust
on pine.

**Plate 226.** *Hypoxylon* canker on oak.

**Plate 228.** Powdery mildew on dogwood.

**Plate 229.** Powdery mildew on crape myrtle.

**Plate 230.** Fire blight on loquat.

**Plate 232.** *Rhizoctonia* web blight on pittosporum.

**Plate 231.** Fire blight on apple.

**Plate 234.** Hyphal strands of aerial *Rhizoctonia.*

**Plate 233.** Web blight on juniper.

**Plate 235.** Algal spot on camellia.

**Plate 236.** *Cercospora* spot on nandina.

**Plate 237.** *Cercospora* spot on pittosporum.

**Plate 238.** *Cercospora* spot on sweetgum.

**Plate 239.**
*Entomosporium*
spot on
photinia.

**Plate 240.** *Entomosporium* spot on Indian hawthorn.

# Photography Credits

Dr. Robert J. Black: Plates 28 - 37, 42, 49 and front cover
(Adam's needle, beach morning glory, daylily)

Dr. Timothy K. Broschat: Plates 2 - 13, 26, 27, 40, 41, 45, 51 and 52.

Dr. James L. Castner:  Plates 65 - 81, 86 - 103, 105 - 137, 139 - 168, 170 - 180, 182 - 193 and 205.

Dr. Ann Chase: Plate 21

Dr. Charles Chellman: Plate 84.

James De Filippis: Plates 14, 16 and 17.

Dr. Wayne Dixon: Plate 82.

Dr. Robert A. Dunn:  Plates 194 - 197 and 199 - 202.

Foliage Education and Research Foundation: Plates 85, 169 and 181.

Dr. Robin Giblin-Davis: Plates 18 - 20.

Dr. Dale H. Habeck: Plate 104.

Dr. Nigel Harrison:  Plates 23 - 25.

Dr. Richard W. Henley: Plate 203.

Dr. Forrest Howard: Plate 15.

Dr. James Kimbrough:  Back cover (*Clathrus columnatus*).

Jack Miller: Plate 1.

Donna Mitchell: Plates 54 - 57, 59 - 64, front cover (magnolia bud) and back cover (fern spores, Spanish moss, Chinese elm bark, dodder, ball moss, lichen and mistletoe).

Daniel Mullins: Plate 198.

Dr. Jeffrey G. Norcini: Plate 58.

Dr. Donald E. Short: Plates 83 and 138.

Dr. Gary Simone: Plates 22, 204 and 206 - 240.

Dr. Thomas H. Yeager:  Plates 38, 39, 43, 44, 46 - 48, 50 and 53.

# General Index

## Index of Common Names

## Index of Botanical Names

*cape*

# ARE THESE SERIOUS PROBLEMS?

1. **NO.** **Stink horns** are mushroom-like fungi that live on decaying organic matter in the soil. Although they do no damage to existing plants, they give off a distinctly unpleasant smell. The stink horns commonly found in Florida usually appear in the cooler months and vary in appearance from the brown-capped white-stemmed *Dictyophora ravenelli* to the spike-shaped orange *Mutinus caninus* to the red-orange and inside-out *Clathrus columnatus* (pictured). Stink horns rely on carrion beetles and greenflies to distribute their spores. Other than removing them by hand, the only effective control for stink horns is tilling the organic matter in the soil. The more you till the soil, the sooner the stink horns will disappear, usually in 5 to 8 years.

2. **NO.** These **spore cases** contain dust-like **fern spores**. Spore cases usually appear as rows of symmetrical dots on the undersides of fern leaves. Ferns do not bear flowers and have no seeds; they propagate themselves by releasing the tiny fern spores to fall to the ground. Under the right conditions, the spores develop into new plants.

3. **NO.** **Spanish moss** is an epiphyte, which means that it derives all its nutrients and water from the air and NOT the plant to which it is attached. Because the amount of Spanish moss increases as a tree declines, some people believe the moss is killing the tree. In fact, the tree is dying from stress caused by such factors as disease or construction related activity. As the tree declines, it loses foliage, and more sunlight penetrates the canopy. It is this increase in light that stimulates the growth of Spanish and ball moss. Although their presence, when abundant, indicates a weakened tree, they are not the *cause* of poor tree health. Spanish moss need only be removed if it is *extremely* thick as it may shade leaves or break limbs.

4. **NO.** The **peeling or exfoliating bark** on this Chinese elm (*Ulmus parvifolia*) is a natural characteristic that is often considered decorative. Several other species of tree also have ridged or peeling bark on their trunks and branches. When a plant's appearance seems unusual, find out if perhaps you are witnessing a normal occurrence in that species.

5. **YES.** **Dodder** has specialized roots that become attached to a host plant and then cease to function. At this point, dodder is a parasite, deriving its nourishment from the host plant. Climbing and vine-like, dodder twines about other plants and occasionally smothers them.

6. **NO.** **Ball moss**, like Spanish moss (above), is an epiphyte and does not parasitize trees.

7. **NO.** **Lichens** are organisms that commonly grow on trees and rocks. A lichen is comprised of a fungus and an algae living in association with one another to give the appearance of a single plant. Like ball and Spanish mosses, lichens are found in abundance on declining trees but are not the cause of plant damage. Lichens come in many sizes, shapes and colors; growths are often crusty gray, green, yellow or white. Some lichens are leaf-like while others resemble tufts of horse hair hanging from the branches. Lichens manufacture their own food.

8. **YES.** **Mistletoe** is a parasite commonly seen in trees from New Jersey to Florida. Its rubbery, leathery leaves and translucent berries are often used in holiday decorations. The berries are considered poisonous. Many times this parasite goes unnoticed until fall or winter when deciduous trees lose their leaves. An evergreen, mistletoe then appears in large, lacy clusters high among the bare tree branches.